Criminal Law & Criminal Justice
An Introduction

Noel Cross

Los Angeles | London | New Delhi
Singapore | Washington DC

First published 2010

Apart from any fair dealing for the purposes of research or private study, or criticism or review, as permitted under the Copyright, Designs and Patents Act, 1988, this publication may be reproduced, stored or transmitted in any form, or by any means, only with the prior permission in writing of the publishers, or in the case of reprographic reproduction, in accordance with the terms of licences issued by the Copyright Licensing Agency. Enquiries concerning reproduction outside those terms should be sent to the publishers.

SAGE Publications Ltd
1 Oliver's Yard
55 City Road
London EC1Y 1SP

SAGE Publications Inc.
2455 Teller Road
Thousand Oaks, California 91320

SAGE Publications India Pvt Ltd
B 1/I 1 Mohan Cooperative Industrial Area
Mathura Road
New Delhi 110 044

SAGE Publications Asia-Pacific Pte Ltd
33 Pekin Street #02-01
Far East Square
Singapore 048763

Library of Congress Control Number: 2009924975

British Library Cataloguing in Publication data

A catalogue record for this book is available from the British Library

ISBN 978-1-84787-086-5
ISBN 978-1-84787-087-2 (pbk)

Typeset by C&M Digitals (P) Ltd, Chennai, India
Printed in Great Britain by TJ International, Padstow, Cornwall
Printed on paper from sustainable resources

Mixed Sources
Product group from well-managed
forests and other controlled sources
www.fsc.org Cert no. SGS-COC-2482
© 1996 Forest Stewardship Council
FSC

Criminal Law & Criminal Justice

Contents

Acknowledgements

Many thanks go to my parents, my colleagues on the Criminal Justice team at Liverpool John Moores University, and Caroline Porter at Sage for their help and encouragement along the long and winding road from developing the idea for the book to publication. The book is dedicated to Helen Paton, for her constant love and support during the time in which it was put together.

Part One

General principles of criminal law

1
Introduction

Chapter Aims

After reading Chapter 1 you should be able to understand:

- The basic principles of criminal law
- The basic principles of criminal justice
- The key theories which try to explain what the criminal law does
- The key theories which try to explain what criminal justice does
- Which individuals and groups of people play a role in criminal justice
- How crime is socially constructed, and what this means

Introduction and rationale: why study criminal law if you're a criminology or criminal justice student?

This book is about criminal law in England and Wales, and the difference between the criminal law as it is defined in law books, and the criminal law as it is used by agencies in the criminal justice process. It is designed to show not only how the current law defines criminal behaviour, but also how people and organisations working in criminal justice use and interpret that law in the approaches they take to responding to crime in practice.

One answer to the question in the section title above is simple – without criminal law there would be no crime and no criminology (Nelken 1987)! It is the criminal law which 'labels' certain kinds of behaviour as being unlawful, and sets out the rules for deciding when a crime has been committed. The organisations who have responsibility for responding to crime use these rules as guidelines for using the state's power to respond to crime.

The question then is: to what extent do the criminal justice organisations stick to the rules set out by the criminal law? Some criminologists have argued (e.g. McBarnet 1981) that the police and other criminal justice organisations use their own power, discretion and 'working rules' far more than they use the criminal law itself. It is this gap between the 'law in the books' and 'the law in action' (Packer 1968) which is the main subject of this book. To understand criminology and criminal justice fully, it is necessary to compare the criminal law with criminal justice practice. In other words, this book aims to bridge the gap between criminal law and criminal justice, to provide a better understanding of both subject areas.

The next section of this chapter introduces criminal law in England and Wales.

Criminal law: what is it?

DEFINITION BOX 1.1

CRIMINAL LAW

Law which defines certain types of behaviour as being criminal, and allows those types of behaviour to be punished in some way by the state.

Substantive criminal law is the part of the law that deals with behaviour which is defined as criminal, and results in punishment by the state when a person is found to be guilty of breaking the law. It is separate from what Uglow (2005: 448) calls procedural criminal law, which defines and regulates the powers of criminal justice agencies to investigate, prosecute and punish crime. Substantive criminal law is also separate from civil law, which deals with other forms of behaviour that result in some form of compensation (often payment of money) after a finding of guilt. A key difference between substantive criminal law and civil law lies in the standard of proof needed to find guilt in each case. For criminal law, guilt is proved by evidence of guilt beyond reasonable doubt. For civil law, guilt is proved by evidence of guilt on the balance of probabilities, which requires a lower standard of proof, and therefore less evidence indicating guilt, than proof beyond reasonable doubt. Linked to this is the idea of the burden of proof being on the prosecution (*Woolmington v DPP* [1935] AC 462). This means that the defendant in a criminal case (defendants will be referred to from now on in the book as 'D') is innocent until the police and prosecutors have enough evidence to prove beyond reasonable doubt in court that D is guilty of all the different elements of the criminal charge(s) brought against them. Traditionally, this means that they will have to prove the guilty conduct (*actus reus*) specified by the definition of the offence, and also the guilty state of mind (*mens rea*) which is specified. The principle is the foundation of the adversarial system of criminal justice that has been established in England and Wales, where the prosecution and defence compete against each other to persuade the courts that their evidence is more convincing than the other side's.

Related to the rule regarding the burden of proof is the principle of the rule of law, which is equally fundamental to understanding criminal law and criminal justice in England and Wales. Under the rule of law, no one can be punished unless they have breached the law as it is clearly and currently defined, and they have been warned that the conduct they have been accused of is criminal (*Rimmington* [2006] 1 AC 459); the breach is proved in a court of law; and everyone (including those who make the law) is subject to the rule of law, unless special status is given by the law itself (Simester and Sullivan 2007: chapter 2).

Criminal law in England and Wales, under the rule of law, comes from three main sources. The first is known as common law. This is law which is made and developed by judges when they decide cases, in line with the rules on precedent. Precedent means that a particular court has to follow an earlier court's decision which is based on the same law and the same facts as the case it is currently deciding, and which was made at a higher court level or (usually) at the same level as itself, but it does not have to follow decisions made at lower levels. Figure 1.1 shows how court decisions are appealed to higher courts in England and Wales, and how precedent works.

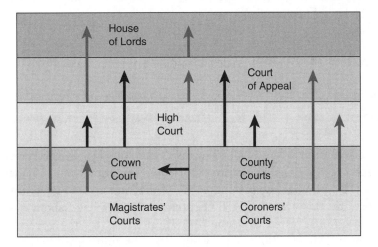

Figure 1.1   The court appeal system in England and Wales

The second source of criminal law is known as statute law. This is law which is created by Parliament, and implemented in the form of Acts of Parliament, or statutes. Statute law is often used to decriminalise old offences, create new offences, redefine or change criminal offences which already exist, or bring together old pieces of legislation on the same topic. All new criminal offences must now be created by statute law, not by the courts through the common law (*Jones and Milling* [2007] 1 AC 136), although courts used to be able to use common law to create offences, and some offences are still defined by common law today, such as murder. However, even where a criminal offence has been defined by statute, courts will often decide the details of that offence through their own case-by-case decisions, especially where there is some confusion over what a statute (or part of a statute) means in practice.

The third source of law is law which is developed from the obligation of substantive criminal law to comply with European human rights law as contained in the European Convention on Human Rights ('ECHR' from now on in this book). Since Parliament passed the Human Rights Act 1998, individuals have the right to complain to courts in England and Wales where they feel that their human rights have been breached by substantive criminal law. The occurrence of miscarriages of justice, for example, where a person is convicted and punished for a criminal offence which they did not commit, involves serious breaches of human rights (e.g. Walker and Starmer 1999). As a result of the Human Rights Act, courts must interpret statute law in a way which is compatible with human rights legislation (s. 3). If this cannot be done, the courts must make a declaration of incompatibility regarding the piece of law being challenged, and pass the issue on to Parliament so that it can redefine the law in a compatible way (Buxton 2000). Section 6 of the Human Rights Act requires public authorities, including the police, the Crown Prosecution Service and the courts (see below), to act in a way which is compatible with the ECHR, and also allows common law to be changed in line with the ECHR (*H* [2002] 1 Cr App Rep 59).

STUDY EXERCISE 1.1

List three features of the substantive criminal law as it operates in England and Wales.

Substantive criminal law, in all its forms, is developed by the decisions of individuals and organisations. Therefore, what counts as 'crime' can and does change over time. The criminal law-making policy of the New Labour government since 1997 illustrates this very clearly. By September 2008, New Labour had created 3,605 new criminal offences – one for almost every day the government had been in power (Morris 2008). The criminalising of hunting wild mammals with dogs, under the Hunting Act 2004, is just one high-profile (and controversial) example of a crime created by New Labour. On the other hand, there are types of behaviour which used to be crimes, but which no longer are – such as the Sexual Offences Act 1967, which partially decriminalised homosexual behaviour between adult men. From these examples it can be seen that crime itself is a 'social construct' (Muncie 2001). No behaviour is criminal until an individual or group of people decides to make it criminal (Christie 2004). As a result, the boundaries of criminal behaviour have changed constantly over time, in line with changes in public opinion, political parties' views, and social and economic conditions (Lacey 1995). This has often caused confusion and inconsistency in the criminal law.

STUDY EXERCISE 1.2

Using Internet resources and statute books, find three examples of offences which have been decriminalised, and three examples of offences which have been created since 1997 by the New Labour government. Why do you think each of these offences has been criminalised or decriminalised? Do you agree with the decision to criminalise or decriminalise each one?

This book is about criminal law and criminal justice in England and Wales, but it is important to note that Scotland has its own, separate criminal law framework, which differs from the one in England and Wales. Scottish criminal law has the same basic sources as the criminal law in England and Wales, but relies more on common law, and less on statutory law, than the law in England and Wales. Scottish common criminal law also relies more on using the underlying principle justifying a law as a precedent, and less on using previous 'example' cases, than English and Welsh law (Christie 2003: 1–6). Not all statutory law that is implemented in England and Wales applies to Scotland – so that, for example, Scottish criminal law still has a common law definition of rape, rather than the statutory definition introduced in England and Wales as part of the Sexual Offences Act 2003, and a common law definition of theft rather the statutory English and Welsh definition under the Theft Act 1968 (McDiarmid 2006). Also, since the Scottish courts have developed their own common law principles, some criminal offences have different names, and different offence requirements, from their equivalents in England and Wales. For example, Scotland has an offence of culpable homicide instead of the offence of manslaughter, and has general offences of assault and aggravated assault, and theft and aggravated theft, rather than the more specific violent and property offences in the English and Welsh law (Jones and Christie 2008). Finally, it should be noted that the Scottish Parliament has the power, under the Scotland Act 1998, to implement its own criminal law legislation applying only to Scotland, and has implemented statute law of this kind since its creation (Hamilton and Harper 2008). Readers are directed towards the sources cited in this paragraph for more information on Scottish criminal law.

The next section introduces criminal justice in England and Wales.

Criminal justice: what is it?

DEFINITION BOX 1.2

CRIMINAL JUSTICE

The individuals, groups of individuals and organisations which have the authority to respond to crime in various ways, including the power to force people to do things (or not do things).

Davies et al. (2005: 8) state that 'the content of the criminal law provides the starting point of the criminal justice system by defining behaviour that is to be regulated through the use of the criminal law'. However, this statement by itself does not reflect the complex reality of criminal justice, as Davies et al. go on to argue, for a number of reasons. First, just as the criminal law itself is built and developed socially and politically, often in a more disjointed way than it first appears, so the criminal justice process of enforcing the law is not carried out equally for all crimes and all criminal offences. Critical criminologists have argued that some types of criminal behaviour are more likely to be investigated and prosecuted than others, and that this prioritising reflects the interests of powerful people in society, rather than the level of harm caused to society (e.g. Tombs 2005). Secondly, although criminal justice is sometimes referred to as a 'system', some have questioned whether it is organised and unified enough to be called a 'system' at all (e.g. Wilson 2004). Criminal justice is made up of a variety of agencies and organisations, each with its own responsibilities and areas of decision-making authority. Based on the analysis of Chapman and Niven (2000: 4), all of the following agencies have a role to play in the process of criminal justice:

- The police, who have the power to stop, search, arrest, interrogate and charge suspects;
- The Crown Prosecution Service, whose role it is to decide whether there is sufficient evidence and public interest to prosecute a suspect, and, if there is enough evidence, to prosecute the case in court;
- The magistrates' courts, who hear and sentence all summary offences, as well as some triable either way offences – in total magistrates deal with 98% of all cases which come before the courts (Ministry of Justice 2007a: 160);
- The Crown Courts, who hear and sentence all indictable only offences as well as some triable either way offences;
- And agencies who deal with those who have been sentenced by the courts, such as Youth Offending Teams (who work with offenders aged between 10 and 17), the National Probation Service, and HM Prison Service.

Even this is not a complete list of those involved in criminal justice. There are also agencies which assist the victims of crime during their case's progression through the process, such as Victim Support (Maguire and Corbett 1987).

Defence solicitors and barristers represent defendants in courts, and present arguments in favour of the defendant being found not guilty of the charges brought against them. The government has a great deal of influence over criminal justice policy, which in turn influences criminal justice practice day to day in various ways (Newburn 2003). The government controls policy directly, through government departments which are responsible for different parts of criminal justice (like the Ministry of Justice and the Home Office), and also indirectly, through organisations which are linked to government (such as the National Youth Justice Board, which is responsible for directing youth justice policy in England and Wales). The media play a key part, not only in reporting on and shaping people's perceptions of criminal justice, but also in influencing the operation of criminal justice itself (Jewkes 2004).

The public also play a vital role in criminal justice, at every stage of the process. Most crimes come to the attention of the police through reports from the public, rather than investigation by the police themselves (Zedner 2004: 15). Members of the public can, since the Police Reform Act 2002, become community support officers, and in doing so use many of the powers that can normally only be used by full-time police officers (Crawford 2003: 157–8). They can also be Special Constables, who help the full-time police in their day-to-day work. The majority of magistrates sitting in the magistrates' court are lay magistrates – members of the public who, after receiving training, hear and sentence court cases (Department for Constitutional Affairs 2006). Crown Court juries are made up of 12 members of the public. The public also play a range of important roles in working with offenders after they have been sentenced in court – for example, in youth justice as mentors helping young people and volunteers monitoring the behaviour of young people who have been sentenced in court, or as prison visitors in the adult criminal justice process. The public can also be victims of, or witnesses to, crime – reporting crime to police, giving evidence in court, and taking part in restorative justice, which often aims to bring offenders and victims together as part of the offender's punishment after they have been convicted by the courts (Walklate 2007).

Just as Scotland has its own criminal law framework, separate from that in England and Wales (see above), so it also has its own criminal justice process, with some distinctive features, which are briefly summarised here. In England, a court reaches a decision on the basis of facts alleged and proved by prosecution and defence lawyers (see above). However, in the Scottish criminal justice process, it is entirely the responsibility of Advocate Deputes (in the High Court of Justiciary) and Procurators Fiscal (in the Sheriff Court), acting for the Lord Advocate's Department, to prove the case (McCallum et al. 2007a) – the Lord Advocate heads the Crown Office and Procurator Fiscal Service, which is the equivalent of the Crown Prosecution Service in England and Wales. Before a trial, when someone is suspected of committing a crime by the police, a file is passed to the local Procurator Fiscal, who decides whether or not the case should proceed. If the Procurator decides that there is a case, they investigate by taking statements, known as precognitions. The decision to prosecute is independent – there is no right of private prosecution as in England and Wales, and no right of appeal against the Procurator's decision to prosecute or not to prosecute (ibid.). Therefore, no court costs are awarded against offenders as they are in England and Wales. If there is a case, the Procurator also decides what the charge should be, and which court the case should be heard in (see below). There is no right for the accused or magistrates to decide on hearing venue as there is in England and Wales (see Chapter 3).

Scotland also has its own three-tier criminal court system. The High Court of Justiciary is the highest court in Scotland, and there is no right of appeal from it to the House of Lords as there is in England and Wales. The Court itself acts as an Appeal Court, and deals with serious crime generally, but has to deal with a small group of very serious offences, such as murder and rape. The second-tier Sheriff Court is presided over by a district Sheriff, who is a qualified judge. The Sheriff Court has two procedures, solemn and summary. In solemn procedure, the case is heard by a 15-person jury, while in summary procedure, only the Sheriff hears cases. The sentencing powers of a Sheriff are limited, so less serious crimes are heard before this court. Finally, there are the District Courts (currently being replaced by Justice of the Peace Courts under the Criminal Proceedings etc. (Reform) (Scotland) Act 2007), which deal with the least serious offences, such as speeding and breach of the peace, and where cases are heard by either a panel of lay magistrates or one stipendiary magistrate. Judges and juries in Scotland can give three verdicts – guilty and not guilty (as in England and Wales), but also not proven, which allows the defendant to be acquitted in the same way as a not guilty verdict (McCallum et al. 2007b).

The law of evidence is also different in Scotland, in the sense that the principle of corroboration applies generally there – in other words, all evidence has to be backed up by at least one other source (Duff 2004). This is different from the system in England and Wales, where there is no need for corroboration, for example with confession evidence and the recent changes in the rules on hearsay (see Chapter 3).

This section has explained what criminal justice is, and who plays a direct part in how it works. However, this discussion can only be a starting point in understanding criminal justice, for two reasons. First, it does not show exactly how each group of people plays its role within criminal justice, and fits in with the other groups involved. For example, victims play several key roles in the criminal justice process, as shown above, but how satisfied are victims by their treatment in that process (e.g. Christie 1977)? Secondly, to understand whether there are differences between what should happen in criminal law and criminal justice, and what actually does happen in them (and if so, what those differences are), it is important to think about different theories which try to explain what criminal law and criminal justice do. These theories will be introduced next.

Draw a flowchart illustrating the different stages of the criminal justice process, including the individuals and agencies that you think have a say at each stage.

DEFINITION BOX 1.3

MODELS AND THEORIES OF CRIMINAL LAW AND CRIMINAL JUSTICE

Explanations for what criminal law and criminal justice do (or should do) in society, in terms of their priorities and values.

What is the criminal law there for?

Clarkson (2005: 254–67) summarises the key theoretical approaches to the purposes of the criminal law, as follows:

- The 'law and economics' approach, which states that the criminal law is there to deter 'economically inefficient' acts which do not help the economy (e.g. stealing a car rather than buying one), and regulate such behaviour, given that individual offenders choose to commit crime of their own free will;
- The 'enforcement of morality' approach, which states that the criminal law is there to criminalise behaviour which is against the common moral values of society (see Devlin 1965; cf. Hart 1963);
- The 'paternalistic' approach, which states that the criminal law is there to prevent behaviour which causes harm either to offenders themselves, or to others;
- The 'liberal' approach, which states that the criminal law is there only to prevent harm caused by offenders to others (see Feinberg 1984);
- The 'radical' approach, which states that the criminal law is there to protect the interests of the powerful in society, and hide social conflict (e.g. Carlen 1980);
- The 'risk management' approach, which states that the criminal law is there to manage the risk to the public created by dangerous situations or behaviour (Feeley and Simon 1994).

As Clarkson (2005) goes on to explain, these principles offer reasons for allowing different kinds of behaviour to be criminalised which compete with each other. As a result, a criminologist analysing the criminal law must consider the possibility that more than one theoretical approach is capable of explaining the criminal law. One way for criminologists to choose between them is considering what the criminal law should do as well as what it actually does. An approach which considers what the criminal law should do can be added to Clarkson's list:

- The 'rights based' approach – law has to uphold and balance the human rights of individuals and society as a whole, in line with relevant human rights legislation (the European Convention on Human Rights) which is part of the law in England and Wales (s. 3 of the Human Rights Act). Key ECHR provisions which are relevant to criminal law include Article 2 (the right to life), Article 3 (the right not to be subjected to torture or inhuman and degrading treatment), Article 5 (the right to liberty), Article 6 (the right to a fair legal hearing and the presumption of innocence), Article 7 (the right to know exactly what the offence someone is accused of involves in terms of criminal behaviour, and the right not to be convicted under law which was not in effect when the act being punished was done), Article 8 (the right to respect for private life), Article 10 (the right to freedom of expression) and Article 11 (the right to freedom of assembly and association).

Another way for criminologists to understand the different theoretical approaches to the criminal law is to compare them to theoretical approaches to criminal justice itself. These are introduced in the next section.

What is criminal justice there for?

King (1981: 12–31) outlines the key theoretical approaches to the purpose of criminal justice, and the typical features which these theories would produce in practice if they were applied:

- The 'due process' model, shown by equality between the defence and the prosecution in the process, rules protecting the defendant against error or abuse of power, and the presumption of defendants' innocence until they are proven guilty;
- The 'crime control' model, shown by disregard of legal controls, implicit presumption of guilt, support for the police, and a high conviction rate (Packer 1968);
- The 'medical' model, shown by individualised responses to crime (so that each offender receives an intervention package tailored to meet their needs and circumstances), treatment of the social causes behind offending rather than punishment of the offence, and discretion and expertise of decision-makers (Garland 1985);
- The 'bureaucratic' model, shown by the promotion of speed and efficiency, the minimisation of conflict between people working in criminal justice and of money spent on the process, and the importance of and acceptance of records;
- The 'status passage' model, shown by the public shaming of the defendant, court values which reflect (or claim to reflect) community values, and criminal justice agents' control over the process;
- The 'power' model, shown by the reinforcement of class values through criminal justice, the deliberate alienation and suppression of the defendant, the presence of paradoxes and contradictions between the rhetoric and the performance of criminal justice, and the ignorance of social harm caused by inequality in society (e.g. Sim et al. 1987).

In addition to these six models, Davies et al. (2005: 27) add a further two:

- The 'just deserts' model, shown by offenders being punished according to the blameworthiness and harmfulness of their actions, the recognition of offenders' basic human rights, the need for establishment of the offender's blameworthiness before punishment, and the recognition of the right of society to punish those who have offended;
- The 'risk management' model, shown by the monitoring and control of offenders based on the risk they pose to society and their previous offending history, the use of surveillance and supervision to reduce crime and change offending behaviour, and the use of longer sentences for offenders who are seen as being particularly dangerous (e.g. Kemshall 2003).

As previously stated, looking for links between theories explaining the criminal law and theories explaining criminal justice leads to an enhanced understanding of both of these social institutions. It is vital to examine and understand both sets of theories critically because criminal law and criminal justice cannot exist meaningfully without each other. Without criminal justice, criminal law cannot be enforced in practice – but without criminal law, criminal justice has nothing to enforce.

STUDY EXERCISE 1.4

Do any of the law and criminal justice models listed above fit together in your view? If so, which ones, and why do you think this is the case?

Conclusions: a guide to the structure of the book

This introductory chapter has introduced criminal law and criminal justice in England and Wales in terms of what they are, and in terms of different ideas about the functions which they have in society. The rest of this book will use these ideas as a platform for comparing criminal law with its implementation, in the form of criminal justice, in practice in England and Wales. The book aims to answer the following questions through this analysis: what differences are there (if any) between the criminal law in the books and its enforcement, via criminal justice, in practice? Whose interests are protected by the criminal law and by criminal justice? On what theoretical basis (if any) can the approaches taken by criminal law and criminal justice be justified? On what theoretical basis should criminal law and criminal justice be based in the future?

The rest of the book is split into two main parts. The first part (Chapters 2–5) considers general principles of liability in criminal law, and examines how they are implemented in criminal justice practice by using different groups of people within the criminal justice process as examples of how well criminal law and criminal justice values fit together. The second part (Chapters 6–9) considers specific types of criminal offence, again discussing how they are implemented in criminal justice practice. Each of these chapters will be split into two parts: the first part explaining what the criminal law is on a particular issue, and the second part building on this analysis by considering how the law is used in criminal justice practice. The final chapter then returns to the questions raised here, and places the analysis in the context of theoretical approaches to criminal law and criminal justice.

FURTHER READING

Allen, M.J. (2007), *Textbook on Criminal Law* (9th edn): chapter 1. Oxford: Oxford University Press.

Ashworth, A. (2006), *Principles of Criminal Law* (5th edn): chapter 1. Oxford University Press.

Lacey, N. (1994), 'Introduction: Making Sense of Criminal Justice', in Lacey, N. (ed.), *Criminal Justice: A Reader.* Oxford: Oxford University Press.

Lacey, N. (2007), 'Legal Constructions of Crime', in Maguire, M., Morgan, R., and Reiner, R. (eds), *The Oxford Handbook of Criminology* (4th edn). Oxford: Oxford University Press.

Padfield, N. (2008), *Text and Materials on the Criminal Justice Process* (4th edn): chapter 1. London: Butterworths/LexisNexis.

Actus reus

Chapter Aims

After reading Chapter 2 you should be able to understand:

- The basic meaning of *actus reus*
- The key criminal law principles which are included within *actus reus*
- The meaning of factual and legal causation in the criminal law
- How *actus reus* is represented in crime statistics
- How the police use *actus reus* in criminal justice practice
- How the CPS use *actus reus* in criminal justice practice
- How victims of crime who report *actus reus* are treated by the police and CPS
- How the evidence on *actus reus* in the criminal law and criminal justice fits in with the theoretical models introduced in Chapter 1

Introduction

In this chapter, the concept of *actus reus*, or the 'guilty act', will be explained and analysed. In Chapter 1, it was stated that the term '*actus reus*' meant 'guilty act' – 'it identifies the conduct which the criminal law considers harmful' (Herring 2006: 86).

But *actus reus* is not as straightforward as this. The first part of this chapter uses case law and statute law to explain the rules of *actus reus* in more detail. The second part of the chapter discusses the ways in which the concept of *actus reus* is used by criminal justice – using the police and the Crown Prosecution Service (CPS) as examples, as well as considering crime victims' relationship with these agencies.

Actus Reus: The Law

Making sense of *actus reus*

DEFINITION BOX 2.1

ACTUS REUS

The external behaviour or conduct which is prohibited by the criminal law.

Actus reus means more than just 'guilty acts'. It also includes a range of other behaviour requirements, defined in each criminal offence. For example, the *actus reus* of theft is taking someone else's property, and the *actus reus* of murder is unlawfully killing another person. But, as these two examples show, the types of illegal behaviour vary greatly between different types of offence. Clarkson (2005: 13–14) splits *actus reus* up into two types of offence. First, there are conduct crimes, which involve doing or being something illegal – for example, possessing illegal drugs. Secondly, there are result crimes, which involve causing a result which is illegal – for example, causing someone's unlawful death as part of a murder or manslaughter offence. Herring (2006: 85), meanwhile, distinguishes between four different *actus reus* requirements – the 'four Cs':

- *Conduct*. Here, the *actus reus* involves illegal behaviour – for example, perjury, a crime which involves lying when giving evidence in court.
- *Circumstances*. Here, the *actus reus* involves behaviour done in a particular scenario which makes it illegal. For example, the crime of criminal damage involves damaging or destroying property *belonging to someone else*, so the key circumstance here is that the property does not belong to you.
- *Context*. Here, it is an internal or 'state of mind' element which makes the behaviour a criminal offence. For example, the crime of rape involves sexual intercourse, but done without the victim's (from now on referred to by the letter 'V') consent, which makes it illegal. Here, V's consent is not something which can be 'seen'. It is their state of mind that counts.
- *Consequences*. Here, the *actus reus* involves producing an illegal result through behaviour – for example, murder, where conduct causes the unlawful death of someone else. If the consequence was not caused by D's behaviour, the offence is not proved (e.g. *White* [1910] 2 KB 124).

Since the term '*actus reus*' covers so many different types of criminal behaviour in the criminal law, most criminal offences will only have some of the 'four Cs', not all of them. For example, context is not relevant to the crime of murder – D would still be guilty of murder even if V asked, or even begged, D to kill them, as long as all of the *actus reus* and *mens rea* requirements were present.

STUDY EXERCISE 2.1

Using an Internet statute database, find one example of an offence containing a 'conduct' element as part of the *actus reus*, one example of a 'circumstances' offence, one example of a 'context' offence, and one example of a 'consequences' offence.

The next part of this chapter considers some of the key principles of *actus reus* as it operates in practice.

Key *actus reus* principles

No mens rea *without* actus reus

Often, in the criminal law, a crime is committed when there is a combination of *actus reus* and *mens rea* (the guilty mind required for each criminal offence – see Chapter 3 for more details). The *actus reus* for each crime must be established. It is not enough that the *mens rea* for the crime was present, if the *actus reus* was not committed as well (*Hensler* (1870) 11 Cox CC 570; *Deller* (1952) 36 Cr App Rep 184). The main reason for this is that the criminal law in England and Wales, as Clarkson (2005: 20) explains, insists on some expression of someone's criminal thoughts through their actions before it will intervene to punish them.

Voluntary acts

Not all illegal acts count as *actus reus*. Acts must be voluntary before they can be considered as criminal behaviour. If D has no control over their physical actions for some reason, and commits a crime while 'out of control' in this way, then there is no *actus reus*. In *Hill v Baxter* [1958] 1 QB 277, the Court of Appeal stated that if D was attacked by a swarm of killer bees while driving, and the bees caused D to lose control of the car and hit a pedestrian crossing the road, D would not commit any *actus reus* because their actions were not voluntary.

In a situation like this, D is conscious, but has lost control over their physical actions. In other cases, though, D might be either partly or completely unconscious. For example, D may be sleepwalking, or suffering from various medical or psychological conditions, such as hypoglycaemia (Simester and Sullivan 2007). The 'voluntary act' principle can apply in these circumstances to remove the *actus reus*, just as it can where D is fully conscious.

Actus reus *and 'status offences'*

Actus reus does not have to be about doing something. It can also be about status – being something or somewhere that is prohibited by the criminal law, or possessing something that is prohibited. Examples include possession of a prohibited drug (Misuse of Drugs Act 1971 s. 5(1)). Occasionally, the lack of the requirement of voluntary action can lead to what seem to be very unfair convictions under status offences, where D appeared to have no control over the situation. Two good examples of this are *Larsonneur* (1933) 24 Cr App Rep 74 and *Winzar v Chief Constable of Kent* (1983), *The Times*, 28 March.

Actus reus *and omissions*

In a few situations, someone can be convicted and punished for *not* doing something, that is for an omission rather than an act. The courts have made people liable for omissions, where the omission has caused a crime, in the following situations:

- Where D has voluntarily agreed to take care of V, but has failed to take reasonable steps to do so (e.g. *Stone and Dobinson* [1977] QB 354);
- Where D, a parent, has failed to look after their child to a reasonable standard (e.g. *Downes* (1875) 13 Cox CC 111);
- Where it is D's duty to do something as part of their job contract, but D does not do it (e.g. *Pittwood* (1902) 19 TLR 37);
- Where D has duties as part of their public office (e.g. as a police officer), but does not carry them out (e.g. *Dytham* [1979] QB 722);
- Where D has created a dangerous situation accidentally or unknowingly, but then realises that it is dangerous and does not take steps to remove the danger (e.g. *Fagan v Metropolitan Police Commissioner* [1969] 1 QB 438; *Miller* [1983] 2 AC 161; *Santana-Bermudez* [2004] Crim LR 471).

In some cases there seems to be very little difference between an act and an omission. For example, in *Speck* [1977] 2 All ER 859, D was guilty of gross indecency with a child because his failure to stop her doing what she did was an 'invitation to continue' the gross indecency. On the other hand, in *Airedale NHS Trust v Bland* [1993] AC 789, the House of Lords decided that a victim of the Hillsborough disaster who had been in a coma for three years and who had no chance of recovery should be allowed to die by doctors ceasing to feed and medicate him through tubes, and stated that this would be an omission (which would not lead to criminal liability for murder) rather than a deliberate act of killing by the doctors at the hospital (which would lead to liability).

STUDY EXERCISE 2.2

Compare and contrast the arguments of Ashworth (1989) and Hogan (1987) on how far liability for omissions should go in the criminal law. Which argument do you think is better, and why?

Actus reus and causation

DEFINITION BOX 2.2

CAUSATION

The criminal law principles requiring D's actions to be connected to the outcome which is prohibited by the criminal law.

Result crimes require D to cause a prohibited consequence before liability can be proved. There has to be a 'chain of causation' between what D did and the prohibited result. For example, for murder and manslaughter, the prohibited result is the unlawful death of another person. There are two types of causation in the criminal law. These are *factual causation* and *legal causation*. Both factual and legal causation need to be proved before causation can be established.

Factual causation

Factual causation is sometimes known as 'but for' causation because proving it involves asking the question: if D's act had not happened, would the prohibited result have occurred? For example, in *White* D put cyanide into V's lemonade in order to kill her. V died shortly afterwards but the cyanide was not the cause of death – she had had a heart attack. V would have died regardless of D's act, so the factual chain of causation between D's act and V's death was not there. *Dalloway* (1847) 2 Cox CC 273 shows that where D could not have done anything to prevent V's death, they are not guilty because factual causation was not present – even where, as in this case, D's conduct was blameworthy in itself.

For factual causation, D's act does not have to be the only cause of the prohibited result, or even the main cause. It just has to be an 'operating and substantial' cause of the result. In *Pagett* (1983) 76 Cr App Rep 279, the main cause of V's death was the police firing bullets at her, but D was still guilty of manslaughter because he had been using V as a human shield while firing at the police at the time of V's death. If a reasonable act of self-defence, or in the execution of duty, by a third party against D's act causes V's death, then the chain of factual causation is not broken. However, in *Environment Agency v Empress Car Co (Abertillery) Ltd* [1999] 2 AC 22, D was convicted of polluting a river, even though a third party had maliciously and deliberately opened the tap on D's tank of diesel, causing the diesel to leak into the river. The House of Lords said that as the vandalism was foreseeable by a reasonable person, D had still caused the prohibited outcome, despite the voluntary damage caused by the third party here.

Legal causation

Proving legal causation involves asking the question: if factual causation is present, are there any other legal principles which will break the chain of causation, and remove D's liability for the prohibited outcome? First, was there an independent and voluntary act by a third party (i.e. not D) which broke the chain of causation? In *Pagett*, it was the police which directly caused V's death by shooting her. But they only did this because D, who was holding V hostage, had shot at them first. As a result, the Court of Appeal decided that the police's act was only a 'reflex', not a voluntary independent act. The police firing at V did not break the chain of causation and D was still guilty of manslaughter.

A second category of 'third-party intervention' involves V dying after receiving poor medical treatment for injuries which have originally been caused by D. *Smith* [1959] 2 QB 35 stated that if what D did is still a 'substantial and operative cause' of V's death, even poor medical treatment will not break the chain (see also *Cheshire* [1991] 3 All ER 670 and *Malcherek* [1981] 2 All ER 422). On the other hand, doctors' treatment of V in *Jordan* (1956) 40 Cr App Rep 152 did break the causation chain because the court decided that the treatment had been 'palpably bad'. D was therefore not guilty of causing V's death – but *Jordan* was an exceptional case in terms of how bad the doctors' treatment of V was.

STUDY EXERCISE 2.3

Is it ever fair to allow bad medical treatment by doctors to break the causation chain? If so, how bad would the medical treatment have to be?

The third category of 'third-party intervention' cases involves situations where D has assisted V to take drugs in some way, V has voluntarily taken the drugs, and V has died as a result of taking them. On the basis of the discussion above, D should not be guilty of causing V's death because V has taken the drugs of their own free will, and so the chain of causation has been broken. This was what was decided in *Dalby* [1982] 1 All ER 916. After some uncertainty in the law, the House of Lords resolved the confusion in *Kennedy (No. 2)* [2007] 3 WLR 612 by stating that where D prepares drugs and gives them to V to take, and V dies as a result of taking the drugs, D is not guilty of manslaughter as long as V made a 'voluntary and informed' decision to take the drugs.

A fourth category involves V, previously injured by D, contributing to their own death by some kind of neglect or intervention. The basic rule here is that D has to 'take the victim as they find them'. In other words, any physical or psychological characteristics which might make V more vulnerable to being harmed are irrelevant as long as what D did is still a 'substantial and operative cause' of V's death. This principle is illustrated by *Holland* (1841) 2 Mood & R 351, *Blaue* [1975] 3 All ER 446, and *Dear* [1996] Crim LR 595.

Where V is injured, or killed, trying to escape from D, the escape will only break the chain of causation if it was not 'reasonably foreseeable'. So, if an ordinary person who was present at the scene would not have expected V to try to escape, then the chain of causation will be broken (*Pitts* (1842) Car & M 284 and *Roberts* (1971) 56 Cr App Rep 95). However, D must have actually committed a *crime* which caused V to try to escape (*Arobieke* [1988] Crim LR 314). Causation can also be proved where D frightens V to death. D can still be liable for murder or manslaughter in such a case (*Towers* (1874) 12 Cox CC 530 and *Hayward* (1908) 21 Cox CC 692).

Apart from this list of principles of legal causation, there are two other topics that are relevant in this area of the law. These are the issues of *transfer of malice* and *contemporaneity*. These topics will be covered in Chapter 3.

The next step is to examine the relationship between *actus reus* principles and criminal justice practice. The following section uses the roles played by the police and the Crown Prosecution Service as case studies to examine the relationship between *actus reus* in law and in criminal justice. As an introduction, though, the discussion takes a brief look at how crime is defined, and the relationship between the *actus reus* in law and the criminal statistics which form the basis of what is known about crime in England and Wales.

Actus Reus In Criminal Justice Practice

Example I: the construction of crime

As shown in Chapter 1, there is no behaviour which is automatically criminal. Behaviour must be criminalised in either common law or statute law, and a range of individuals, social groups and factors play a part in deciding which behaviour will be outlawed by the criminal law, and become an *actus reus*. The key players in this process are summarised by Lacey et al. (2003: 78–80). First, the public and their opinions play a part, not just in their voting for politicians and governments which introduce new laws, and the importance attached to appealing to public opinion on acceptable and unacceptable behaviour by politicians (Bottoms 1995), but also in terms of how they report some crimes more than others, perceive some kinds of behaviour as being more dangerous than others (Lacey 1995) and fear certain types of criminal behaviour more than others (Hope and Sparks 2000). The media also plays a crucial part in both shaping public opinion on crime and reporting it (Jewkes 2004). Secondly, Parliament, judges, magistrates and their clerks all create and interpret the meaning of *actus reus* in practice. Thirdly, the Home Office and the Ministry of Justice introduce and develop new criminal laws and policies.

Fourthly, the power of the Attorney-General and the Director for Public Prosecutions to allow particular types of prosecution to be brought gives them power to determine what is and is not *actus reus*. Next, the Lord Chief Justice, the senior criminal judge in England and Wales, plays a key role in developing sentencing policy as well as hearing criminal appeal cases – both of these help to determine the shape of *actus reus*. Finally, pressure groups such as Liberty, the pro-human rights organisation, the Law Commission, and the Association of Chief Police Officers (ACPO) all put forward their own views on how the criminal law should look. All of these different individuals and agencies play a key part in the development of *actus reus* and how it is applied in criminal justice practice.

How accurately do the crime statistics that are available from the government (and other sources) reflect the number of '*actus reuses*' which are committed in England and Wales? Crime statistics are published annually by the Home Office. They are taken from two main sources: police statistics – the crimes recorded by the police and then divided up into different types of offence; and the British Crime Survey (BCS) – the results of a survey asking a selected group of adults in England and Wales about their experiences of being victims of crime over the previous year (Coleman and Moynihan 1996). Police statistics for 2006/07 recorded around 5 million crimes in England and Wales, while BCS figures for the same time period recorded around 11 million crimes, a decrease of 42% from the peak BCS figure in 1995 (Thorpe et al. 2007: 18).

These crime statistics are often portrayed as being an accurate representation of all the crime, or all of the '*actus reuses*', that exist in England and Wales at any given time – for example, by the tabloid press – but the reality is very different. As Mayhew (2007) points out, not only do the police not record all of the crime that is reported to them – because they feel it is too minor or too vague to be put into a specific category of crime, for example – but also there is a substantial 'dark figure' of crime which is not reported to the police at all. Also, there have been changes in what crime is actually counted by police – only 'notifiable offences' are included. For example, in 1998, common assaults were counted as 'notifiable offences' for the first time, and each crime was recorded individually for each victim rather than recording only the most serious of a series of crimes between the same offender and victim. Both of these changes had the effect of increasing the amount of crime in the police statistics (Jones 2005: 62). As a result, there is a clear gap between the criminal law and what is known about when it is broken in the criminal justice process, in terms of police statistics.

The British Crime Survey also has its weaknesses in terms of how accurately it measures crime. While the BCS does pick up some of the 'dark figure' of crime which is not reported to the police, there are several other categories of crime which it does not cover – for example, crimes committed against children, 'victimless' crimes such as drug-dealing, and crimes against businesses (Maguire 2007: 268). As a result, neither the BCS nor the police statistics can measure the full extent of *actus reus* being committed. They simply give a partial picture of it, in different ways (because of the different sources of data and the different categories of crime the data is broken down into). Like crime itself, crime statistics are social constructions, and what is counted 'in' or 'out' can and does change over time. This supports the view that both crime and crime statistics reflect not only changes in society's views on what should and should not be criminalised, and liberal views on the maximisation of individual people's freedom to live their lives as they wish, but also the interests of the powerful and their attempts to hold on to their position of power in society (Lacey 2007).

Since the BCS picks up more crime than the police-recorded crime statistics, is there any point in continuing to collect the police statistics? Explain your answer.

The next section of the chapter considers the relationship between *actus reus* and the police, as an example of the role played by *actus reus* in the criminal justice process.

Example II: *actus reus*, the police[1] and PACE

This subsection of the chapter examines how the public police use *actus reus* in criminal justice practice.

Actus reus and the police: PACE powers and the 'gap' between actus reus and criminal justice

The power of the police to intervene in people's lives to enforce the criminal law, in terms of powers to stop, search, arrest, detain and interrogate those it suspects of committing an *actus reus*, is largely governed by the Police and Criminal Evidence Act 1984 (hereafter 'PACE'). PACE sets out the police's powers in legislation, and widened many of them (Ashworth and Redmayne 2005: 9), but also introduced formal 'rights' for defendants for the first time, attempting to reach a balance between crime control and due process.

For example, s. 1 of PACE allows police officers to stop and search persons and vehicles if they have a reasonable suspicion that they will find either stolen or prohibited articles, but PACE Code of Practice A gives protection against its abuse by police. For example, stops and searches must be based on objective evidence, and cannot be carried out merely as a result of prejudice on age, gender, racial or other grounds (Home Office 2005a: para. 2.2). Under s. 110 of the Serious Organised Crime and Police Act 2005, which replaces s. 24 of PACE, a police officer can arrest someone without a warrant for any offence which that person is committing or about to commit, or for any offence which the officer reasonably suspects that person is committing or about to commit. But these powers can only be used where a police officer has reasonable grounds for believing that one of a list of reasons applies, including preventing the suspect from causing injury or damage. PACE Code of Practice G emphasises that the use of the power of arrest must be necessary, and that officers must consider whether less intrusive ways of

---

[1]It should be noted that writers such as Zedner (2004) see 'policing' as involving a wider range of groups and organisations than the public police, including policing activities by the general public, and by private policing and security firms. This discussion focuses only on the public police, what is known about their criminal law enforcement practice, and how it relates to the law itself.

achieving their objectives can be used instead (Home Office 2005b: para. 1.3). Police also have the basic right to detain suspects (PACE s. 41ff.) and question them (s. 66) but, again, PACE limits these powers in various ways. Suspects must be taken to a police station as soon as possible after being arrested. Once they are at the station, they should be brought to a custody officer as soon as is practicable, and suspects can only be detained for a maximum of 36 hours before either being charged or released (Criminal Justice Act 2003 s. 7, amending PACE ss. 41–42). If more time is required, the police can apply to a magistrates' court to detain the suspect for further 'blocks' of 36 hours, up to a maximum of 96 hours (PACE ss. 43–44). Throughout the custody period, the suspect's detention should be reviewed by a custody officer (i.e. a senior police officer), after six hours initially, and then every nine hours after that.

There has been a great deal of debate among criminologists about how well PACE works in terms of balancing crime control and due process. One body of critical research has argued that PACE has done very little to close the gap between criminal law and criminal justice in terms of the response to *actus reus*es that the police are aware of. McConville et al. (1991) argued that PACE had very little impact on the police's behaviour in terms of stretching the concept of criminal behaviour in the form of *actus reus*. Instead, the police's 'working rules', or patterns of using their informal discretion, were what mattered in terms of how the criminal law was used. These working rules were based around the 'crime control' approach to criminal justice, whereby obtaining as many convictions as possible was prioritised, even if this meant some innocent people being convicted along the way. They pointed out that the police were a prosecution agency, and aimed to construct a case for the prosecution focusing on evidence that pointed to guilt, rather than all available evidence (including evidence that suggested innocence). They argued, as a result, that detention of suspects was automatically authorised, as custody officers tended not to question what other officers claimed, and that suspects were either informed of their rights at the police station in a way that they did not understand, or were not informed of their rights at all (ibid.). They also highlighted the key role of confession evidence in the process of crime control, since this removes or greatly reduces the need for supporting evidence indicating guilt (Sanders and Young 2006: 273) as well removing the need for the case to go to trial at court (which in turn saves time and money). On this view, the way in which the police uses *actus reus* in practice could breach s. 6 of the Human Rights Act, which requires them to comply with the ECHR, because of the challenges to Article 3 (the right not to be treated inhumanely, which could be threatened by aggressive interrogation tactics) and Article 5 (the right to liberty, which could be threatened by deliberately keeping suspects in custody in an attempt to obtain confessions).

On the other hand, other criminologists believe that while PACE has faced problems in reducing wrongful use of police discretionary powers, and thereby reducing the gap between *actus reus* and its accurate detection in criminal justice, it has had a positive impact on police practices. Brown (1997), for example, argues that in the first 10 years of PACE's operation, there was an increase in the percentage of suspects receiving free legal advice – to around one-third of all suspects. He also claims that the use of illegal tactics to extract confessions or incriminating evidence appeared to have declined during this time, and that the tape-recording of interviews had become standard practice. This suggests that PACE has not only reduced the amount of police discretion, but has also led to police using their powers to reduce miscarriages of justice and unfair tactics.

Dixon (1997) points out that PACE has had some effects, such as the fact that suspects are almost always informed of their rights on arrival at police station, and so it is overstating things to claim, as McConville et al. (1991) do, that law can do very little to change police culture, attitudes and behaviour. Maguire (2002), meanwhile, while acknowledging the difficulties PACE has had in changing usage of police discretion in practice – for example, in terms of implementing independent checks on police activity while detaining and questioning suspects – points out that PACE has been valuable in introducing a clear legal structure for police activities which was lacking before its implementation. Morgan (1995) also criticises the arguments of McConville et al., claiming that their study deliberately highlights evidence which shows the police (and PACE's influence) in a negative light, and plays down evidence which suggests that PACE had made a difference to police behaviour in their study.

STUDY EXERCISE 2.5

Given the research evidence on PACE discussed in this subsection, do you think current government proposals to allow the police to detain terrorism suspects for 42 days without charge are necessary to fight back against serious crime, or a dangerous limitation of civil liberties which could lead to more miscarriages of justice? Give reasons for your answer.

Actus reus *and the police: causation and criminal investigation*

Causation, as shown above, is an essential element in investigating and detecting the *actus reus* of crimes, especially result crimes. In doing these activities, police must gather evidence that particular suspects have caused an outcome which is prohibited by the criminal law, satisfying the factual causation principles which were discussed earlier in this chapter. There are a range of different types of evidence which the police can use to build a case. Newburn (2007: 605–6) lists the main categories of forensic evidence:

- Fingerprints – either impressions in soft materials, visible fingerprints (e.g. blood or ink stains containing prints), or prints left on a surface (e.g. glass);
- DNA – taken from various sources (e.g. skin or blood), and recovered by swabbing or scraping stains, or by recovering an item suspected to contain DNA;
- The National DNA database which has now been set up.

These add to other types of evidence which the police can gather, such as ballistic evidence to show whether a gun has been fired, documentary evidence such as letters, and 'real' evidence, that is objects which are relevant as evidence.

There is therefore a wide r[...] [...]e can use to establish that an *actus re*[...] [...]e establishment of the National D[...] [...]e database contained 3,785,571 sa[...] [...]he world (Home Office 2006). S[...] [...]nds s. 63 of PACE to allow the p[...] [...]s arrested for a recordable offenc[...] [...]cted. The increased power to gathe[...] [...] convicted of an offence has arguably [...] g substantial and operative factual and le[...] [...]. Government statistics show that in 2004/05, [...] [...]etected as a result of further investigations linked to the [...] [...]n DNA was recovered, and the National Database provided the police with 3,000 case matches per month on average (Home Office 2005c).

Research such as this suggests that new techniques of evidence-gathering are closing the gap between *actus reus*es which are committed and criminal justice. For example, they enable the police to solve 'cold cases' where crimes have been committed years before, but for which no one was convicted, such as the so-called 'Wearside Jack' case in which a phone hoaxer misled police who were investigating the Yorkshire Ripper murders. However, no evidence is 100% reliable in terms of from where or from whom it came. This is the case whether the evidence in question is 'traditional' evidence, such as handwriting or firearms examination, or even apparently more exact sources of evidence, such as fingerprints and DNA, which are often portrayed by those using them as unique and unproblematic (Broeders 2007). An example of DNA evidence leading to an innocent person being wrongly accused of committing an *actus reus* is the case of Raymond Easton, who was charged with burglary in 1999 after his DNA sample matched one taken at the crime scene on six test points, even though it was physically impossible for him to have committed the crime.

It is therefore clear that while advances in evidence-gathering technology have created new opportunities for the police to establish causation, and therefore to match *actus reus*es with the people who committed them, there is still scope for 'wrong turnings' in the establishment of evidence in a case. The strength and reliability of evidence are also key questions when considering the role and practice of the Crown Prosecution Service, discussed in the next section.

Example III: *actus reus* and the Crown Prosecution Service

The Crown Prosecution Service (hereafter 'CPS') decides whether or not a case should proceed to the court stage after the police have charged a suspect, and selects appropriate charges in cases which it does take to court. The police consult their local CPS branch before deciding whether or not to charge a suspect, and pass on details of the case to the CPS. The local Principal Crown Prosecutor then allocates the case to a member of their team, and only the Principal Crown

Prosecutor has the power to decide whether or not to continue with the case. Next, the CPS must provide a constant review of the progress made with each case, in terms of the quantity and quality of evidence obtained. Finally, the CPS makes the decision whether or not to prosecute, using the *Code for Crown Prosecutors* (e.g. Crown Prosecution Service 2004) as a guide. They use two key tests: whether or not there is sufficient evidence to provide a realistic prospect of conviction if the case reaches court, and whether or not prosecution is in the public interest. The CPS's task, in principle, is to 'close the gap' between *actus reus* in the law and criminal justice, in two ways: by ensuring that there is enough evidence to prove that the right person is matched up with an *actus reus*, and ensuring that an appropriate offence charge is found to match the criminal behaviour committed.

HM Crown Prosecution Inspectorate (2005) found that in 2004/05, 98% of prosecuted cases in England and Wales met the evidential test, and that 99% of cases met the public interest test. However, other evidence suggests that the CPS faces operational and institutional problems which limit its effectiveness in bringing *actus reus* and criminal justice closer together. One problem is the *Code for Crown Prosecutors* itself. In theory, it is supposed to provide all of the guidance that CPS workers need to make the decision on whether or not to prosecute. Yet Hoyano et al. (1997) found that the language used in the *Code* has become more and more simplified each time that a new version of the *Code* is published. They identified the lack of clarity in explanations of the policies CPS workers should follow as a key factor for their finding that the *Code* had very little impact on decisions made by the CPS day to day.

The tests used to decide whether or not to prosecute have also been criticised as unhelpful. The *Code* (CPS 2004) defines the 'realistic prospect of conviction' test as being an objective test: is a court more likely than not to convict on the basis of the evidence available, based on the admissibility and reliability of that evidence? Yet this test oversimplifies the wide discretion which courts have to decide on admissibility of evidence, and to decide the facts of the case in different ways. Similarly, the 'public interest' test hides the reality of the greater number of evidential factors in favour of prosecution than against it, the presumption in favour of prosecution unless there are factors present which are against prosecution, and the CPS reliance on (sometimes very limited) police information on whether prosecution would be in the public interest or not (McConville et al. 1991).

Other research indicates that the CPS takes cases which are evidentially weak to court more often than the evidence from HM Crown Prosecution Inspectorate (see above) suggests. In Baldwin's (1997) study, early warning signs about prosecutions ending in acquittal in court were noticed by the CPS in 87.3% of the judge-ordered acquittals,[2] 73.1% of the judge-directed acquittals,[3] and 58.8% of acquittals by a jury in the Crown Court. Problems have also arisen regarding the

---

[2] Where a judge orders that the defendant is acquitted before the jury has been sworn in at the start of a Crown Court trial – for example, because the CPS has offered no evidence to the court.
[3] Where a judge directs the jury to acquit the defendant during the course of a trial.

accountability of the CPS for its decisions. Ashworth and Redmayne (2005) show that weaknesses have been found in terms of recording CPS decisions, and in terms of communication of vital information from person to person within the CPS.

STUDY EXERCISE 2.6

Read the CPS explanation on their website of their decision not to prosecute any police officers in connection with the death of Frank Ogboru on 26 September 2006 (at www.cps.gov.uk/news/press_releases/132_08). Applying the two CPS prosecution tests, do you agree with the CPS decision reached in this case? Explain your answer.

The next section of this chapter considers how victims of crime who report *actus reus*es to criminal justice agencies are dealt with by the police and CPS.

Example IV: *actus reus*, victims of crime and criminal justice

Actus reus, *victims and the police*

The reporting of crime to criminal justice agencies by victims is vital in 'closing the gap' between the occurrence of the *actus reus* and the prosecution, conviction and punishment of people for breaking the law, since most crimes come to the police's attention via the public, and victims of crime play a vital role in giving evidence in court which forms the basis of successful prosecution. As the discussion of crime statistics above showed, there is a gap between the number of *actus reus*es experienced by victims and the number which are recorded by the police. The BCS indicates that when a 'comparable subset' of BCS and police crime categories is considered, only 42% of comparable crime included in the BCS is reported to the police, and only 30% of comparable crime is recorded by the police. Clarkson et al. (1994) identified key reasons for victims not reporting crimes to the police as including the victim's perception that their crime is not detectable, the victim's reluctance to have their own conduct scrutinised, and fear of reprisals.

Some criminologists (e.g. Shapland et al. 1985) argue that the police have traditionally been slow to recognise the needs of victims who report their crimes, especially victims who are vulnerable because of their age, gender, ethnicity, or class. Reeves and Mulley (2000) found that the support and information that police provided to victims varied greatly from police force to police force, depending on other police work and priorities, such as the detection and investigation of crime. Research done into the impact of other police-led initiatives designed to make reporting crime easier for victims has also had mixed results. For example, the Second Victim's Charter (1996) introduced a pilot victim statement scheme, which allowed selected victims to make a statement to police explaining how the crime committed against them had affected their lives. This statement could later be used in court. Sanders et al. (2001) found that of 148 victims who made statements, 77% of victims thought making a statement was the right thing to do at the start of the criminal process, compared with 57% at the end. Sanders et al. concluded from these findings that victims experienced a great deal of dissatisfaction as a result of victim statements, and had often had their expectations falsely raised by statements. However, other research has found more positive effects for victim statements. Chalmers et al.'s (2007) evaluation of a Scottish pilot project based around a written statement made by the victim to the police and passed on to the judge hearing the victim's court case found that while only 14% of eligible victims made a statement, 86% of the victims taking part thought that making a statement was the right thing to do at the end of their case. These conflicting research studies show the impact of police discretion – at individual, force and national level – in deciding how far victims' needs during the giving of information about an *actus reus* will be met, and also show the importance of good communication between police and victims about the processes of criminal justice.

▬▬▬▬▬▬▬▬▬▬ STUDY EXERCISE 2.7 ▬▬▬▬▬▬▬▬▬▬

Read the articles by Sanders et al. (2001) and Chalmers et al. (2007). On the basis of the research findings reported in these two articles, would you make a victim statement if you had the opportunity to do so?

▬▬▬▬▬▬▬▬▬▬▬▬▬▬▬▬▬▬▬▬▬▬▬▬▬▬▬▬▬▬▬▬

Actus reus, *victims and the CPS*

Measures have recently been introduced that try to improve communication between the CPS and victims, and aim to make victims a central part of criminal justice. For example, CPS *Codes for Crown Prosecutors* from 2000 onwards (e.g. CPS 2004) state that the CPS must take the victim's views into account when deciding whether or not to prosecute in a particular case, and the *Attorney-General's Guidelines on the Acceptance of Pleas*, issued to all CPS workers, states that the victim's interests must also be considered before the prosecution accepts a guilty plea from a defendant in court (Attorney-General's Office 2005).

However, the victim's interest must be balanced against the CPS's main two tests for deciding whether or not to prosecute a case – that is the public interest in prosecution and the prospect of a realistic conviction. These tests will take priority over the interests of the victim and, if there is a conflict between the two, would be decisive in reaching a decision on prosecution. Also, as Sanders (2002) points out, these guidelines do not cover victims whose cases are handled by other prosecution agencies, such as the Health and Safety Executive, rather than by the CPS.

Discussion and Conclusions

Actus reus has been developed and portrayed as a way of holding individual people responsible for behaviour that the criminal law states is wrong. The emphasis on acts being voluntary and requiring *mens rea* to go with them, for example, points to the criminal law view of *actus reus* being a liberal one – only blaming people for behaviour which has been a conscious decision to break the law, allowing all other conduct to go unpunished, and allowing individuals to remain free from any social or political interference as long as they do not break the law (Norrie 2001). This also fits in with the law and economics approach, which emphasises that people commit crimes of their own free will.

However, *actus reus* can also involve being somewhere or possessing something which the criminal law will not allow, even where, as in *Larsonneur* or *Winzar*, there was no voluntary decision to go to the 'forbidden' place. Similarly, the criminal law also punishes people for omissions, in certain limited circumstances – for example, where someone fails to protect a vulnerable person in their care (*Downes, Stone and Dobinson*), or where someone does not do what their job requires them to do (*Pittwood, Dytham*). None of these scenarios would be punished under an entirely liberal criminal law. Instead, they offer evidence that *actus reus* can also be used paternalistically, to protect vulnerable people in society from being harmed by others who do not do what is expected of them. But these social uses of *actus reus*, which depend on ties between people being wrongly broken, are hidden by the general liberal principles commonly associated with *actus reus* (Norrie 2001).

If causation is re-examined, *actus reus* is again not as liberal as it first appears. Factual, 'but for' causation is a liberal idea – people are only held responsible for their *actus reus* if the prohibited outcome would not have happened if they had not done what they did. If D voluntarily changes the course of V's life, for example by killing or injuring V, then it is right to hold D responsible in the criminal law for what happens to V as a result of their actions, unless a third person's voluntary act intervenes to break the chain (Hart and Honoré 1985). However, as Norrie (2001) points out, this does not take into account the social circumstances that shape the decisions and actions made and done by individual people in their everyday lives. It does not try to understand *why* the individual has done what they have done.

Considering legal causation, the liberalism of *actus reus* is limited even further. The courts have decided that doctors should not be held liable for breaking the causation chain between D and V, even where they treat V very badly (*Smith, Cheshire*), unless their treatment was 'palpably bad' (*Jordan*). This shows that *actus reus* is about something more than protecting the vulnerable in society. It is also about regulating the social order, and making moral judgements about the behaviour of certain types of 'socially acceptable' people, regardless of their liability under liberal principles (Norrie 2001). Overall, then, the core of *actus reus* may claim to be liberal and individualistic, but in fact this hides a variety of criminal law aims, some of which contradict each other and promote divisions and discrimination in society (Norrie 2005).

Turning now to criminal justice, there is a considerable gap between every *actus reus* that occurs in England and Wales and the response to them from criminal justice. As well as crime itself being a social construction, the criminal statistics that claim to measure the number of crimes are in no way an accurate representation of crime, due to limitations on what is reported to and recorded by police and the

BCS. Again, therefore, the liberal and positivist view of crime statistics as being an accurate picture of crime hides a range of social issues which decide which *actus reus* will be included in criminal statistics and which will not.

In terms of how the police and the CPS use the rules on *actus reus* set out in the liberally-centred criminal law, and how they use the rules for deciding when to use the power of criminal justice against the public, there is a body of evidence, spearheaded by McConville et al. (1991), that argues that the legal rules (such as PACE), which claim to structure what the police and the CPS do, have very little impact in practice. The evidence of McConville et al. suggests that police and CPS work is more about crime control than due process and human rights. Others, such as Choongh (1997), argue that the police use their power to extend social control and social exclusion as far as possible. However, work such as that by Dixon (1997) argues that due process-based law can have, and has had, an impact on criminal justice practice by structuring that practice according to a set of rules, and reducing the misuse of power. This suggests that criminal justice, like criminal law, has a conflicting set of aims in terms of how it uses *actus reus*. Sometimes due process wins, but at other times criminal justice practice is characterised by the crime control or power models. On this view, criminal justice is best characterised as 'a related but not entirely co-ordinated set of practices geared to the construction and maintenance of social order' (Lacey 1994: 28). This conflict and confusion is particular significant for victims, who have a set of needs of their own when they inform criminal justice of an *actus reus* that has affected their lives, but who must fit in with the wider aims of the criminal justice process as reflected in the daily practice of the police and the CPS – aims which can be very different from their own, and the conflict over which can lead to victims' expectations being frustrated in their dealings with the police and CPS.

The next chapter applies the same analytical approach to *mens rea*, in terms of its legal and criminal justice context.

FURTHER READING

Allen, M. (2007), *Criminal Law* (9th edn): chapter 2. Oxford: Oxford University Press.

Ashworth, A., and Redmayne, M. (2005), *The Criminal Process* (3rd edn). Oxford: Oxford University Press.

Dignan, J. (2005), *Understanding Victims and Restorative Justice*. Maidenhead: Open University Press.

Sanders, A., and Young, R. (2006), *Criminal Justice* (3rd edn). Oxford: Oxford University Press.

Simester, A.P., and Sullivan, R. (2007), *Criminal Law: Theory and Doctrine* (3rd edn): chapter 4. Oxford: Hart.

Mens rea

Chapter Aims

After reading Chapter 3 you should be able to understand:

- The meanings of intent in the criminal law
- The meanings of recklessness in the criminal law
- The role of negligence as *mens rea*
- The individuals and agencies which play a key role in the court trial process
- How these key players use *mens rea* in criminal justice practice
- How victims of crime who give evidence on *mens rea* in court are treated by the court process
- How the evidence on *mens rea* in the criminal law and criminal justice fits in with the theoretical models introduced in Chapter 1

Introduction

Chapter 3 continues the explanation of the basic rules of criminal liability in England and Wales. Here, the concept of *mens rea* will be explained and analysed. The first part of this chapter uses case law and statute law to explain the rules of *mens rea* in more detail. The second part of the chapter then uses the key legal principles as a platform for discussing and analysing the ways in which the concept of *mens rea* is understood and applied by the criminal justice process. Here, the focus will be on criminal courts and their operation.

Mens Rea: The Law

Making sense of *mens rea*

DEFINITION BOX 3.1

MENS REA

The internal mental thoughts or attitude which have to be present in the mind of D, at the time they are committing the *actus reus*, to prove guilt for particular criminal offences.

Literally, '*mens rea*' means 'guilty mind'. It refers to the internal thoughts which, when combined with *actus reus*, make up the definition of the most serious crimes – in other words, what D is thinking or planning at the time when they are committing the offence. Not all crimes require *mens rea*, though. Crimes which are known as strict liability offences only require *actus reus* for at least one element of the offence. These will be discussed further in Chapter 5. The different meanings of *mens rea* in the criminal law will be explained next.

Intent

DEFINITION BOX 3.2

CRIMINAL INTENT

The type of *mens rea* which is defined *either* by D's planning of or decision to commit the *actus reus*, *or* by D's foresight of the *actus reus* occurring as a result of their actions as a virtually certain consequence.

Direct and oblique intent

Some offences can only be committed with intent as *mens rea*, for example, murder or theft. There are two types of intent in the criminal law. The first is *direct intent*. This occurs where D aims, desires, or makes the decision to bring about a particular consequence which is prohibited (*Mohan* [1976] QB 1). Where there is evidence beyond reasonable doubt that D wanted to commit a particular crime, or tried or made an effort to make the crime happen, they have direct intent, and intent is proved.

However, intent also has another meaning in the criminal law in England and Wales. This is known as either *indirect intent* or *oblique intent*. This is proved where there is evidence beyond reasonable doubt that D did not have direct intent, but did foresee a chance that the crime might happen as a result of what they did. The question is: how much of a chance of the crime happening does D have to foresee before intent is proved? This is a vitally important question where the crime which D is accused of can only be proved with intent as *mens rea*, such as murder. If D does not have enough foresight of the prohibited consequence, they cannot be found guilty of the crime.

The House of Lords have struggled to define the boundary between indirect intent and recklessness in the murder cases of *Moloney* [1985] 1 AC 905, *Hancock and Shankland* [1986] 1 AC 455, and then *Nedrick* [1986] 1 WLR 1025, which tried to consolidate the guidelines set out in the two previous cases. It said that juries were only entitled to find indirect intent where D foresaw the prohibited outcome as *virtually certain*, taking into account the 'naturalness' of the prohibited outcome as a result of D's actions (from the *Moloney* test) and the level of probability of the prohibited outcome as a result of D's actions (from the *Hancock* test). If D realised the outcome was 'almost inevitable', that would be strong evidence that indirect intent was there. But foresight of death or GBH was still only *evidence* – it was still up to the jury to decide whether or not it actually amounted to intent in each case, on the basis of the evidence that had been presented to them during the trial.

The House of Lords attempted to confirm the *Nedrick* guidelines in *Woollin* [1998] 3 WLR 382, but Lord Steyn appeared to define the scope of indirect intent in two different ways at different points in his speech. First, he said that foresight of virtual certainty is intent in itself, so that the jury has no discretion on this issue, and must find intent and convict if they find evidence of this level of foresight. But later he said that foresight of virtual certainty is only evidence from which a jury *can* infer intent, but do not *have* to – so on this reading the jury's discretion is still there. *Matthews and Alleyne* [2003] 2 Cr App Rep 30 decided that *Woollin* did not take away the jury's discretion on finding intent, so that foresight of virtual certainty is only evidence from which juries can infer intent, but do not have to. As the law currently stands, therefore:

- The lower limit of indirect intent is foresight by D of the prohibited outcome as a virtually certain result of their actions;
- If D does not have this level of foresight, there cannot be any intent;
- But even where foresight of a virtual certainty is proved, the jury do not have to convict;
- And if a jury finds that D has foreseen the prohibited outcome as a 'morally certain' outcome of their actions (meaning that the level of foresight is higher than a virtual certainty), then under *Moloney* they have to convict.

STUDY EXERCISE 3.1

How easy does the law's current definition of intent make it for juries to understand what intent means legally?

Intent and motive

DEFINITION BOX 3.3

CRIMINAL MOTIVE

D's reason(s) for intentionally committing the *actus reus* of a crime.

The criminal law has stated that D's good motive is irrelevant as long as they have the intent required, so that D would still be guilty if they intentionally committed a crime for a good reason. In *Yip Chiu-Cheung v R* [1995] 1 AC 111, it was decided that an undercover police officer, if he had been prosecuted, would have been guilty of conspiracy because he had planned to smuggle drugs with D, even though the police officer only did this in an attempt to trap and arrest D in the act of smuggling the drugs (see also *Sood* [1998] EWCA Crim 254). But in *Steane* [1947] KB 997, it was decided that D was not guilty of assisting the enemy during wartime even though he intentionally made radio broadcasts for the Nazis during the Second World War because his intention was judged to be saving his family from being sent to a concentration camp, rather than assisting the enemy.

STUDY EXERCISE 3.2

Should the law ever take good motive into account? If so, in what circumstances should it be considered?

Transfer of malice
Where D has the right *actus reus* and *mens rea* for a particular criminal offence, but the offence has a different 'target' (either a person or property) from the one that D intended to hit, then D is still guilty of the offence (*Latimer* (1886) 17 QBD 359). This is known as the transfer of malice principle. However, the principle does not work where D has the *actus reus* of one crime but the *mens rea* of another because they have missed the 'target' (*Pembliton* (1874) LR 2 CCR 119).

Contemporaneity
Generally, the *actus reus* and the *mens rea* of an offence must happen at the same time in order for D to be guilty of that offence. However, if the *actus reus* is a continuing act and D has the right *mens rea* during that continuing act, then D can still be guilty. In *Thabo-Meli* [1954] 1 WLR 228, D was guilty of murder where he attacked V with a wooden club and then threw V over a cliff, thinking V was already dead. In fact V died later from exposure at the bottom of the cliff. D's *actus reus* was held to be continuing from when he first attacked V until after he had thrown V over the cliff, and as he had the right *mens rea* (intent to do grievous

bodily harm or kill) during this continuing act, he was guilty of murder. This principle has also been applied to unlawful act manslaughter in *Church* [1966] 1 QB 59 and *Le Brun* [1991] 4 All ER 673, and to non-fatal assaults in *Fagan v Metropolitan Police Commissioner* [1969] 1 QB 439 and *Santana-Bermudez* [2004] Crim LR 471. Both of these offences will be discussed later in this book. In *Attorney-General's Reference (No. 4 of 1980)* [1981] 1 WLR 705, one of several acts committed by D caused V's death, but it could not be confirmed which one actually had. The court said that this did not matter as long as each act was enough to establish a conviction for manslaughter, which was true in this case.

Next, the discussion will consider the meaning of recklessness in the criminal law.

Recklessness

DEFINITION BOX 3.4

CRIMINAL RECKLESSNESS

The type of *mens rea* that is defined by D's taking of an unjustifiable risk which causes an *actus reus* to occur.

Some crimes, as shown above, need intent as *mens rea*, but other crimes can be committed either intentionally or recklessly. Recklessness is not about aiming or meaning to commit a crime, but instead only requires taking a risk that the crime will be committed as a result of D's actions. Not every risk of a crime being committed will be punished by the criminal law, though. The risk needed for criminal liability must be unjustifiable. Whether a risk is justifiable or not is decided based upon how socially beneficial taking that risk is (Ormerod 2008: 108).

The law on criminal recklessness is there to punish people who take 'stupid risks' which end up causing damage or harm. There are two specific types of recklessness that need to be distinguished. The first type of recklessness is *subjective recklessness*. Subjective recklessness is proved where D foresaw a risk of the *actus reus* of the crime occurring (damage, injury, etc.), but took that risk anyway, resulting in the causing of the *actus reus*. This type of recklessness was used in the case of *Cunningham* [1957] 2 QB 396. The second type of recklessness is *objective recklessness*. Objective recklessness is proved where a reasonable person in D's position would have foreseen an *obvious* and *serious* risk of the *actus reus* occurring as a result of the risk that D took. It also includes subjective recklessness as described above. This type of recklessness was defined in the cases of *Caldwell* [1982] AC 341 and *Lawrence* [1982] AC 510. The objective type of recklessness labels a wider range of behaviour as being criminally blameworthy than the subjective type because there is no need for D to have actually foreseen the risk of causing the *actus reus* under the objective test, as long as a reasonable person in D's position would have seen an obvious and serious risk. Under the subjective test, if D did not foresee a risk of the *actus reus* being caused, there can be no recklessness.

Before *Caldwell*, the courts applied the subjective recklessness test to cases of assault (*Cunningham* itself) and criminal damage (*Stephenson* [1979] 1 QB 695; cf. *Parker* (1976) 63 Cr App Rep 211) as well as to other crimes which could be committed recklessly. After *Caldwell*, the courts began to apply the wider objective recklessness test instead of the subjective recklessness test for offences such as criminal damage. But G [2003] 3 WLR 1060 overruled *Caldwell* for cases of criminal damage. In this important case, the House of Lords gave a range of reasons for preferring the subjective recklessness test to the objective recklessness test. These included:

- Subjective recklessness is based around what Ds were actually thinking about at the time of the offence, or their 'blameworthy' thoughts. This makes punishing people for crimes on the basis of their recklessness fairer, especially for serious crimes, because they have seen the risk of what could happen as a result of their behaviour, but continued with that behaviour regardless.
- Subjective recklessness avoids discrimination against those who cannot see the risks they create for reasons that are not their fault, such as children and the mentally ill. Both of these groups were convicted and punished under objective recklessness (e.g. *Elliott v C* [1983] 1 WLR 939, *Bell* [1984] 3 All ER 842) because although they could not understand the 'obvious and serious' risks which they were taking, a reasonable person in their position would have seen those risks – so again, bringing back the subjective recklessness test would be fairer on vulnerable people in society, in terms of not punishing them for taking risks which they did not realise they were taking. Such an approach could meet concerns about the criminal law breaching Article 6 of the ECHR (the right to a fair hearing) by convicting the vulnerable on the basis of risks which they could not have foreseen.
- Subjective recklessness also avoids the confusion of a necessary feature of objective recklessness – the so-called 'lacuna'. This is another way of saying that there is a 'loophole' in the law allowing some Ds to escape liability. Here, what the lacuna means is that where D sees the risk but thinks they have eliminated it completely (but in fact have not done so), then they cannot be objectively reckless because they have foreseen the risk, but they cannot be subjectively reckless either because they have not 'gone ahead' with the risk. The loophole was never successfully used to avoid liability in a case, but in cases like *Chief Constable of Avon and Somerset v Shimmen* (1986) 84 Cr App Rep 7 its applicability was considered.
- Finally, juries (and presumably magistrates too) can be trusted to tell whether a D is telling the truth or not if they claim not to have seen the risk, based on the evidence of D's actions.

However, objective recklessness has not disappeared completely. If D is voluntarily intoxicated because they have taken alcohol or other drugs of their own free will, and committed a crime while intoxicated, then they are treated in law as having foreseen the risk and gone ahead anyway, even if their intoxication meant that they did not actually see the risk themselves (*Bennett* [1995] Crim LR 877). This was decided by *Caldwell* itself because in that case D was drunk at the time he committed the criminal damage, and this part of the *Caldwell* decision is still the law even though the case was overruled by G in terms of the law on criminal damage (Herring 2006: 168).

Next, the law on negligence as *mens rea* will be discussed in more detail.

Make a list of the advantages of subjective and objective recklessness. Which do you think should be used by the criminal law, and why? Should the law use them both together, and if so, which should be used in which circumstances?

Negligence

▰▰▰▰▰▰▰▰▰▰▰▰▰▰▰▰▰ DEFINITION BOX 3.5 ▰▰▰▰▰▰▰▰▰▰▰▰▰

CRIMINAL NEGLIGENCE

The type of *mens rea* that is defined by D's behaviour falling below what a reasonable person in D's position would have thought was a reasonable thing to do (or not do), and causing an *actus reus* to occur as a result.

Negligence is about what D does not think about rather than what D does. In other words, negligence is about an objective standard of behaviour, which D falls below and is liable for a criminal offence as a result. It was not formerly used as the *mens rea* for crimes, except for particular categories of offence, such as some driving offences and gross negligence manslaughter. But in recent times, as Clarkson (2005: 74) points out, negligence has been used as the *mens rea* for an increasingly wide range of crimes, especially offences that have become statutory, such as rape under the Sexual Offences Act 2003, and new statutory offences, such as harassment under the Protection from Harassment Act 1997. Negligence also plays a role in the criminal law in relation to strict liability offences, which will be discussed in detail in Chapter 5. Many statutory strict liability offences provide a defence where D has exercised 'due diligence'. In other words, if D can prove that they were not negligent, they will be acquitted.

The second part of this chapter considers how *mens rea* is used in criminal justice practice, using the court process as an example.

Using an Internet statute database, find five other offences which require negligence as *mens rea*. Do you agree that all of the offences that you have found should have this type of *mens rea*?

Mens Rea and Criminal Justice

Example I: *mens rea* and the court trial process

This section uses the example of the pre-sentence court process, and how it operates, to show how *mens rea* works in practice. It takes as the starting point the principle of

Woolmington v DPP [1935] AC 462 that defendants in the court process are innocent until proven guilty beyond reasonable doubt using evidence of their responsibility for an offence in court, and that everyone is treated equally under court justice.

Court trials and pleas

Sanders and Young (2006: chapter 8) show that over 90% of cases in the magistrates' court end up with the defendant either pleading guilty or being found guilty in their absence, and that only around 25% of cases in the Crown Court actually reach the jury trial stage. One reason for the low rate of trials is the problem of so-called 'cracked trials', when the defendant changes their plea to guilty on the day when the trial is due to start, or when the prosecution offers no evidence at this point, and 'ineffective trials', when a trial does not go ahead as planned due to delays caused by the prosecution, defence or the court, and a new hearing has to be scheduled. In 2006, 12.5% of trials in the Crown Court were ineffective and 39.2% were cracked (Ministry of Justice 2007a: 97), while in the magistrates' court, 19.4% of trials were ineffective, and 36.9% were cracked (ibid.: 127). A key factor in the number of cracked trials is the number of last-minute guilty pleas by defendants. In 2006, 53% of the cracked trials in the magistrates' courts were caused by a last-minute change of plea to guilty (ibid.: 127), and 64% of trials in the Crown Court were cracked for the same reason (ibid.: 103). In the Crown Court in 2006, 66% of defendants pleaded guilty (Ministry of Justice 2007b: 12), although 66% of those who did not plead guilty were acquitted (ibid.: 22). In the magistrates' courts in 2006, 74% of defendants whose cases came to court pleaded guilty (ibid.: 26), and 97% of those who pleaded not guilty were convicted, giving a conviction rate of 84% overall (ibid.: 18).

In order to explain the high rate of guilty pleas, some criminologists have argued that in the magistrates' court, the emphasis is on processing cases as quickly as possible, and maintaining social power over the 'criminal classes', rather than making sure that defendants' guilt is proved beyond reasonable doubt (e.g. McBarnet 1981). Parker et al. (1989) pointed to the emphasis on local 'court culture' in magistrates' decision-making rather than on application of the formal rules, and argued that the magistrates in their study tended to be heavily in favour of the prosecution case and conviction. Brown (1991) argued that in deciding on defendants' innocence or guilt in cases, magistrates often stereotyped and depersonalised the facts of each individual offence and offender, to speed up the process of justice.

Sanders and Young (2006) argue that the main reason for the high number of guilty pleas is the amount of pressure that is put on defendants to plead guilty – not only by the prosecution, but also by the defence solicitor or barrister. This pressure can come in the form of plea-bargaining (where a defendant is offered a less serious sentence in exchange for pleading guilty) or charge-bargaining (where the defendant is offered a less serious charge in exchange for pleading guilty). Such pressure could be seen as a breach of the ECHR, particularly Article 6 (the right to a fair hearing). Pressure can be put on defendants by both prosecution and defence lawyers, both to choose a magistrates' rather than a Crown Court trial on the grounds of more lenient sentences, less delays and fewer cost penalties, and to plead guilty even where there are doubts about their legal guilt (Baldwin and McConville 1977). In some court cases, the defendants will be factually guilty of the offence with which they have been charged, and will plead guilty to reflect their responsibility through *mens rea* (and *actus reus*), so as to take advantage of the sentencing discount that an early guilty plea offers them. But research evidence suggests that the court process overall offers the scope for an individual to be put under pressure to plead guilty to an offence for which they did not have the required *mens rea*, through the process of plea-bargaining (McConville 2002). The high rate of guilty pleas is a clear challenge to the idea that a defendant's *mens rea* must be proved beyond reasonable doubt in a court before they can be convicted.

▨▨▨▨▨▨▨▨▨▨▨▨▨ STUDY EXERCISE 3.5 ▨▨▨▨▨▨▨▨▨▨▨▨▨

Spend a morning or afternoon observing cases in a magistrates' court near you. Do you agree with McBarnet (1981) that magistrates are more concerned about resolving cases quickly than about proving defendants' guilt beyond reasonable doubt? What factor(s) influenced your answer?

Bail

Although bail decisions can be made by the police at three points earlier in the criminal justice process (see Hucklesby 2002), the focus here will be on court bail decisions, which again can be made at three different points in the process: when a case is awaiting trial, after conviction but before sentencing, and awaiting the outcome of an appeal against conviction or sentence.

The Bail Act 1976 states that there is a presumption in favour of bail, and contains the grounds which courts must use when restricting or denying bail (in Schedule 1 of the Act). For imprisonable offences, the court must have substantial grounds for believing that if released on unconditional bail, D would fail to attend court, re-offend while on bail, or interfere with witnesses or obstruct the course of justice. For non-imprisonable offences, a court can restrict or deny bail where D has previously failed to comply with bail conditions and the court thinks that this is likely to happen again. The court must provide reasons to support the ground(s) which they have relied on to restrict or deny bail. The Criminal Justice Act 2003 restricts the right to bail in certain circumstances.

The significance of bail legislation and policy for the discussion here is that the restriction or denial of bail presents a direct challenge to the idea that people will not be punished in court until their individual responsibility, in the form of *mens rea*, has been proved in a trial beyond reasonable doubt. Where bail is restricted or denied while someone is awaiting trial, this process has clearly not occurred. As Newburn (2007: 647) points out, the restriction and denial of bail is the limitation of liberty to prevent things happening in the future, rather than punishment for crimes which have already happened, which involves a prediction of behaviour and so increases the chances of getting the decision wrong (Ashworth and Redmayne 2005). This in turn could breach Articles 5 (the right to liberty) and 6 (the right to a fair legal hearing) of the ECHR. Although 72% of cases in the magistrates' court do not require any bail period at all (Ministry of Justice 2007b: 84), in February 2008, 15.3% of the prison population in England and Wales, or 12,646 people, were on remand (Ministry of Justice 2008a: 2).

Not all of those remanded in custody go on to receive a custodial sentence. In fact, in 2006, 52% of cases in the magistrates' courts or Crown Courts received a custodial sentence, while 13% received a community sentence, 17% were acquitted or not proceeded with, and the rest were dealt by fines, discharges or suspended sentences (Ministry of Justice 2007b: 82). Other potential problems in this context include the fact that remand prisoners face the most overcrowded and squalid conditions in prison (Cavadino and Dignan 2007); many bail decisions are made by courts in just a few minutes, suggesting that the evidence is not considered thoroughly; and research has shown that courts making bail decisions are more influenced by the recommendation of the CPS and local decision-making 'court culture' (i.e. the patterns of decision-making which particular individuals or groups of magistrates rely on when considering guilt in cases) than by the bail rules themselves (Hucklesby 1997), although the standardised magistrates' training introduced in England and Wales by the Courts Act 2003 may reduce the influence of 'court culture' in future years.

▬▬▬▬▬▬▬▬▬▬▬▬▬▬▬▬▬▬▬▬▬ STUDY EXERCISE 3.6 ▬▬▬▬▬▬▬▬▬▬▬▬▬▬▬▬▬▬

What kind of bail decision would you make in this case? Focus on the grounds and reasons for your decision under the Bail Act.

Jane is a 38-year-old woman who has been charged with s. 20 GBH. She has no previous criminal convictions. She claims that at the time of the alleged offence she was defending herself against a violent attack from her husband, who has three convictions for assaults against her. Shortly before her arrest she and her 8-year-old son moved out of the family home and are now staying with friends.

▬▬▬

Mode of trial decisions

Of all cases, 98% are tried and sentenced by magistrates in the magistrates' court (Ministry of Justice 2007a: 160), but 91,900 'triable either way' cases were committed for trial to the Crown Court in 2006/07, plus another 20,695 which were committed to Crown Court just for sentencing (Crown Prosecution Service 2007: 87). In fact, around 70% of cases in the Crown Court each year are triable either way, and as Newburn (2007: 650) points out, Crown Court cases take much longer and cost much more than magistrates' court cases, as well as having a high acquittal rate for those pleading not guilty – 66% in 2006 (Ministry of Justice 2007b: 22).

For all these reasons, government policy in recent years has tried to encourage more triable either way cases to be heard at magistrates' courts. Newburn (2007: 650) outlines the key arguments regarding why this development can be seen as challenging the idea that a defendant's *mens rea* will always be judged fairly in court. First, he points to evidence that cases against black defendants tend to be weaker than those against white defendants, and are often charged at a higher level (Phillips and Brown 1998). Therefore Crown Court trials can be seen as a defence against the social harm caused by racial discrimination. Secondly, he points to the 'rather cursory' nature of justice in magistrates' courts (see below). There is also evidence that magistrates' courts can be heavily influenced by local 'court culture' on mode of trial decisions, based around punitive attitudes rather than a straightforward application of the due process rules (Cammiss 2007).

Legal representation in court

As Lacey et al. (2003: 93) note, both prosecution and defence lawyers have considerable influence over the course of the court process, not just through their use of plea-bargaining and charge-bargaining (see above), but also their knowledge of the criminal law itself and the reactions of particular judges or juries, their questioning of witnesses during examination of their own witnesses and cross-examination of the other side's witnesses, and the quality of their preparation for a case. It is the defence solicitor or barrister who has the responsibility of ensuring that the prosecution proves that the defendant has the required *actus reus* and *mens rea* for an offence beyond reasonable doubt.

In terms of preparation for cases, the evidence on its quality is mixed. McConville et al. (1994), for example, found that some defence practices in their study encouraged or created guilty pleas against their client's wishes, or used language in court which made it clear to magistrates that their client was guilty. The solicitors who took this approach did so because they believed certain clients or social groups were guilty, or because they did not want to upset the police or the courts with which they worked. Therefore, there was no point in defending their clients to the full extent.

McConville et al. highlighted poor training as a key reason for defence solicitors not defending their clients' rights strongly enough. Legal aid, the financial support available to defendants to help them secure legal representation in court, has not been used effectively enough by solicitors – an issue which has become more important as the legal aid budget has been cut by the government recently, reducing the number of solicitors which offer legal aid services to defendants (Bridges 2002). While this evidence does not suggest that all defence solicitors ignore due process in their work, it does point to the fact that in practice, court justice has the potential to move away from a pure consideration of a defendant's responsibility for crime through *mens rea*, in favour of saving time and money.

The role of National Probation Service workers who prepare pre-sentence reports (PSRs) must also be mentioned here. PSRs provide magistrates and judges with information about the circumstances of the offender and the offence as well as recommending a sentence. Courts do not have to request a PSR for adult offenders if they do not think it is necessary, and around 15% of adults offenders are sent to prison without one (Charles et al. 1997). PSR proposals for custody doubled between 1990 and 2000 (Cavadino and Dignan 2007: 109). More will be said about probation work in Chapter 5.

Evidence

Evidence plays a crucial role in understanding the links between *mens rea* in the criminal law and how it is used in criminal justice practice, especially because, as Davies et al. (2005: 279) point out, *mens rea* involves what is going on in D's head at the time of the offence, and the easiest way to prove this is through evidence of D's external behaviour at that time. Both the prosecution and the defence can call and examine witnesses on their side, as well as cross-examining witnesses on the other side, to help them to disprove the other side's version of events. Newburn (2007: 653) and Davies et al. (2005: 277–8) identify a number of different types of evidence which can be given in court:

- Oral testimony on the witness stand, which is traditionally seen as being the best and most reliable form of evidence in an adversarial system (Goodey 2005: 134);
- Documentary evidence, such as witness statements;
- Exhibits, such as weapons and clothing;
- Audio and photographic materials, such as CCTV footage;
- Eyewitness testimony from an observer of the facts;
- Confession from D, often made while being interviewed by the police;
- Expert testimony by psychiatrists or doctors on specialist matters;
- Evidence of alibi, indicating that D could not have been at the place claimed;
- Character evidence about a witness's history and background;
- Circumstantial evidence from which inferences can be drawn about matters relevant to the case.

Juries and magistrates have to consider the relevancy, admissibility and weight (reliability) of evidence. In terms of relevance, facts are only admissible as evidence if they are 'facts at issue' or relevant to facts at issue. Facts at issue are facts which have to be proved by the prosecution to establish that D has committed the offence, or facts which are needed to prove that D is entitled to use a legal defence which they have raised.

In terms of admissibility, hearsay evidence, that is the use of statements made outside the court as evidence relating to a relevant fact, is generally not admissible because the person who made the statement cannot be cross-examined, but can be admissible if one of a series of exceptions stated in ss. 115–118 of the 2003 Criminal Justice Act applies. These include situations where a witness cannot be available in court, so that their evidence is read out, or where the evidence is a document created in the course of business. It is the judge's role to decide what is and is not hearsay, and to tell the jury which evidence is admissible. Another rule relating to admissibility is evidence of D's previous convictions. Under s. 101 of the 2003 Act, evidence of D's bad character, including their previous convictions, can be admissible where all parties agree to admit it, and where, for example, the evidence is relevant to a matter which the prosecution and defence are disputing.

As Newburn (2007: 653) points out, the prosecution has to disclose its case to the defence in Crown Court cases, and also has to disclose all the evidence it is planning to rely on in a magistrates' court case. In addition, it must disclose major items of evidence which it is not going to use in serious cases, in case these items are useful to the defence. Under ss. 33–36 of the Criminal Justice Act 2003, the defence must make a disclosure statement to the court within a specified time, and the prosecution can make adverse inferences in court (i.e. question the reliability of the defence case) if the defence fails to make this statement.

Evidence plays a vital role in proving a person's criminal liability in terms of *mens rea* (and *actus reus*) beyond reasonable doubt. The move towards subjective *mens rea*, for example, may encourage the police and courts to place too much emphasis on confession evidence which may have been obtained illegally at the police station, despite the regulations of the Police and Criminal Evidence Act 1984 outlawing this practice. On the other hand, the use of objective recklessness effectively asks magistrates and juries to ask themselves, as 'reasonable people', what risk they would have foreseen in a particular situation – something which would arguably be easier to do than to rely on court evidence relating to what D was thinking about at the time of the offence.

This may only be possible through judging D's physical actions at the time, or gaining evidence on *mens rea* through *actus reus*.

Rules such as the restrictions on hearsay evidence, as Davies et al. (2005: 278) point out, have developed to protect defendants from being convicted on the basis of fabricated or unreliable evidence. The relaxation of the restrictions on hearsay evidence in the Criminal Justice Act 2003 can be seen as a move towards allowing a greater range of evidence to be used by the prosecution, and increasing the risk that innocent people will be wrongly convicted. It could also be seen as a breach of Article 6 of the ECHR (the right to a fair hearing). Similarly, allowing the prosecution to make adverse inferences about the defence's case in court where the defence has not complied with the disclosure rules set out in the 2003 Act arguably gives the prosecution an unfair advantage in court, given the advantages of state resources in the criminal process over limited defence time and legal aid funding (Leng 2002). However, Redmayne (2004) found widespread non-compliance with the disclosure rules by defence lawyers.

Expert and scientific evidence plays a crucial role in how evidence is used in court. Roberts (2002) points out that while evidence from these sources has undoubtedly benefited criminal justice by securing rightful convictions in many cases, it can wrongly be seen as being conclusive by juries and magistrates simply because it has come from experts or scientists. This can lead to miscarriages of justice, and so evidence interpretation by the court process is vital. Roberts also shows that scientific evidence can have a number of limitations, particularly from the point of view of proving *mens rea*, since even clear evidence such as fingerprints or DNA does not tell the court anything about the *mens rea* involved in the crime – for example, whether it was committed intentionally, recklessly, negligently or accidentally.

━━━━━━━━━━━━━━━━ STUDY EXERCISE 3.7 ━━━━━━━━━━━━━━━━

Find a report of a court case where misleading expert evidence led to a miscarriage of justice. How did the miscarriage occur, and do you think that anything could have been done to prevent it from occurring in the first place?

Appeals

As Pattenden (2002: 488) shows, appeals can be made against conviction on three different grounds: an error in how the judge or clerk applied the law, an error of fact such as a conviction on unsafe evidence, and an error in the trial process, such as a biased summing up to the jury by the judge. Figure 1.1 in Chapter 1 shows which court(s) hear appeals at which stages in the criminal process. According to Ashworth and Redmayne (2005: 343–4), around 10% of appeals were granted from Crown Court decisions by the Court of Appeal in 2003, and the rate of appeal against verdict from the magistrates' court to the Crown Court in 2000 was only 0.4%. Of the appeals heard by the Court of Appeal Criminal Division in 2006, 32% were allowed against conviction and 71% against sentence (Ministry of Justice 2007a: 7).

Sanders and Young (2006) point to the inconsistency of the appeals process as well as its failure to uncover enough miscarriages of justice due to criminal justice agencies' breaking of the rules. The appeals process is a double-edged sword in terms of how *mens rea* is proved. On the one hand, it provides a potential way of restoring someone's legal innocence if their *mens rea* has been mistakenly 'proved' in their original court case. But on the other hand, it could also mean that people who really did have *mens rea* could be wrongly set free due to a mistake in the court process.

Example II: victims, *mens rea* and criminal justice

Victims play a crucial role in criminal justice by giving evidence at the court stage which proves criminal responsibility, in the form of *mens rea* as required by criminal offences, beyond reasonable doubt. This is particularly vital in cases involving offences where the victim was the only witness to what happened. However, the adversarial court process and the emphasis on the principle of oral evidence focus on the circumstances of the individual offence, and take away the social context of events, such as the relationship between the defendant and victim and the experience of repeat victimisation (Rock 1993). All of these factors make giving evidence more difficult for victims.

Shapland et al. (1985) pointed to the fact that victims were often taken for granted in the court process, with their needs often being ignored. Research has shown that vulnerable victims, such as victims of sexual offences, children and the mentally disordered, felt 're-victimised' and traumatised by the giving of evidence under cross-examination, due to the hostile adversarial attitudes of solicitors and barristers (e.g. Temkin 2002). Shapland and Bell (1998) found that 76% of Crown Courts and 53% of magistrates' courts made victims sit in the public gallery, potentially exposing them to abuse and intimidation from the defendant's family and friends. Finally, Whitehead (2000) found that 9% of victims had to wait for four hours or more before giving evidence, but 40% of victims in the study were not asked to give evidence despite attending court.

Recently, government policies and legislation have attempted to take victims' needs into account before and during the trial. The Witness Service, which gives victims support at courts pre-trial, was extended from Crown Courts to cover all magistrates' courts in England and Wales in 2002. Also, as McEwan (2002) shows, Part II of the Youth Justice and Criminal Evidence Act 1999 introduces a range of measures for vulnerable victims and witnesses giving evidence in court. These include screens so that the defendant and the witness cannot see each other in court, video-recorded evidence and cross-examination evidence from the witness to remove the need to give evidence 'live' in court, and witnesses giving evidence via video link from another room. Evidence on the effectiveness of these measures has been mixed. Hoyle and Zedner (2007: 475) report that the introduction of 165 'one-stop shop' Witness Care Units in 2003 to provide a single point of contact for victims at court in terms of information and support, whereby the police and CPS work together, resulted in a 20% improvement in witness attendance at court, reduced witness-related trial adjournments by 27%, and reduced cracked trials by 17%.

Goodey (2005: 161), however, argues that the Youth Justice and Criminal Evidence Act 1999 measures do nothing to address the fundamental issue of the traumatic experience of cross-examination for victims. Birch (2000) agrees, additionally arguing that the Act is based around the view that conditions can only be made better for victims by making them worse for defendants. Burton et al. (2006), meanwhile, found that the measures for vulnerable witnesses had not been fully implemented nationwide, and that the police and the CPS had great difficulty in identifying who was and was not 'vulnerable' and eligible for the special measures under the 1999 Act, excluding many victims who really were vulnerable in the process. Overall, the measures designed to make things easier for victims giving evidence may damage due process for defendants, by excluding some evidence which they could otherwise have used to disprove the charges against them, while not making giving evidence in court easier for victims.

▬▬▬▬▬▬▬▬▬▬▬▬▬▬▬▬▬ STUDY EXERCISE 3.8 ▬▬▬▬▬▬▬▬▬▬▬▬▬▬▬

If you could make three changes to the court process to make things easier for victims of crime who are giving evidence, what would those changes be?

Discussion and Conclusions

This chapter shows a range of conflicts between how criminal law and criminal justice claim to approach the issue of *mens rea*, and how they actually do approach it in practice. The liberal view of criminal law states that it is not fair to punish people for their behaviour unless individual responsibility through having the right *mens rea* is proved (Hart 1968). In terms of intent, the law reinforces the idea of factual individual responsibility by stating, in cases such as *Moloney*, that the idea of intent has an ordinary meaning which everyone can understand, so the law does not need to define it. However, as Lacey (1993) has pointed out, intent includes not just cases where people have aimed or planned to do what they did, but also cases where people did not aim or plan the offence, but did foresee the prohibited outcome as a moral or virtually certain outcome of their actions (*Nedrick, Woollin*). Therefore criminal intent has no 'everyday meaning'. Norrie (2001: 46–58) argues that the law has included foresight within the scope of intent, while leaving magistrates and juries to decide whether it applies case by case, to cover up the difficult social and moral decisions that have to be made on whether someone deserves to be held criminally responsible for the consequences of their actions. The law wants to be able to convict people whom it wants to blame for what they have done, while still being able to acquit people whom it thinks do not deserve to be punished for having criminal intent (*Steane*). On this view, intent in the criminal law is not just about liberal and economic principles, which relate to individual responsibility for crime that deserves to be punished. It is also about having the discretion to make moral judgements about individuals' responsibility in a way which reflects attitudes about society and reinforces social inequality.

Criminal recklessness can be analysed in a similar way. In G [2003], the House of Lords supported a subjective view of recklessness which again made the criminal law look liberal, by only blaming people for their recklessness where they saw the risk themselves and went on to take that risk anyway. But, as Clarkson (2005) has argued, sometimes it is right to blame people who did not think about the risks they were taking, especially where the risks are obvious and dangerous. The objective reckless-ness test set up in *Caldwell* allowed the law to do this, but meant that people who were not capable of appreciating the risks that they were taking (e.g. *Elliott v C, Bell*) were still blamed for their actions. This was one of the key reasons why G [2003] overruled *Caldwell* – punishing defendants like this made the law look less liberal.

However, it is arguable that the criminal law on recklessness is still trying to make moral judgments about the behaviour of particular defendants by mixing together subjective and objective recklessness. This can be seen in G [2003] itself, where the stated exception to the subjective recklessness test is where D cannot see the risk of their actions because they are voluntarily intoxicated. Describing this as an 'exception' to the recklessness rule ignores the clear links between alcohol and crime. The 2006/07 British Crime Survey found that victims believed offenders to be under the influence of alcohol in 46% of all violent inci-dents, or 1,087,000 incidents altogether (Jansson et al. 2007: 65). So, the objec-tive recklessness test has not disappeared from the criminal law as G [2003] claimed. Similarly, the use of negligence as *mens rea*, another objective test, has spread from minor offences to serious crimes such as rape. It could be argued that, given the social harm that overuse of alcohol and sexual violence clearly cause, this is a positive step for the law to take. However, the law is not being honest about the purpose of recklessness. As with intent, the move towards sub-jective recklessness fits in with a liberal view of what the criminal law is there for, but the reality of objective recklessness as it is still used by the law tells a dif-ferent story, one which deals with social issues, sometimes in a way that benefits society, sometimes in a way that makes social divisions greater.

In criminal justice, the traditional view of how *mens rea* is dealt with is again one which promotes liberalism and due process. For example, the prosecution must prove the defendant's responsibility for an offence, in terms of *actus reus* as well as *mens rea*, beyond reasonable doubt, otherwise the defendant must be found not guilty. Also, defendants have the right to choose a jury trial in the Crown Court for triable either way offences, and have a presumption in favour of bail where a case is adjourned.

However, the consistently high rate of guilty pleas bypasses the due process procedures for proving *mens rea*. This feature of criminal justice practice could partially be explained by current government criminal justice policy, which has attempted to prevent defendants from being able to choose their mode of trial; reversed the presumption of bail in a range of situations; allowed some offend-ers to be sentenced to prison without a pre-sentence report; and allowed a wide range of previously inadmissible evidence to be considered in courts. In addition, it has prioritised efficiency in terms of saving time and money in dealing with court cases, not just as a way of achieving justice and due process, but as a goal in its own right. This has encouraged court cultures to develop, which stereotype decisions on bail and guilt to speed up the process of justice, but which mean that due process is not taken seriously enough. Cutbacks in the availability and quality of legal aid work as well as the time available to prepare a defence case have increased the risk of due process not being fully upheld in court, even by the defence. In addition, a large number of defendants voluntarily give up their right to have their criminal responsibility tested in a court, after being offered a range of incentives and coercive tactics to plead guilty, such as lesser charges and sentencing discounts. These developments, particularly the last one, threaten to breach the human rights of defendants. There is also clear evidence of the status passage model playing a key role in the court process. Decisions are made in court by people who claim to represent the views of the community in their judgments (magistrates and judges), and the layout of magistrates' and Crown Courts isolates defendants by making them sit or stand separately from the rest of the court, in a dock or behind a screen (King 1981: 113–14).

Finally, although the reforms introduced in the Youth Justice and Criminal Evidence Act 1999 and the Criminal Justice Act 2003 to improve the experiences of vulnerable victims in court have to some extent promoted the theory that the criminal justice process has the prevention of social harm as one of its aims, they have tried to increase victims' rights mainly by taking rights away from defendants. These reforms have not improved conditions for all vulnerable victims in court, and have failed to address the fundamental issue of victims having to give evidence and be cross-examined in court orally. Overall, they have removed further due process from the courts in terms of thorough proof of the defendant's *mens rea* and criminal responsibility, while not improving the social justice of the court process for all of those who need it the most.

As a result, although the framework of due process remains in the court setting, and can still potentially be enforced by such measures as jury trials, models explaining the rise in bureaucracy, which in turn allows crime control to dominate criminal justice practice, such as Cavadino and Dignan's (2007) 'punitive managerialism', are better at explaining how criminal justice really deals with *mens rea*. Due process still survives, but has been eroded by managerialist and crime control concerns in recent times.

FURTHER READING

Brown, S. (1991), *Magistrates at Work*. Buckingham: Open University Press.

Goodey, J. (2005), *Victims and Victimology: Research, Policy and Practice*. Harlow: Pearson.

McConville, M., and Wilson, G. (eds) (2002), *The Handbook of the Criminal Justice Process*. Oxford: Oxford University Press.

Norrie, A. (2001), *Crime, Reason and History* (2nd edn): chapters 3 and 4. London: Butterworths.

Ormerod, D. (2008), *Smith and Hogan's Criminal Law* (12th edn): chapter 5. Oxford: Oxford University Press.

4

General defences in the criminal law

Chapter Aims

After reading Chapter 4 you should be able to understand:

- Which excusatory defences are available in the criminal law, and how they work
- Which justificatory defences are available in the criminal law, and how they work
- How criminal sentencing reflects responsibility for crime in different ways
- The difference between retributive and reductivist approaches to sentencing, and the strengths and weaknesses of each approach
- How these approaches have been used in recent sentencing legislation
- How these approaches have influenced sentencing in practice
- How the evidence on defences in the criminal law and sentencing in criminal justice fits in with the theoretical models introduced in Chapter 1

Introduction

Chapter 4 follows on from previous discussion of the basic foundations of criminal liability by looking at defences in the criminal law. This chapter considers the range of general criminal defences in the law and how they work, as well as their context in criminal justice. In the criminal justice section of the chapter, the links between the role and aims of defences in the criminal law and the role and aims of sentencing in criminal justice will be examined as a case study.

Criminal Defences: The Law

DEFINITION BOX 4.1

GENERAL CRIMINAL DEFENCES

Conditions defined in the criminal law which, if they apply in a particular case, remove D's liability for a range of criminal offences, even though D has the *actus reus* and *mens rea* requirements for that offence.

Making sense of criminal defences

Defences are ways in which people can avoid criminal liability, even though they have the *actus reus* and *mens rea* for the offence with which they have been charged. There are different types of defence in the criminal law. Some are specific to certain offences (such as murder), but this chapter deals with general defences. The legal team for the defence has to raise evidence that a particular criminal defence applies in each case. Then, for most of the common law defences discussed in this chapter, the prosecution has to prove beyond reasonable doubt that the defence does not apply, otherwise the defendant has to be acquitted. D must know the facts that justify them being able to use the defence at the time of the crime which they claim is covered by the defence, otherwise they cannot use it (*Dadson* (1850) 4 Cox CC 350).

Some general defences are excusatory, based on an excuse or internal characteristic which is special to D. Other defences, however, are justificatory, based on an external factor or situation which D has to face, and which makes D behave in a way for which the criminal law does not blame them. The excusatory defences will be considered first, followed by the justificatory defences.

Excusatory defences

Infancy

DEFINITION BOX 4.2

INFANCY

The excusing of D's liability for an offence because they are seen by the criminal law to be too young to be held responsible.

The infancy defence excuses criminal conduct because D is below the age of criminal responsibility for England and Wales. The minimum age of criminal responsibility in England and Wales is currently 10 (Children and Young Persons Act 1933 s. 50). For children aged between 10 and 13, the principle in the law called *doli incapax*, which set up a rebuttable presumption that a child did not know that they were committing the crime with which they had been charged, has now been abolished by the Crime and Disorder Act 1998 s. 34. In *T* [2008] EWCA Crim 815, the Court of Appeal stated that the abolition of the presumption was intended to abolish the concept of *doli incapax* completely, not just reverse the presumption so that the defence could still be used.

STUDY EXERCISE 4.1

Find out what the minimum age of criminal responsibility is in other European countries. Why do you think different countries have different minimum ages? What do you think the minimum age of criminal responsibility should be, and why?

Insanity (insane automatism)

DEFINITION BOX 4.3

INSANITY

The excusing of D's liability for an offence because, at the time of the offence, they had a defect of reason, caused by a disease of the mind, so that they did not know what they were doing in relation to the crime, or did not realise what they were doing was a crime.

The legal definition of the requirements of the insanity defence is in *M'Naghten* (1843) 10 Cl & Fin 200. First, D must have been suffering from a 'defect of reason'. This means that at the time of the offence D must have been unable to use their ability to think and use the brain to make decisions, rather than just failing to use the power to reason because they were absent-minded or distracted temporarily, for example. The defect of reason can be temporary as well as permanent (*Clarke* [1972] 1 All ER 219).

Secondly, this defect of reason must have been caused by a 'disease of the mind'. *Quick* [1973] QB 910 shows that the disease must be an *internal* factor. It must be something that is only 'inside D's head'. *Sullivan* [1984] AC 156 shows that the disease can have an 'organic' or a 'functional' cause, so it can be something physical, such as brain damage or some other medical condition such as epilepsy, or psychological, like a nervous condition. *Sullivan* also says that the condition can be temporary as well as permanent. *Burgess* [1991] 2 QB 92 stated that there did not have to be any danger of the disease recurring – the condition could be a 'one off' and still count for the purposes of insanity. Examples of the insanity defence being used successfully due to the presence of 'diseases of the mind' that were decided to be relevant, include *Kemp* [1957] 1 QB 399; *Sullivan*; *Hennessy* [1989] 2 All ER 9; and *Burgess*.

Thirdly, the defect of reason caused by a disease of the mind must have had such an effect on D that *either* D did not know what they were doing *or*, if D did know what they were doing, that D did not know what they were doing was wrong. In terms of proving that D did not know what they were doing, D has to show that at the time of the offence they did not understand the physical consequences of what they were doing, or the circumstances surrounding it (*Codere* (1916) 12 Cr App Rep 21). If D is trying to prove that they did not know what they were doing was wrong, this mean that D did not know what they were doing was *legally* wrong (i.e. that it was a crime), as opposed to *morally* wrong (*Windle* [1952] 2 QB 826).

The insanity defence works differently from other common law defences because the defence has to prove that D is legally insane on the balance of probabilities, rather than just raising evidence of the defence which the prosecution then has to disprove. However, the defence only has to prove insanity if the prosecution has already proved beyond reasonable doubt that D committed the *actus reus* of the offence they have been charged with. If the prosecution cannot prove the *actus reus* in this way, then D has to be acquitted anyway (*Attorney-General's Reference (No. 3 of 1998)* [2000] QB 401).

STUDY EXERCISE 4.2

Do you think that (a) sleepwalkers, (b) hyperglycaemic diabetics and (c) epileptics should be labelled by the criminal law as 'insane'?

Automatism (non-insane automatism)

DEFINITION BOX 4.4

AUTOMATISM

The excusing of D's liability for an offence because, at the time of the offence, they were not in voluntary control of their physical actions which comprised or caused the crime.

Bratty v Attorney-General for Northern Ireland [1963] AC 386 defines automatism as an act which is done physically, but without any mental control, or which is done during a loss of consciousness. The law is not always consistent about how much of a loss of control is required for there to be automatism, though. For example, for driving offences there has to be a 'total destruction of voluntary control' (*Attorney-General's Reference (No. 2 of 1992)* [1994] QB 91) before automatism is proved, implying almost total unconsciousness. However, in cases involving assault, Ds have been allowed to claim automatism where they were semi-conscious and could remember what they had done to some extent (e.g. *Charlson* [1955] 1 All ER 859; *Quick*).

Under *Quick*, the factor causing automatism must be external to the defendant (see insanity above). Examples of automatism are given in *Hill v Baxter* [1958] 1 QB 277, *T* [1990] Crim LR 256, *Quick*, and *Bailey* [1983] 2 All ER 503. Where D has recklessly caused the automatic action in some way, though, self-induced automatism is a defence to 'specific intent' offences if the automatism was caused by voluntary intoxication, but not a defence to 'basic intent' offences (see further discussion of 'specific intent' and 'basic intent' in the context of voluntary intoxication below). If the automatism was due to something other than voluntary intoxication, it was a defence even for basic intent offences, *unless* D was subjectively reckless, that is D saw the risk that whatever they did or did not do would make them behave aggressively or uncontrollably, and went ahead anyway (*Bailey*). Other examples of 'reckless automatism' include *Gray v Barr* [1971] 2 QB 554, where the Court of Appeal decided that 'automatic' accidents caused by recklessness or negligence still make D liable, and *Marison* [1996] Crim LR 909, which shows that in cases of careless driving, a D who goes into a diabetic coma or falls asleep at the wheel is still guilty, and cannot use the automatism defence, if they were reckless in the sense that they realised or should have realised that there was a real risk they might become unconscious, but drove or carried on driving anyway.

STUDY EXERCISE 4.3

Should people who have successfully used the defence of automatism always be allowed to go free without any intervention in their lives to control their behaviour? Explain your answer.

Voluntary intoxication

DEFINITION BOX 4.5

VOLUNTARY INTOXICATION

The excusing of D's liability for an offence because, at the time of the offence, they were so intoxicated, through alcohol or drugs taken of their own free will, that they did not have any *mens rea* in relation to the offence.

The voluntary intoxication defence deals with situations where D has voluntarily taken alcohol or drugs, and has later committed a crime while under the influence of them. Mostly, voluntary intoxication cannot be used as a defence to any crime.

Under *Sheehan and Moore* [1975] 2 All ER 960, drunken intent is still intent. So, as long as D actually formed the *mens rea* needed for the offence with which they have been charged, they will be guilty no matter how intoxicated they were. It is the magistrates' or jury's job to decide, on the basis of all the relevant evidence, whether D actually did form the intent needed (cf. *Sooklal* [1999] 1 WLR 2011 and *McKnight* (2000) *The Times*, 5 May, where the courts tried to use the test of whether D was not *capable* of forming intent because of their intoxication, which is harder to prove than the test of whether D actually *did* form the intent). Under *Attorney-General for Northern Ireland v Gallagher* [1963] AC 349, the only time voluntary intoxication can ever be a defence is where D was so intoxicated that they had no *mens rea* at all. This case also shows that if D uses intoxication for 'Dutch courage', then their intoxication is no defence to any crime they commit as a result.

What happens in situations where D has no *mens rea* at all due to voluntary intoxication was explained further in *DPP v Majewski* [1977] AC 443, where the House of Lords distinguished between specific intent and basic intent offences. Voluntary intoxication can be a defence to specific intent crimes, but not basic intent ones. In *Heard* [2007] 3 All ER 306, the Court of Appeal narrowed the scope of specific intent offences by saying that a specific intent offence was one where, to satisfy the *mens rea* requirements, D needed ulterior intent about the consequences of their actions rather than just intent in the normal sense of planning or desiring to do something.

Lipman [1970] 1 QB 152 applies the rules on voluntary intoxication to crimes committed under the influence of drugs. In this case, D was acquitted of murder, a specific intent offence, because he had not formed intent to kill or do grevious bodily harm (GBH). However, because D had killed V by doing an unlawful and dangerous act (assault), and this was the basis of liability for manslaughter, a basic intent offence, it did not matter that D did not have *mens rea* – he only lacked *mens rea* because of his intoxication, and so he was convicted of manslaughter. If, on the other hand, the drugs which have intoxicated D are not known to cause aggression or violence in the people who take them, then *Bailey* and *Hardie* [1985] 1 WLR 64 shows that D can use voluntary intoxication as a defence. The exception to this rule is where D saw the risk of behaving dangerously when they took the drugs, that is, D was subjectively reckless as to the risk of dangerous behaviour. In this situation, the voluntary intoxication defence cannot be used due to D's recklessness in intoxicating themselves.

STUDY EXERCISE 4.4

Should we replace the current voluntary intoxication defence with a new offence of 'criminal intoxication' which carries a lesser sentence than the one for the full offence which D has been charged with?

Involuntary intoxication

DEFINITION BOX 4.6

INVOLUNTARY INTOXICATION

The excusing of D's liability for an offence because, at the time of the offence, they were so intoxicated, through alcohol or drugs not taken of their own free will, that they did not have any *mens rea* in relation to the offence.

The involuntary intoxication defence deals with situations where D has unknowingly taken alcohol or drugs, and has later committed a crime while under the influence of them. Situations where this could happen include D taking a medically prescribed drug without realising what the side-effects would be, or D drinking a soft drink which, unknown to them, has been spiked with alcohol or drugs.

Involuntary intoxication, like voluntary intoxication, is only a defence where D has not formed the *mens rea* at all. Unlike voluntary intoxication, though, it can be used with either basic or specific intent offences. The scope of the defence is very narrow, however. In *Allen* [1988] Crim LR 698, D's drinking of alcohol, which was stronger than D thought it was, did not entitle D to use the involuntary intoxication defence. In *Kingston* [1995] 2 AC 355, the House of Lords confirmed that as long as D has the required *mens rea*, they are guilty, even if their intoxication was involuntary. So even though it was only the drugs which had been used to spike D's drink that caused D to form the intent to commit the offence in *Kingston*, D's conviction stood.

STUDY EXERCISE 4.5

Do you think the House of Lords' decision in *Kingston* was fair? Explain your answer.

Justificatory defences

Self-defence

DEFINITION BOX 4.7

SELF-DEFENCE

The justification of D's liability for an offence because, at the time of the offence, they were using proportionate and necessary defensive force, on the facts as they were or as D believed them to be, to prevent unjustified harm (to D or another person) or unjustified damage to D's property.

Common law self-defence allows the use of defensive force to prevent unjustified harm to the person using the force, their property, or another person. Under the Criminal Law Act 1967 s. 3, defensive force can also be used to prevent crime, or to make (or help others to make) a lawful arrest of offenders or suspected offenders.

Under *Williams* [1987] 3 All ER 411, the force D uses must be *necessary*. The necessity of the force used is judged on the facts of the situation as D believed them to be. This means that D is allowed to make an honest mistake about the facts that lead to the force being used (even if the mistake is not reasonable). But D cannot rely on any mistake made due to voluntary intoxication (*O'Grady* [1987] QB 995; *Hatton* [2006] Crim LR 353).

D's response must be also *reasonable* and *proportionate* to the threat as it was, or as D honestly believed it to be (*Palmer v R* [1971] 1 All ER 1077). The response does not have to be exactly proportionate to the threat – the jury or magistrates should take a liberal approach, including consideration of the time available to D for reflection on the situation. Under *Owino* [1996] 2 Cr App Rep 128, the force used must be *objectively reasonable* in the circumstances as D honestly believed them to be. So it is not enough that D believed subjectively that the force used was reasonable in the circumstances as they believed them to be – the force must be *objectively* reasonable in those circumstances. There has been some uncertainty in the law recently regarding how the level of danger which D is in should be judged. *Shaw v R* [2001] 1 WLR 1519 stated that the facts and level of danger must both be assessed subjectively, that is as D believed them to be, including any honest mistakes. But in *Martin* [2003] QB 1, although the facts D was facing had to be assessed subjectively, the level of danger D was facing had to be assessed objectively.

The threatened harm which D is facing, or which D honestly believes they are facing, must be *imminent*, that is about to happen. But D can 'get in there first' and use necessary, reasonable and proportionate force against an attack which is about to happen imminently, before it actually does (e.g. *Attorney-General's Reference (No. 2 of 1983)* [1984] QB 456). D is also under no duty to retreat from the situation, that is to show unwillingness to fight, 'back away' from the threat and seek help, although if D does so, it would be seen as evidence that their actions were necessary and reasonable (*Bird* [1985] 1 WLR 816).

Section 76 of the Criminal Justice and Immigration Act 2008 restates the principles of self-defence explained above with the aim of 'clarifying their operation' (s. 76(9)). All of the common law principles explained above are included in the statutory law. One notable feature is s. 76(7), which emphasises that 'a person acting for a legitimate purpose may not be able to weigh to a nicety the exact measure of any necessary action', to encourage courts to give the benefit of the doubt to Ds who use slightly too much force in self-defence.

STUDY EXERCISE 4.6

Read an account of the *Martin* case using a newspaper archive website. Do you think he should have been allowed to use self-defence? Why?

Duress through threats (duress per minas)

DEFINITION BOX 4.8

DURESS THROUGH THREATS

The justification of D's liability for an offence because, at the time of the offence, they had received threats of immediate death or grievous bodily harm (or reasonably believed they had received such threats) which were directed either at D themselves or at someone else whom D reasonably felt responsible for, where D reasonably believed they had to commit their crime as a result of the threats, the threats were a good cause for D's fear, and a reasonable person would have reacted in the same way that D did.

This defence can be used where someone is threatened with harm unless they commit a crime. *Hudson and Taylor* [1971] 2 QB 202 shows that only threats to kill or do GBH (serious injury) are enough to allow a defence of duress. *M'Growther* (1746) Fost 13 shows that threats to damage property also cannot be used as a basis for duress through threats. However, if the threats made to D involve non-relevant threats and threats to kill or do GBH together, then the relevant threats can still be considered (*Valderrama-Vega* [1985] Crim LR 220). *Safi* [2004] 1 Cr App Rep 14 shows that the threat of death or GBH does not actually have to exist, as long as D reasonably believes that it exists. There is some uncertainty in the law about how specific the threats made to D have to be. *Cole* [1994] Crim LR 582 stated that duress could only be used where the person making the threats specified exactly not only which offence to commit, but also which victim to target. However, in *Ali* [1995] Crim LR 303, the Court of Appeal thought that as long as the person making threats nominates a particular crime, duress can still be used where no particular victim was nominated.

The next issue is who has to receive the threats of death or GBH. *Wright* [2000] Crim LR 510 states that the threats do not have to be made to D in order for D to use the duress through threats defence. The threats can also be made to those for whom D reasonably considers themselves to be responsible – for example, a close family member or a partner.

The third issue is how soon the threat of death or GBH must be capable of being carried out. In *Hasan* [2005] 2 WLR 709, the House of Lords emphasised the importance of immediacy, rather than imminence in the sense of being able to be carried out soon but not necessarily straight away. The offence must be carried out immediately or almost immediately after the threat was made for the duress through threats defence to be allowed. Under *Hasan*, a day between the threat and the crime would be too long.

The fourth issue is what happens if D had the chance to remove the threat for some reason, or could be held responsible for getting into the situation which resulted in them being threatened. *Hudson and Taylor* stated that even if there was a chance for D to ask for police help, the threat could still be counted, depending on D's characteristics (e.g. age), the circumstances of the case, and any risks involved in seeking help. Where D has voluntarily joined a criminal gang, though, the scope for using duress through threats is severely limited. *Hasan* stated that if D has voluntarily joined a violent criminal association, and D saw, or should have seen, the risk of being put under duress by threats of violence against them, D cannot later use duress through threats as a defence. The association D joins does not have to be violent at the time of joining, as long as D foresees the risk of violence, and the threats of violence are later made. D also does not have to foresee the exact type of crime they will be forced to commit, as long as D, when they began to associate voluntarily with the group, knew that by doing so they were likely to be pressured by threats of violence to commit *any* crime.

The fifth issue is how the impact of the threat on D is assessed. The rules for this are found in *Graham* [1982] 1 All ER 801, which lays down a *mixed subjective and objective* test in three parts: (a) whether D *reasonably* believed they had to do what they did because of the threat; (b) whether the belief was a *good cause* for D's fear; and (c) whether a *sober person of reasonable firmness* would have reacted in the same way as D did. If the answer to all three of these questions is yes, then D is allowed to use the duress through threats defence. The more serious the crime, the more resistance is expected from D in terms of not committing it. *Bowen* [1996] 4 All ER 837 lists the characteristics that can be included in assessing the reasonableness of D's response to the threat – in other words, which of D's characteristics can be taken into account as being things which reduced D's ability to resist the threat. The following characteristics are relevant here: D's age and (maybe) gender, pregnancy, serious physical disability, or a recognised mental illness or psychiatric condition. However, characteristics which are present due to D's self-induced alcohol or drug abuse cannot be taken into account, and neither can suggestibility, vulnerability, nervousness, neuroticism or evidence of sexual abuse in childhood, which does not amount to a recognised psychiatric disorder.

The final issue is the range of crimes for which duress through threats can be used. It is a general defence, so it applies to most crimes, even strict liability offences where no *mens rea* is required for one or more parts of the *actus reus* (e.g. *Eden DC v Braid* [1999] RTR 329). However, *Howe* [1987] AC 417 shows that it is not a defence to murder, whether D is being charged as a principal offender or as a secondary offender (see Chapter 5 for details of what these terms mean). In *Wilson* (2007) *The Times*, 6 June, the Court of Appeal emphasised that duress was not available, even where D is a child who is a secondary party to the murder and is only acting out of fear of an adult principal offender. In addition, *Gotts* [1992] 2 AC 412 shows that duress through threats is not a defence to attempted murder either.

STUDY EXERCISE 4.7

Should duress be a defence to murder and attempted murder? Why do you think the law decided that duress should not be available for these crimes?

Duress of circumstances

DEFINITION BOX 4.9

DURESS OF CIRCUMSTANCES

The justification of D's liability for an offence because, at the time of the offence, D was forced to commit their crime because of objective dangers (or objective dangers which D reasonably believed existed) facing D or someone else whom D felt reasonably responsible for, where D had good cause to fear death or grievous bodily harm, and where a sober person of reasonable firmness would have reacted in the same way as D did.

Duress of circumstances can be used when D commits crime to avoid 'objective dangers' threatening themselves or others. The threat does not have to come from a person – it can come from a natural source, such as a fire – but it can come indirectly from a person, as in *Pommell* [1995] 2 Cr App Rep 607. For duress of circumstances, the threat does not have to be verbal and direct as a threat relating to duress through threats has to be. The threatening circumstances also do not have to involve committing a crime, as is the case with duress through threats, as *Willer* (1986) 83 Cr App Rep 225 and *Conway* [1989] QB 290 illustrate. However, the threats do have to be external, and able to be examined objectively by a court (*Rodger and Rose* [1998] 1 Cr App Rep 143).

The test for assessing the impact of the threat in terms of the duress of circumstances defence was set out in *Martin* [1989] 1 All ER 652. The questions to be asked are: (a) whether D was forced to act because of what happened, or what D reasonably believed to be happening (*Cairns* [1999] 2 Cr App Rep 137); (b) whether D had good cause to fear death or serious injury, either to D themselves or to someone else; and (c) whether a sober person of reasonable firmness, sharing D's characteristics, would have responded by acting in the same way that D did. If the answer to these questions is yes, a defence of duress of circumstances should be made available to the jury or magistrates to decide on the facts. Where D has started to commit the offence, but then the threat which they are responding to ends, D must stop committing the offence as soon as they reasonably can in the circumstances, according to *Pommell*.

The other principles of duress through circumstances are similar to the principles of duress through threats discussed above. *Abdul-Hussain* [1999] Crim LR 570 shows that there must be a close and direct link between the threatening circumstances and the offence being committed; *Hasan* states that the offence has to follow the threat more or less immediately; and *Pommell* emphasises that the defence could apply to any crime, subject to the exceptions to the availability of duress through threats set up in *Howe* and *Gotts*.

Necessity

DEFINITION BOX 4.10

NECESSITY

The justification of D's liability for an offence because, at the time of the offence, D was forced to commit their crime to avoid something even worse than the crime from occurring.

The defence of necessity is similar to duress of circumstances, but wider in its scope, because it is not tied to a particular identifiable threat in the same way as duress of circumstances is. The idea behind necessity is that, in a crisis situation, D commits a crime because doing so is the 'lesser of two evils'. Committing the crime, in other words, means that D prevents something which is worse than the crime from happening.

The existence of the necessity defence in the criminal law in England and Wales is controversial. It was not allowed for murder in *Dudley and Stephens* (1884) 14 QBD 273. However, necessity has reappeared, either in arguments made by Ds in court or in court judgments, in various cases since then which have not involved murder. For example, in *A* [2001] 3 All ER 1, Brooke LJ set out three requirements for the use of necessity: (a) the act must be needed to avoid inevitable and irreparable evil; (b) no more should be done than is reasonably necessary for the purpose to be achieved; and (c) the evil inflicted must not be disproportionate to the evil avoided. However, since *A* [2001] the necessity defence has not been allowed in *Shayler* [2001] 1 WLR 2206, *Quayle* [2005] 2 Cr App Rep 527, and most recently in *Jones and Milling* [2007] 1 AC 136. It is therefore still uncertain whether the necessity defence actually exists in the criminal law.

STUDY EXERCISE 4.8

Why do you think the courts will not allow a general defence of necessity to be used?

The second part of this chapter considers how defences relate to criminal justice, using the sentencing process as a case study.

Criminal Defences and Criminal Justice

Example I: sentencing processes in criminal justice

As Norrie (2001) points out, criminal defences limit the central liberal principle of the criminal law, which is that people are held responsible for the crimes they commit. The aim of this section is to introduce the key approaches to criminal justice sentencing and the recent legislation that has influenced sentencing in England and Wales, and then to compare these sentencing principles and policies with how sentencing is carried out by the courts in practice. In this way, the discussion will examine whether or not the nature and scope of criminal defences can be explained by approaches to sentencing theory, policy and practice – in other words, whether the justifications given for sentencing people match up with the justifications for *not* sentencing them, in the form of defences.

To understand how sentencing works, it is necessary to briefly consider the key theories of sentencing. These can be broken down into two groups: retributivism and reductivism. Retributivism justifies punishment through sentencing on the ground that it is deserved by the offender. On this view, punishment is justified because people have made the choice to commit crime (Cavadino and Dignan 2007: 44). However, it also used incapacitation as a ground for sentencing violent and sexual offenders to punishments which were longer than proportionate, and allowed other sentencing aims, such as rehabilitation, to be taken into account in certain circumstances. These aims are collectively known as reductivism. Whereas retributivism 'looks back' to the type of offence committed, reductivism 'looks forward'. It justifies punishment through sentencing on the ground that it helps to reduce the incidence of crime (Easton and Piper 2008: chapter 4) through deterrence (making punishment so unpleasant that offenders or others avoid crime so as to avoid being punished), rehabilitation (preventing crime through reforming or curing the offender) and incapacitation (physically preventing the commission of crime through punishment). A third theory, reparation, or restorative justice, is different from both retribution and reductivism as a sentencing strategy. The aims of reparation are varied and sometimes vague. Even so, a few key principles can be identified. First, reparation focuses on the offender making amends in some way to the victim of the offence for the harm which the victim has suffered. It aims to bring the offender and victim together to work out how to resolve the conflict caused by the crime (Johnstone 2001). It therefore 'looks back' to the harm caused by crime, but also 'looks forward' to how that harm can be repaired, and how the offender can be reintegrated into society after being 'shamed' for committing the offence (Braithwaite 1989).

The discussion begins by critically discussing the development of sentencing policy in England and Wales since 1998.

Sentencing legislation: a critical overview

The Crime and Disorder Act 1998 introduced a new type of incapacitative and deterrent sentence in the form of the anti-social behaviour order (ASBO). The ASBO is a civil order which can be imposed on any person who has acted in an anti-social manner and can include any prohibition which the court feels is necessary to prevent further anti-social behaviour. Breaching an ASBO can be prosecuted as a criminal offence and carries a maximum sentence of five years' imprisonment if dealt with in the Crown Court (Burney 2005: chapter 5).

The ASBO is particularly relevant to sentencing practice because since the Police Reform Act 2002 ASBOs can be imposed alongside a criminal conviction (CRASBOs).

Most recently, the Criminal Justice Act 2003 has introduced a new set of sentencing principles. There are some elements of retribution and proportionality in this Act, which have been carried over from the previous sentencing principles in the Criminal Justice Act 1991. For example, under ss. 142, 152 and 153 there are custody and community sentence thresholds, so that before a court can pass a custodial sentence it must be satisfied that the offence is 'so serious' that only prison can be justified, and before it can pass a community sentence it must be satisfied. The sentence must also be proportionate to the offence (Easton and Piper 2008: 77). But the Act (s. 142) also states that court must have regard to five different sentencing aims: punishment or retribution, reduction of crime or deterrence, the reform and rehabilitation of offenders, the protection of the public or incapacitation, and reparation by offenders. These sentencing aims conflict with each other so it is no wonder that Ashworth (2005: 99) describes the new structure as 'ambiguous' and 'incoherent'.

Elsewhere in the Act, deterrence and incapacitation are clearly the main influences. For example, s. 225 introduces a new mandatory indeterminate custodial sentence of imprisonment for public protection (IPP), for anyone over age 18 who has been convicted of one of a list of serious offences where the court thinks there is a significant risk to the public of serious harm from the offender's future re-offending. Similarly, ss. 227 and 228 introduce extended periods of supervision in the community in addition to custodial sentences for violent and sexual offenders which the court must impose if it thinks that the extended supervision is necessary to protect the public from serious harm in the future. Three other key changes introduced by the 2003 Act should also be noted. First, community orders (s. 177) replaced the previous range of community sentence options with one generic community sentence which had to include at least one of a menu of 12 requirement options (Cavadino and Dignan 2007: 135). Secondly, suspended sentence orders (ss. 189–94) replaced the earlier suspended sentence with a new scheme whereby courts could impose a fixed prison sentence of between 28 and 51 weeks, and suspend that sentence for between six months and two years, but could also include one or more of the 12 community order requirements as part of the package (ibid.: 156). Finally, the Act introduced a new Sentencing Guidelines Council, whose job it is to improve consistency in sentencing by setting guidelines for particular offences and types of offence.

Table 4.1 below gives an outline of which sentences are currently available for adults aged 18 and over in England and Wales.

Looking at sentencing legislation in England and Wales since 1998, there seems to have been a retreat from principles of proportionality and just deserts, and a move towards the exclusion, based on incapacitation and deterrence, of those considered to be a 'danger to society' (Faulkner 2006: chapter 9). The rules in the Criminal Justice Act 2003 about proportionality between the offence and the sentence, and thresholds which had to be met before different types of sentence could be given, are based around the retributive just deserts approach to

Table 4.1 Currently available sentences for adults* in England and Wales (adapted from Cavadino and Dignan, 2007: 133)

CUSTODIAL PENALTIES

Determinate immediate prison
Indeterminate immediate prison – mandatory life sentence
Indeterminate immediate prison – imprisonment for public protection
Suspended sentence order (custody 28–51 weeks, suspended for 6 months–2 years)

COMMUNITY PENALTIES

Community order (max. length 3 years) including one or more of:
- Exclusion requirement
- Curfew requirement
- Residence requirement
- Mental health requirement
- Drug rehabilitation requirement
- Alcohol requirement
- Unpaid work requirement
- Programme requirement
- Activity requirement
- Prohibited activity requirement
- Attendance centre requirement
- Supervision requirement

FINANCIAL AND ADMONITORY PENALTIES

Fine
Compensation order
Conditional discharge
Bind-over
Absolute discharge

*Discussion of sentencing for young people, and issues relating to youth justice generally, is outside the scope of this book. For more details on youth justice sentencing, see Easton and Piper (2008: chapter 8); and on youth justice policy and practice generally, see Smith (2007).

sentencing. However, the sentencing framework in the 2003 Act allows a range of sentencing principles to be taken into account, some of which contradict others. As a result, it is difficult to say which sentencing principles now drive sentencing in England and Wales. Norrie (2001: 218) argues that this outcome is inevitable, because no one sentencing theory can explain sentencing generally, and in fact they all conflict with one another. But, on the other hand, Norrie argues that all of the sentencing theories are concerned with the same process of removing social factors from sentencing – by either blaming individuals for crime or trying to control and cure their criminal behaviour.

The next subsection turns to the evidence on trends in sentencing in practice, to look for further indications on which principles drive the sentencing process day to day.

STUDY EXERCISE 4.9

Why do you think the government made the decision, in the Criminal Justice Act 2003, to allow courts to take a range of sentencing objectives into account when sentencing, instead of just requiring sentences to be proportionate, as the Criminal Justice Act 1991 had done?

Sentencing in practice: historical trends and the current picture

Cavadino and Dignan (2007: 140) provide a useful historical overview of the changing trends in the usage of different sentences. According to their data, in 1975, the proportion of sentenced adult indictable[1] offenders who were sent to prison was 13.4%, but rose steadily to 28.6% in 2004; the proportion sentenced to penalties involving supervision, such as probation, community service and curfew orders, was 7.5% in 1975, and increased to 28.1% in 2004; and non-supervisory penalties, such as fines, and absolute and conditional discharges, was 79.1% in 1975, but declined noticeably to 43.1% in 2004. In 2006, these trends stayed largely the same, with 24% of indictable offenders being sent to prison, 34% receiving a community sentence, and 22% receiving a fine in the magistrates' court, compared with 2% in the Crown Court (Ministry of Justice 2007c: xii–xiii).

These figures point to a clear trend of greater use of custody and more intrusive community penalties, and lesser use of non-intrusive penalties such as fines and discharges. This, in turn, can be seen as a move away from retributivism and just deserts in sentences, and a move towards reductivist aims such as deterrence and incapacitation. This move towards risk-based sentencing is made particularly clear by evidence that the use of indeterminate custodial sentences rose by 31% in 2006 alone (Padfield 2007), and that the use of suspended sentence orders (which combine the threat of custody with the option of intensive community punishment) rose by nearly 200% in 2006 (Ministry of Justice 2007c: 31). The use of ASBOs and CRASBOs provide more evidence of moves towards deterrent and incapacitative sentencing. ASBOs can be imposed for behaviour which is not defined as a crime, and CRASBOs can be imposed as an 'add-on' to the main court sentence. Both of these policies therefore represent a removal of the proportionality between crime and sentence. They punish based on excluding people from activities or places seen as being 'anti-social', trying to deter them with the threat of prison if they do not comply, and incapacitating them in prison if they are convicted of a breach, even where their actual behaviour was either not an imprisonable offence, or not a criminal offence at all, in the first place (Burney 2005).

However, reductivist aims have not taken over sentencing completely. The Criminal Justice Act 2003 has held on to the requirement of proportionality between crime and sentence, and non-supervisory sentences are still used more than custody or supervisory penalties. Nor should the continuing role of discretion in sentencing be overlooked. There has been a range of evidence to suggest that sentencers in the Crown and magistrates' courts have a great deal of discretion in practice. In particular, it has been shown that sentences can depend on the individuals or groups of people doing the sentencing as much as on the law

---

[1]Note that the category 'indictable offences' includes all offences which are triable either way or triable only on indictment, but it does not include summary offences which can be dealt with only in the magistrates' court.

itself (Parker et al. 1989), that irrelevant factors such as offenders' race can play a part in sentencing (Hood 1992), and that even where sentencing guidelines have been introduced, sentences can still be inconsistent without explanation (Tarling 2006). But the move towards reductivism is still a significant feature of current sentencing in England and Wales.

STUDY EXERCISE 4.10

How would you fit ASBOs into Table 4.1 above, in terms of being a custodial, community or admonitory penalty? Explain your decision.

Discussion and Conclusions

General defences in the criminal law provide an exception to the liberal principle that people are held criminally responsible for their actions where it can be proved that they had the right *actus reus* and *mens rea* for the offence. Excusatory defences are based around liberal principles – that people should not be held responsible for their actions if something about them makes it morally unacceptable to blame them for their criminal actions. But the law has tried to limit these excuses in recent times. For example, in terms of infancy, the abolition of *doli incapax* in 1998 ignores the extensive psychological evidence that children's brains – and therefore their ability to reason and see consequences – are still developing at the age of 10, and continue to do so throughout most of the teenage years on average (Haines and Drakeford 1998). Similarly, the definition of the insanity defence not only allows the law to ignore the significant over-representation of people with recognised mental illnesses in criminal justice, and deny even some people suffering from psychosis any excuse for their criminal behaviour (Peay 2007), but conversely allows people who are seen as being socially dangerous (such as epileptics and sleepwalkers as in *Sullivan* and *Burgess* respectively) to be unfairly labelled as 'mad'. Most insanity cases result in some form of supervision, either in hospital or in the community (Mackay et al. 2006). Under s. 24 of the Domestic Violence, Crime and Victims Act 2004, where D is found not guilty by reason of insanity, the judge must make one of three orders. The options are a hospital order (with or without a restriction order limiting the ability of D to be released from hospital) under s. 37 of the Mental Health Act 1983, a supervision order, or an absolute discharge. However, where D has been charged with murder and found to be insane, the judge must make a hospital order, and attach a restriction order without a time limit. But those who are allowed to use the automatism defence receive no further intervention in their lives.

Finally, given the apparent links between alcohol abuse and crime (e.g. Finney 2004), the criminal law could argue that it is justified in severely limiting the ability of offenders to excuse their behaviour through drunkenness, most recently in

Heard. But the current government has also increased the availability of alcohol by extending licensing hours, removed obstacles to new pubs and bars opening even in areas already overcrowded with licensed premises (both via the Licensing Act 2003), and allowed the alcohol industry to regulate itself rather than being regulated by the government – all in the knowledge of the massive social harm caused by binge-drinking (Hadfield 2006). It could therefore be argued that the law's approach to intoxication is somewhat hypocritical, allowing the powerful in society to make profit from alcohol consumption, but not allowing the less powerful to use it as an excuse for crime. The intoxication defence looks even more unfair when involuntary intoxication is considered. Here, it is difficult to argue that an offender should be held responsible for their actions when they have become intoxicated through no fault of their own, unless they have absolutely no *mens rea* at all. It is perhaps significant that the case where this principle was confirmed – *Kingston* – involved paedophilia at a time when sexual offences were being re-politicised in England and Wales.

In justificatory defences, the law is again presented in liberal, retributive and proportionate terms – D is allowed to use a defence if the set of circumstances which D found themselves in at the time of the offence justified the crime(s) that they committed, because they did not have a fair opportunity to avoid breaking the law (Hart 1968), as with duress through threats. But the law has retreated from this approach to make moral, deterrence-based judgments about particular types of duress scenario – most notably in *Howe* and *Gotts*, where the House of Lords decided that no threat could morally justify intentionally taking a life, or attempting to. But this distinction makes little sense in practice because, as Norrie (2001: 168) points out, it is often a matter of luck whether or not someone who has been seriously injured dies as a result. If they survive, duress is a defence to GBH under s. 18 of the Offences against the Person Act 1861. If they die, duress becomes unavailable on a murder charge. However, murder carries with it a social significance and 'fear factor' that GBH does not. The *Howe* and *Gotts* exceptions could be seen as a breach of Article 6 of the ECHR (the right to a fair trial) because of the potential role that luck could play in whether the defence was available or not.

On self-defence, the law is again based on liberal views on proportionality between threat and action, and individual responsibility. But in *Martin*, a case which attracted widespread publicity and debate, the Court of Appeal made an artificial distinction between D's perception of the facts of the scenario and D's perception of the danger involved to ensure that Tony Martin's conviction was not overturned. This could be seen as a decision aimed at holding on to law's power in the face of what was seen as the threat of social unrest resulting from public sympathy for Tony Martin shooting intruders who were threatening his property. Leverick (2002) has also argued that the current law on self-defence to homicide does not comply with a human rights approach either because the European Court of Human Rights has interpreted Article 2 of the ECHR (the right to life) so that only necessary and strictly proportionate force can be used, rather than 'reasonable' force as under the current law, and so that only a reasonable mistake can be relied on, rather than a merely honest one as under the current law.

Finally, the courts have been extremely reluctant to allow anyone to use a defence of necessity. Norrie (2001: 172–3) argues that this is because the law does not want to acknowledge the inequality in society – in terms of poverty and unemployment especially – which narrows down the choice people have not to commit crime.

In the criminal justice section of the chapter, the issue of individual responsibility for crime was approached from another angle – the perspective of sentencing, which is based around the justification for allowing people to be punished by the state. The question here was whether, just as criminal law moves away from the idea of individual responsibility in some situations, criminal justice also moves away from individual responsibility when it punishes the legally guilty. Although the retributive principle of proportionate sentencing which was the basis of the Criminal Justice Act 1991 is still part of criminal justice (Ashworth 2005), new policies based on crime control, deterrence and incapacitation have also been introduced, most noticeably in the Criminal Justice Act 2003 (Cavadino and Dignan 2007). The results – more custodial sentences, the blurring of custodial and community punishment through suspended sentence orders, greater use of preventive orders such as ASBOs that can attract criminal conviction and sentencing if they are breached and could be seen a breach of Article 6 of the ECHR, and harsher and more intrusive punishments generally – are a clear reflection of the move towards reductivism in sentencing. But this move ignores evidence on the limited effectiveness of deterrence (von Hirsch et al. 1999). The role of discretion in sentencing should also not be ignored. It would be simplistic to say that sentencing has shifted from retributivism to reductivism overall when individual magistrates and judges still have the power to hide their true reasons for giving a particular sentence behind vague legal statements such as 'this offence is so serious that only custody can be justified', if they wish to do so.

Finally, it is also significant that deterrence and incapacitation responses, like retributivism, generally focus on individual responsibility for crime. It has been far harder for reparative sentencing, which at least brings the opportunity for a more social and community-based approach to responding to crime, to become established in sentencing practice. This is true even where legislative measures have been introduced to encourage reparative justice, such as reparation orders in the Crime and Disorder Act 1998, and referral orders in the Youth Justice and Criminal Evidence Act 1999. Even the use of compensation orders, which are designed to make the offender give reparation to their victim for loss suffered in the form of financial compensation, has more than halved in magistrates' and Crown Courts since 1990, and has been restricted by courts' greater use of custody and wrongful prioritisation of court costs and fines over compensation orders (Cavadino and Dignan 2007: 143–4). More will be said about the nature of punishment in practice in the next chapter, which looks at other ways in which the criminal law moves away from the liberal concept of individual responsibility for crime.

════════════════ **FURTHER READING** ════════════════

Ashworth, A. (2007), 'Sentencing', in Maguire, M., Morgan, R., and Reiner, R. (eds), *The Oxford Handbook of Criminology* (4th edn). Oxford: Oxford University Press.

Easton, S., and Piper, C. (2008), *Sentencing and Punishment: The Quest for Justice* (2nd edn). Oxford: Oxford University Press.

Hudson, B.A. (2003a), *Understanding Justice: An Introduction to Ideas, Perspectives and Controversies in Modern Penal Theory* (2nd edn). Buckingham: Open University Press.

Jefferson, M. (2007), *Criminal Law* (8th edn): chapters 7–9. Harlow: Pearson.

Norrie, A. (2001), *Crime, Reason and History* (2nd edn): chapters 8–10. London: Butterworths.

5

Alternative forms of criminal liability

Chapter Aims

After reading Chapter 5 you should be able to understand:

- The meaning of strict liability in the criminal law, and which principles decide whether or not an offence is strict liability
- The principles governing corporate and vicarious liability in the criminal law
- Which forms of complicity liability exist in the criminal law, and what the *actus reus* and *mens rea* requirements are for each form
- How the law defines a joint unlawful enterprise
- Which forms of inchoate liability exist in the criminal law, and what the *actus reus* and *mens rea* requirements are for each form
- Which approaches the different forms of punishment currently available in England and Wales take in terms of how they punish people
- How the evidence on the forms of liability in the criminal law which are discussed in this chapter and the nature of punishment in criminal justice fits in with the theoretical models introduced in Chapter 1

Introduction

Chapter 5 continues the discussion of the basic rules of criminal liability by discussing three particular ways of committing crime which stand out from the traditional individual *actus reus/mens rea* scenario: strict liability, complicity and inchoate offences. Following an explanation of the law in each of these areas, the key legal principles will be set in the context of how they operate in criminal justice practice. This chapter uses two examples: first, the particular issues faced by criminal justice in imposing corporate and strict liability on businesses and corporations; and secondly, whether the different forms of punishment available in criminal justice punish offenders on the basis of their individual responsibility, or whether other approaches are used instead.

The chapter begins by introducing and explaining the law on strict liability.

Alternative Forms of Criminal Liability: The Law

Strict liability: the law

DEFINITION BOX 5.1

STRICT LIABILITY OFFENCES

Criminal offences which require a particular *actus reus*, but which do not require *mens rea* to be present for one or more parts of that *actus reus*.

Strict liability offences only require *actus reus* to be proved to secure a conviction, not *mens rea*. This immediately raises questions about whether strict liability offences breach Article 6 of the ECHR (the right to a fair trial). Strict liability is mostly used for statutory offences, that is offences which have been created by Parliament under statute law. Where the *mens rea* requirements for these offences are not clear in the original statute, the courts have had to decide whether the offence is completely strict liability, partly strict liability, or not strict liability at all, based on the words of the statute. The aim of this section is to explain how the courts make this decision, by examining the series of guidelines they have used.

It is important to remember three preliminary points about strict liability. First, some offences can be strict liability for one or more parts of the *actus reus*, but require *mens rea* for other parts of it. A good example of how this works can be found by contrasting the cases of *Hibbert* (1869) LR 1 CCR 184 and *Prince* (1875) LR 2 CCR 154 – two cases involving the same offence but resulting in different outcomes because some parts of the offence's *actus reus* were held by the courts to require *mens rea*, whereas other parts were held to be strict liability. Secondly, other parts of the *actus reus* still have to be proved even if no *mens rea* is needed, including causation. The courts have, however, taken a wide view of what counts as causation for strict liability offences (see the discussion of *Environment Agency v Empress Car Co* [1999] 2 AC 22, which involved a strict liability offence, in Chapter 2). Thirdly, sometimes Parliament will intervene with new legislation to make an offence strict liability even though the courts have said that it requires *mens rea*, as they did with a range of sexual offences in the Sexual Offences Act 2003 (see Chapter 7).

Taking these points into account, the principles which help the courts to decide when to use strict liability will now be discussed in turn.

Presumption in favour of mens rea

Generally, in the criminal law there is a presumption that an offence will require *mens rea* (*Sweet v Parsley* [1970] AC 132). Under *B v DPP* [2000] 2 AC 428, there needs to be a 'compellingly clear' or 'necessary' implication that the statute is strict liability, that is that strict liability was clearly what Parliament had in mind when it created the legislation.

However, the courts still have discretion to decide one way or the other where the legislation is not completely clear on whether an offence is strict liability or not. There are some statutory words which, when used in legislation, point towards *mens rea* being needed (such as 'knowingly') or towards strict liability (such as 'sell'). Offences involving possessing something, such as controlled drugs, are normally partially strict, in the sense that once the prosecution has proved that D knows about possessing a particular item, such as a box or container, then D is held to possess whatever is contained inside that item, such as drugs, even if D does not know about what is inside (*Warner v MPC* [1969] 2 AC 256).

'Truly criminal' offences

If the offence is 'truly criminal', that is serious enough to involve a 'breach of morality', it is more likely to need *mens rea* than if it is just a regulatory offence designed to improve societal behaviour (*Gammon Ltd v A-G for Hong Kong* [1985] AC 1).

The punishment available for the offence

The more serious the offence is, the more serious the punishment for it will be, and the more likely it is that *mens rea* will be needed (*B v DPP*). But in *Howells* [1977] QB 614, the offence was possession of a firearm which carried a maximum punishment of five years' imprisonment – however, the offence was strict liability. Even if an offence can be punished with a prison sentence, it does not necessarily mean it will be held to require *mens rea*. In *Blake* [1997] 1 All ER 963, the offence was 'truly criminal' because it carried a two-year maximum prison sentence, but in *Harrow LBC v Shah* [1999] 3 All ER 302 the same maximum sentence did not make the offence 'truly criminal'. These two cases show how different guidelines can take priority over one another in different case scenarios.

Protection of the public

If the offence regulates public safety in some way – for example, by protecting the public against contaminated food or water – it is more likely to be considered as strict liability (*Gammon*). For example, *Blake* [1997] was held to be a strict liability case because the public could be put at risk by the emergency services not receiving 999 calls because of pirate radio stations blocking their radio transmissions. Similarly, *Smedleys v Breed* [1974] AC 839 and *Hobbs v Winchester Corp* [1910] 2 KB 471 were both cases which involved Ds contaminating food, and both offences (more exactly, the right to civil compensation for food being destroyed in *Hobbs*) were held to be strict; *Bezzina; Codling; Elvin* [1994] 3 All ER 964 were cases involving the offence of failing to control dangerous dogs – again this was a strict liability offence due to the public safety issue; and finally, *Alphacell v Woodward* [1972] AC 824 and *Southern Water Authority v Pegrum* [1989] Crim LR 442 both involved water pollution, and in both cases the offences were strict.

Vulnerable victims

The more vulnerable the likely victims of the offence are, the more likely the offence is to be held to be strict liability. The contaminated food and pollution cases (see above) are good examples of this because everyone needs food to eat and air to breathe, but has very little protection against people and organisations who harm them through damaging these 'essentials'. Another example is *Harrow LBC v Shah*, where the offence of selling lottery tickets to under-16s was held to be strict to protect children from the dangers of gambling.

But vulnerability of victims is not conclusive in terms of whether an offence is strict liability. In *Sheppard* [1981] AC 394, an offence of wilful neglect of a child was held by the House of Lords to require *mens rea*; and in *B v DPP* the offence of inciting a child under the age of 14 to commit gross indecency was held to require *mens rea*, so that D was not guilty if he made an honest mistake about the girl's age. In *B V DPP*, the House of Lords pointed out that although the statute was sometimes used to protect vulnerable children from paedophiles, it could also involve (as in fact it did in this particular case) children of similar ages sexually experimenting with one another consensually. The case was followed in *K* [2002] 1 AC 462, which also involved a sexual offence (indecent assault) and a mistake as to age. The offences in these cases were later made strict liability by statute, in the Sexual Offences Act 2003. However, the points made in *B* and *K* about the effect of vulnerable victims and the balancing of different strict liability principles in the same case are still important.

Ease of compliance with the law

The easier it is for D to comply with the requirements of the statutory offence, the more likely it is that that offence will be held to be strict liability. *Lim Chin Aik v R* [1963] AC 160, *Bowsher* [1973] RTR 202, and *Matudi v R* [2003] EWCA Crim 697 are examples of this principle in operation. Similarly, if the offence is aimed at regulating people who are in a particular business or profession, rather than at regulating the behaviour of the general public, then it is more likely to be strict liability. In *Sweet v Parsley* the offence was aimed at the public, and this was one reason why the offence required *mens rea*; but in *Pharmaceutical Society of Great Britain v Storkwain* [1986] 1 WLR 903 the offence was aimed at a particular industry, and was strict.

The next section of this chapter considers two related forms of liability which can involve D being convicted of a crime without any *mens rea* on their part – corporate liability and vicarious liability.

STUDY EXERCISE 5.1

Simester (2005) argues that it is fair to impose strict liability for offences where there is no social stigma attached to the criminal offence, but that it is not fair to impose it where stigma exists. Do you think the current law on strict liability fits in with Simester's argument?

Corporate liability: the law

DEFINITION BOX 5.2

CORPORATE LIABILITY

Criminal offences which allow a whole business or company to be criminally liable for that offence, rather than just one or more individuals.

Corporate liability involves the conviction and punishment of whole companies or organisations for particular offences, rather than just individuals. However, corporate liability can only be proved in certain circumstances. The basic rule for establishing corporate liability is what is known as the 'identification principle', under *Tesco v Nattrass* [1972] AC 153. This means that to establish corporate liability the prosecution must prove that there was a 'directing or controlling mind' which had the right *actus reus* and *mens rea*. In other words, there must be one person in charge of the organisation who has both the *actus reus* and *mens rea* required for the offence before the whole company can be convicted. If no one involved with the company has the right *actus reus* and *mens rea*, then the company cannot be liable for the offence. The *mens rea* of more than one person cannot be put together to create the *mens rea* which is needed for a corporate offence (*Attorney-General's Reference (No. 2 of 1999)* [2000] QB 796).

A recent example of legislation imposing corporate liability for a particular offence can be found in the Corporate Manslaughter and Corporate Homicide Act 2007, which deals with the offence of corporate manslaughter. This offence will be discussed in more detail in Chapter 8.

Do you agree with the identification principle being used to determine corporate liability? If not, what principle(s) would you use instead?

Vicarious liability: the law

████████████ DEFINITION BOX 5.3 ████████████

VICARIOUS LIABILITY

Criminal offences which allow D to be criminally liable for an offence where someone whom D employs has the right *actus reus* and *mens rea* for that offence.

Vicarious liability is based around D's responsibility for an offence because of another person's *actus reus* and *mens rea*, not D's own. Often vicarious liability is imposed for strict liability offences, so these areas of the law are also linked. As with strict liability, it is often statutes that the courts have to interpret to decide whether or not vicarious liability should be imposed, based on the words used in that statute.

Certain words used in statutes are taken by the courts to indicate that vicarious liability should be imposed. For example, statutes prohibiting the 'selling' of certain goods in certain situations are often held to include vicarious liability, as in *Tesco v Brent LBC* [1993] 2 All ER 718, where an employer was held responsible for D (one of its employees) selling an 18 certificate video to a child under the age of 18. But vicarious liability can only be imposed where D, an employee, is acting within the scope of their authority as part of the job. So, in *Adams v Camfoni* [1929] 1 KB 95, D was not vicariously liable for his employee selling alcohol outside the permitted hours because the employee in question had no authority to sell alcohol as part of his job.

The offences to which vicarious liability can be attached are not always strict liability, though. Where the offence does require *mens rea*, the employer must have the right *mens rea*, as well as the employee, to be vicariously liable. The exception to this is where the employer is held to have fully delegated their responsibilities to the employee, so that the employee has completely taken the place of the employee at the time of the offence (*Vane v Yiannopoullos* [1965] AC 486). In such a case, the employer is still vicariously liable. If not all of the responsibilities have been delegated, the employer will not be vicariously liable.

████████████ STUDY EXERCISE 5.3 ████████████

Is it ever fair to impose vicarious liability on employers for offences which they themselves have not committed?

Complicity: the law

DEFINITION BOX 5.4

COMPLICITY

D's criminal liability for an offence which D has helped, assisted or encouraged someone else to commit, or which D has committed together with another person, with the right *mens rea*.

The law on complicity deals with who is responsible (and what they are responsible for) when more than one person is involved in the same crime. There are three basic points to note about complicity. First, the law differentiates between main, or principal, offenders and secondary offenders. The main offender is the person who directly commits the crime, that is the one who causes it. The secondary offender is the person who helps or encourages the main offender to commit the crime. However, it is not always easy to tell the difference between a main and a secondary offender, especially where they are committing the same offence at the same time. In this section of the chapter, the secondary offender in a case will be referred to as D, and the main offender will be referred to as P.

Secondly, if the *actus reus* of the main offence is not committed, then D cannot be guilty. Secondary liability is based upon what is called *derivative liability*. D's liability for the offence is based upon P's liability, so if P is not liable, then D cannot be liable either (*Thornton v Mitchell* [1940] 1 All ER 339). Similarly, D cannot be liable for any offence unless and until P commits the main offence. However, in a small group of cases, secondary offenders have been convicted despite the main offender not having the right *mens rea* or *actus reus* – a situation which threatens to breach D's right to a fair trial. Examples include *Bourne* (1952) 36 Cr App Rep 125, where D was convicted of aiding and abetting even though P had a defence to the crime; *Cogan and Leak* [1976] QB 217, where P did not have the *mens rea* for the offence, and D was convicted as the main offender even though he could not physically have committed the *actus reus* of rape (as the offence was defined at that time); and *Millward* [1994] Crim LR 527, where D was convicted of secondary liability (procuring) when only the *actus reus* of the main offence had occurred, and P did not have the *mens rea* – so D's *mens rea* was 'added' to P's *actus reus*.

Thirdly, the legislation which defines secondary offender liability (s. 8 of the Accessories and Abettors Act 1861 and s. 44 of the Magistrates Act 1980) states that secondary offenders can be punished as if they were main offenders. Defendants can therefore receive the same sentence, up to and including the maximum sentence allowed for each offence, as Ps. For example, Ds guilty of murder must be sentenced to life imprisonment in the same way as Ps because life imprisonment is the only sentence which can be passed for murder under the Murder (Abolition of Death Penalty) Act 1965 s. 1.

Next, the chapter considers the *actus reus* requirements for secondary liability.

Secondary liability – actus reus

The basic *actus reus* required for secondary liability is an act (or omission) which assists or encourages the main crime. There are four types of secondary liability in the relevant legislation – aiding, abetting, counselling and procuring. D only has to commit one of the four types of *actus reus* to be guilty (*Ferguson v Weaving* [1951] 1 KB 814). The *actus reus* requirements for each of these offences will now be explained.

Aiding means D giving some kind of help or support to P. This can occur in a wide variety of ways. In *Bainbridge* [1960] 1 QB 129, D was convicted of aiding burglary when he supplied blowtorch equipment to P, which P then used to open the safe at the bank which was burgled. Aiding can be done either before or during the commission of the main offence (*Coney* (1882) 8 QBD 534).

The causation requirements for aiding differ slightly from the normal criminal law causation principles which were discussed in Chapter 2. For aiding, there is no need for D's actions to be the 'but for' cause of the main offence. But there does have to be some kind of 'causal link' between D helping and P committing the main offence (*Bryce* [2004] 2 Cr App Rep 35). This is a question for the jury or magistrates on the facts. However, D's act must actually do something to help P (*Attorney-General v Able* [1984] QB 795). Help can be in the form of verbal encouragement as well as more physical forms of help, such as supplying equipment for use in crime. D is still guilty even if P does not know about, or does not want, the help that D has given.

Under *Coney*, D's presence at the scene of the crime without doing or saying anything can only be evidence suggesting that the *actus reus* for aiding has been committed, but not conclusive proof – although D can aid through either unplanned or planned presence at the scene of the crime, in terms of encouraging the crime to continue. Aiding, as well as abetting and counselling, can be done by omission. *Tuck v Robson* [1970] 1 WLR 741 shows that if D has a legal duty to stop someone doing something illegal, and does not fulfil that duty, then D is liable as a secondary offender.

The *actus reus* of abetting and counselling both involve some kind of help or encouragement being given by D to P, either by words, actions or omissions occurring before or during the main offence. Counselling implies helping through words rather than physical actions, although this does not have to be the case. There is no need for 'but for' causation (*Attorney-General v Able*), but there must be a causal link between the actions of D and the actions of P (*Bryce*), as with aiding. For D to be guilty of abetting or counselling, P must know that they are acting within the scope of D's encouragement or approval (*Calhaem* [1985] QB 808) – this differentiates the *actus reus* for these forms of secondary liability from that for aiding (see above). The law on whether D can abet or counsel simply by being present at the scene of the crime is similar to that for aiding. Under *Clarkson* [1971] 1 WLR 1402, there has to be 'encouragement in fact'. Not much 'encouragement' is required in order for D to be liable, however – shouting or clapping would be enough under *Clarkson*.

Procuring means 'to produce by endeavour' (*Attorney-General's Reference (No. 1 of 1975)* [1975] QB 773). To procure a main offence, D must cause it in some way. A causal link between D's actions and P's crime is therefore needed for the *actus reus* of procuring. The causation requirement was widely drawn in *DPP v Blakeley and Sutton* [1991] Crim LR 763, though, where the court said that D procures if they foresee the offence as a possible consequence of their behaviour, which effectively removes the requirement for a physical causal link between what D does and the main offence. No consensus between D and P is needed for procuring (*Attorney-General's Reference (No. 1 of 1975)*).

▓▓▓▓▓▓▓▓▓▓▓▓▓▓▓▓▓▓▓▓ STUDY EXERCISE 5.4 ▓▓▓▓▓▓▓▓▓▓▓▓▓▓▓▓▓▓▓▓

Should the four separate types of secondary liability *actus reus* be scrapped and replaced with one general *actus reus*? If so, how would you define this new offence in terms of *actus reus* requirements?

Secondary liability – mens rea

Mens rea requirements for secondary liability can be split up into two categories: the requirements for aiding, abetting and counselling (which are the same for all three offences), and the requirements for procuring. The requirements for aiding, abetting and counselling will be discussed first.

First, D has to intend to encourage or assist the main offence (*National Coal Board v Gamble* [1959] 1 QB 11). D's motive for helping is not relevant. As long as D intends to help P, and knows the essential facts of the main offence (see below), D will be guilty. Secondly, D has to realise that their acts are capable of assisting or encouraging P *(Bryce)*. Thirdly, D must have knowledge of the key elements of the main crime. In other words, D must also have *mens rea* regarding the consequences of the help that they are giving. This means that P's *mens rea* must be examined as well as D's. *Powell; English* [1999] 1 AC 1 decided that D does not have to *intend* that P commits the crime. D only has to foresee a real (substantial) risk (i.e. be subjectively reckless) that P will commit the crime, and will have the right *mens rea* while committing it. Fourthly, D must know the essential facts of the offence which P commits (*Ferguson v Weaving*). In *Carter v Richardson* [1974] RTR 314, it was stated that 'knowledge of the essential facts' of the main offence includes being subjectively reckless as to whether the facts which make up the main offence exist, that is seeing the risk that P will commit the offence in a particular way and going ahead with help or encouragement anyway. In terms of how much D has to know about the main offence, *DPP for Northern Ireland v Maxwell* [1978] 1 WLR 1350 says that D is only liable if the main crime committed is on a 'shopping list' of crimes which D foresaw might be committed. So, in *mens rea* terms:

- if D knows about the offence, D is guilty;
- if D knows one or more of a range of offences will take place, D is guilty if one or more of these offences occur;
- if D foresees one particular offence occurring, but another similar crime occurs instead, D is not guilty;
- and if D knows the general class of offence, but not the specific one, D is guilty.

Where the aiding, abetting or counselling is committed by omission, D's *mens rea* must include the following characteristics:

- knowledge that P was committing the crime;
- deliberately 'turning a blind eye' to the crime;
- and knowledge that by doing so D was encouraging P to commit the crime (*JF Alford Transport Ltd* [1997] 2 Cr App Rep 326).

The *mens rea* for procuring, on the other hand, has traditionally been seen as different from the *mens rea* for the other secondary liability offences because procuring effectively means doing something to cause or bring about the main offence. As a result, the *mens rea* for procuring has been judged to require a direct intention to bring about or cause the main crime (*DPP v Blakely and Sutton*). However, in *Rook* [1993] 1 WLR 1005 and *Bryce* the courts doubted whether the *mens rea* for procuring was any different to the *mens rea* for aiding, abetting and counselling, and thought that intent should not be required. Therefore, the *mens rea* requirements for procuring remain uncertain.

The discussion now turns to a special kind of secondary liability, known as joint unlawful enterprise liability.

STUDY EXERCISE 5.5

How easy do you think it is for juries and magistrates to understand the *mens rea* requirements for secondary offenders? Do you think the law could be simplified in this area without letting blameworthy people get away with criminal behaviour? If so, how could it be simplified?

Joint unlawful enterprises
A joint unlawful enterprise means that there is an express or implied agreement to commit crime together between two or more people (*Anderson and Morris* [1966] 2 QB 110). The case which defines the legal requirements for a joint unlawful enterprise is *Powell; English*, which decided that where there is a joint unlawful enterprise, everyone involved in it is liable for the crimes which result from the plan. However, if P acts outside the plan, by using a different type of weapon to the one the Ds planned to use during the attack, for example, then the others are not liable for the crime P commits, *unless* the others intended or foresaw the risk that P would commit the offence that they committed in the way that they committed it. There is therefore an 'all or nothing' approach to D's liability – either they are guilty of whatever happens under the joint unlawful enterprise or they are guilty of nothing (cf. *Gilmour* [2000] 2 Cr App Rep 407). *Concannon* [2002] Crim LR 213 confirmed that the law on joint unlawful enterprises did not breach Article 6 of the ECHR (the right to a fair trial) because Article 6 only regulated the fairness of individual criminal trials, not the fairness of the law itself. This is a narrow reading of the courts' obligation to comply with human rights law.

It is the jury's or magistrates' role to decide whether or not there has been a joint unlawful enterprise, who was involved in it if there has been, and whether one or more people have acted outside the enterprise when they committed the crime. *Rook* shows that for joint unlawful enterprises, it is not necessary for D to be present at the scene of the crime as long as the unlawful agreement has taken place, and D either has the intention that P will commit the crime in the way in which P in fact commits it, with the right *mens rea*, or foresees the risk that this will happen.

The principles in *Powell; English* were recently clarified in *Rahman* [2007] EWCA Crim 342, which gave the following guidelines for juries deciding whether to convict of murder in joint unlawful enterprise cases:

> In order to convict D of murder the jury must first be sure that P unlawfully caused the death of V intending to kill them or cause them really serious bodily harm, and secondly be sure that D played some part in the attack on V. The route to a verdict could then be:
>
> 1. Is the jury sure that D intended that one of the attackers would kill V intending to kill them or that D realised that one of the attackers might kill V with intent to kill them? If yes, D is guilty of murder. If no, go to question 2.
> 2. Is the jury sure that either:
>
>   (a) D realised that one of the attackers might kill V with intent to cause V really serious bodily harm; or
>   (b) D intended that serious really bodily harm would be caused to V; or
>   (c) D realised that one of the attackers might cause serious bodily harm to V intending to cause V such harm?
>
>   If no, D is not guilty of murder. If yes, go to question 3.
>
> 3. What was P's act which caused the death of V (e.g. stabbing, shooting, kicking, beating)? Go to question 4.
> 4. Did D realise that one of the attackers might do *this* act? If yes, D is guilty of murder. If no, go to question 5.
> 5. What act or acts is the jury sure D realised that one of the attackers might do to cause V really serious harm? Go to question 6.
> 6. Is the jury sure that this act or these acts (which D realised one of the attackers might do) is/are not of a fundamentally different nature from P's act which caused the death of V? If yes, D is guilty of murder. If no, D is not guilty of murder.

In the House of Lords hearing of *Rahman* ([2008] UKHL 45), Lord Brown stated that D would not be guilty where they knew nothing about P's weapon, and P's weapon was more lethal than any weapon that D contemplated P or any other participant might be carrying, *even if* D, P or any other participant might be carrying, *even if* D foresaw that P might kill with intent to either kill or inflict grievous bodily harm, therefore widening the exception to the rule in *Powell; English* in one respect. On the other hand, this suggests that D cannot rely on the 'fundamental change' principle at all where they are aware that P has a weapon, even if D does not foresee the possibility that P might use it – therefore narrowing the exception in another respect.

Powell; English and *Rook* were cases which involved planned violence, but *Uddin* [1999] QB 431 applied the *Powell; English* principles to spontaneous group criminality. The case set out a number of guidelines to help juries decide who is guilty of what, when a group of people violently attack V, and they all intend to commit grievous bodily harm. If, during spontaneous violence, one offender (P) produces a 'surprise' weapon which the other offenders do not know about and have not foreseen a risk that P would use, attacks V with it, and the others carry on attacking V, they are all guilty of murder if V dies. However, if V's death was caused by actions or a weapon which are entirely different from what the other offenders intended or foresaw the risk of, then only P is guilty of murder. The others may still be guilty of lesser offences (wounding, for example) in a scenario like this, based on their own *actus reus* and *mens rea*.

It is also possible for someone to withdraw from a joint unlawful enterprise and avoid liability for the crimes which result from that enterprise later. To successfully withdraw from a planned joint unlawful enterprise, D has to give a clear warning of withdrawal to the others involved in the plan (*Becerra and Cooper* (1976) 62 Cr App Rep 212), or do something to try to stop the others carrying out their plan, such as calling the police (*Grundy* [1977] Crim LR 543). As *Rook* shows, the withdrawal from the enterprise must be clear and unambiguous.

The law on withdrawal is slightly different where the joint unlawful enterprise is unplanned and spontaneous – a group of people suddenly and violently attacking an individual, for example. *O'Flaherty* [2004] Crim LR 751 states that in a situation like this D does not need to say clearly to the others that they are withdrawing from the enterprise. All D needs to do is to leave the scene of the crime. Again, it is a question of fact for the jury or magistrates to decide in cases like this whether, first, there has been one continuing joint unlawful enterprise or two separate ones, and secondly, whether D has done enough to withdraw from the enterprise based on all the available evidence.

The next section of this chapter moves on to look at the law on inchoate offences.

STUDY EXERCISE 5.6

Why do you think the law sometimes lets people withdraw from joint unlawful enterprises?

Inchoate offences: the law

Making sense of inchoate offences

DEFINITION BOX 5.5

INCHOATE OFFENCES

D's criminal liability for an offence which D has not completed fully in terms of the *actus reus* and *mens rea* required, but which D has attempted to commit, conspired to commit with one or more other people, or has helped or encouraged someone else to commit, with the right *mens rea* in each case.

Inchoate offences are a specific group of types of liability, covering situations where D has not completed the full *actus reus* and *mens rea* for a particular offence, but has taken some steps towards completing the *actus reus* and *mens rea* required. The key question here is how far the criminal law allows people to go towards committing the full offence before it criminalises their behaviour. The *actus reus* and *mens rea* requirements for different types of inchoate liability will now be explained.

There are three different types of inchoate offence – attempt, conspiracy and incitement. Attempt and conspiracy 'attach' to individual offences, so that D has to be charged with, for example, attempted burglary rather than simply attempted crime generally. However, incitement can be charged independently as 'encouraging or assisting crime' under the Serious Crime Act 2007. All three inchoate offences are now defined mostly by statute law. The discussion of the law will begin by taking a closer look at criminal attempts, followed by conspiracy and incitement.

Attempt – actus reus

An attempt means that D has tried to complete the *actus reus* and *mens rea* for a particular offence, but has not fully succeeded. The question is how far D has to go towards completing the *actus reus* of the offence before their conduct counts as a criminal attempt. The *actus reus* of attempt is defined by the Criminal Attempts Act 1981. Section 1(1) of the Act states that the *actus reus* of attempt is any act which is 'more than merely preparatory to the commission of the offence'. This issue, as the Act states, is a question of fact, so juries and magistrates have to decide on a case-by-case basis whether D has gone beyond what is 'merely preparatory' in committing an offence, taking the circumstances of the case into account. The discretion given to courts in deciding what is and is not an attempt has led to contrasting decisions since the Criminal Attempts Act was introduced. So, for example, the Ds were convicted of attempts in *Jones* [1990] 1 WLR 1057, *Attorney-General's Reference (No. 1 of 1992)* [1993] 1 WLR 274, and *Tosti* [1997] Crim LR 746. On the other hand, the Ds were not guilty in *Campbell* (1991) 93 Cr App Rep 350 and *Geddes* [1996] Crim LR 894. *Gullefer* [1990] 1 WLR 1063 stated that D had to have 'embarked on the crime proper' in order to be guilty of a criminal attempt.

Attempt – mens rea

The Criminal Attempts Act 1981 s. 1(1) states that intention to commit the full offence is the *mens rea* required for attempts. So, for murder, only an intention to kill is enough *mens rea* – not intention to do GBH as with the full offence (*Pearman* (1985) 80 Cr App Rep 259). Where there is more than one element to the *actus reus* of the offence which needs *mens rea*, *Khan* [1990] 1 WLR 813 stated that there must be intent to commit the 'core act' in the *actus reus*, and that the same *mens rea* is needed as for the full offence for the other parts of *actus reus*. *Attorney-General's Reference (No. 3 of 1992)* [1994] 1 WLR 409 stated that D must 'intend to supply whatever is missing from the completion of the offence'.

Attempt and impossibility

Sections 1(2) and 1(3) of the Criminal Attempts Act 1981 show that even if an offence is factually impossible to commit in the circumstances, D can still be convicted of attempt. It is possible for D to do something thinking that it is an offence, but circumstances which D does not know about means that in fact what D is doing is not a crime. *Shivpuri* [1987] AC 1 decided that impossible attempts like this are still attempts in the criminal law.

STUDY EXERCISE 5.7

Should the law convict people of attempting impossible crimes, or is this just prosecuting 'thought crime'?

Conspiracy – actus reus

The *actus reus* for most conspiracies is defined by the Criminal Law Act 1977. A few common law conspiracies still exist in the law for specific criminal offences – for example, conspiracy to defraud (see *Wai Yu-Tsang v R* [1992] 1 AC 269) and conspiracy to corrupt public morals (see *Knuller v DPP* [1973] AC 435). Section 1(1) of the 1977 Act states that the *actus reus* for a statutory conspiracy is 'an agreement by two or more people' to follow 'a course of conduct *necessarily* amounting to the commission of an offence by one or more of them'. The offence is completed once the agreement has been formed. There has to be proof of a definite agreement, however. Proof of ongoing discussions working towards an agreement to commit the full offence is not enough (*Walker* [1962] Crim LR 458). Various situations where there cannot be a criminal conspiracy can be found in s. 2(2) of the 1977 Act.

Conspiracy – mens rea

There are three elements in the *mens rea* for statutory conspiracy, according to *Saik* [2006] 2 WLR 993. First, there must be intention to make the agreement. Secondly, under s. 1(1) of the Criminal Law Act 1977, there has to be an intention to do the act which is prohibited by the full offence. Thirdly, under s. 1(2), there has to be intention or knowledge that a fact or circumstance which is necessary for the commission of the substantive offence will exist when the agreement is carried out.

Each person involved in the conspiracy must have intention that the full offence will be carried out (*Yip Chiu-Cheung v R* [1995] 1 AC 111). The parties to the conspiracy are only liable for the intended consequences of their planned course of conduct (*Siracusa* (1990) 90 Cr App Rep 340). D does not have to intend to play an active role in the planned course of conduct as long as the intention that the full offence will be carried out is present, and D intends to go along with the other parties' activity in pursuing the course of conduct without doing anything to prevent them following it (*Siracusa*; cf. *Anderson* [1986] AC 27).

If there is a conditional agreement to carry out an offence if something else happens, then the parties still have the *mens rea* for conspiracy as long as the offence is the aim of the agreement, and the offence would necessarily be committed if the conspiracy was carried out (*Jackson* [1985] Crim LR 442). However, if the aim of agreement is something else other than the offence, and something which does not necessarily involve the commission of an offence, the parties do not have the *mens rea* for conspiracy, even if the offence is foreseen as a possible way of bringing about the agreement (*Reed* [1982] Crim LR 819).

Conspiracy and impossibility

Section 1(1)(b) of the Criminal Law Act 1977, which was inserted by s. 5 of the Criminal Attempts Act 1981, states that impossibility is no defence to a statutory conspiracy. In this way the law on impossibility in relation to statutory conspiracy is the same as it is in relation to attempt.

STUDY EXERCISE 5.8

Do you think the current conspiracy laws give a reasonable prospect of convicting the leaders of terrorist organisations such as Al-Qaeda?

Incitement – actus reus

The common law on incitement has recently been replaced by provisions in the Serious Crime Act 2007, which introduces new offences of 'encouraging or assisting crime'. Under s. 49(1) of the Act, the *actus reus* for these offences is proved as soon as the encouragement or assistance has taken place with the right *mens rea*. It does not matter whether or not the full offence is actually committed later.

The basis of the *actus reus* under the new legislation is doing an act or omission which is factually capable of assisting or encouraging a criminal offence (ss. 44–45) or which is factually capable of assisting or encouraging more than one criminal offence (s. 46). D has a defence if they can prove that they had knowledge of circumstances, and that their actions were reasonable in the light of these circumstances; or if D can prove that they had a reasonable belief in the existence of certain circumstances, and that their actions were reasonable in the light of the circumstances as D believed them to be (s. 50). So in this case, the normal burden of proof switches from the prosecution to the defence.

Incitement – mens rea

The offence under s. 44 of the Serious Crime Act 2007 requires *mens rea* of intention to assist or encourage the commission of the full offence. The offence under s. 45 (which has the same *actus reus* as the one under s. 44) requires the lesser *mens rea* of belief that the full offence will be committed, and belief that the act will assist or encourage the commission of the full offence. Similarly, the offence under s. 46 (assisting or encouraging more than one offence) requires *mens rea* of D's belief that one or more offences will be committed, and D's belief that the act will assist or encourage the commission of one or more of the offences.

In proving for the purposes of this section whether an act is one which, if done, would amount to the commission of an offence, there are varying *mens rea* requirements depending on the *mens rea* for the full offence. If the full offence requires proof of fault, it must be proved that either:

- D believed that, if the act was done, it would be done with that fault;
- D was reckless as to whether or not it would be done with that fault; or
- D's state of mind was such that, if D did carry out the act, it would be done with that fault.

In addition, if the full offence also requires proof of particular circumstances or consequences (or both), it must be proved that either D believed that, if the act was done, it would be done in those circumstances or with those consequences; or that D was reckless as to whether or not it would be done in those circumstances or with those consequences.

Incitement and impossibility

Under s. 49(1) of the Serious Crime Act 2007, D is still guilty of incitement even if the offence is factually impossible to commit in the circumstances, as long as D believes that the full offence will be committed and that what D does will encourage or assist that offence.

STUDY EXERCISE 5.9

Find a discussion of the old law on incitement. Make a list of three differences, in terms of *actus reus*, *mens rea* and impossibility, between the old law and the new law under the Serious Crime Act 2007.

Alternative Forms of Criminal Liability and Criminal Justice

Example I: the aims of punishment in practice

The aim of this case study is to examine the types of sentence which were introduced in Chapter 4 in more analytical detail. This will be done in order to investigate whether punishment in practice reflects individual responsibility for crime, or whether it has different aims in terms of how and why it deals with offenders, just as criminal law moves away from the idea of individual fault-based responsibility for crime in the form of alternative types of criminal liability such as strict liability, complicity and inchoate offences.

Financial and admonitory penalties

The discussion here starts with the fine. As Bottoms (1983) noted, the fine is the ultimate liberal, individualised form of punishment. It does not need any supervision of the offender, and it can easily be adjusted to reflect the seriousness of the offence being punished. But the 'pure punishment' view of fines hides some of the issues which have been faced when imposing them in practice. Crow et al. (1989), for example, have illustrated that courts have been reluctant to use fines for unemployed offenders because magistrates and judges do not see the point in fining the unemployed a small amount to reflect the fact that they do not have much disposable income. In addition, Raine et al. (2004) found that non-payment of fines was more to do with courts not obtaining enough information about offenders' ability to pay, and not doing enough to help offenders to pay before criminalising non-payment, than with offenders deliberately not paying fines. They also found wide variations between different courts in terms of how much fine money was recovered, and how long it took courts to recover fines which are owed, with 39% of fines in 2001/02 (£149m) being either written off or cancelled by courts. Therefore, the evidence on fine enforcement in practice suggests that it can be both unfair on certain groups of offenders and also inefficient in terms of the unnecessary costs of enforcement and fine default.

The main admonitory penalty to be considered here is the ASBO. It was noted in Chapter 4 that ASBOs are best explained in sentencing terms as a risk-based preventative measure. Examined from the angle of what ASBOs tend to involve in punishment terms, the focus again seems to be on risk-based punishment. As Burney (2005) points out, the minimum length of time for which an ASBO can last is two years, and they can last indefinitely. Burney goes on to show that the concept of 'anti-social behaviour' is vaguely defined. As a result, ASBOs can be imposed for behaviour which is not a criminal offence in itself, but which is seen as anti-social behaviour. Since ASBOs can be punished with a prison sentence on breach, this in turn means that people can be imprisoned for behaviour which is not a crime, or which is not normally an imprisonable crime. It could therefore be argued that ASBOs breach several ECHR provisions – Article 5 (the right to liberty, which is restricted by ASBOs obtained without proof of guilt beyond reasonable doubt in court), Article 6 (the right to a fair trial, which is bypassed by removing the need to bring offenders to court) and Article 7 (the right to know exactly what the offence someone is accused of involves in terms of criminal behaviour, which is not provided by the vague definition of 'anti-social behaviour' in the law on ASBOs). Burney shows that the number of ASBOs being imposed in England and Wales rose rapidly after a slow start when they were first made available, although the number of ASBOs issued in 2006 declined by a third compared with 2005, while the breach rate rose to 49% (Ford 2008).

There is also evidence which suggests that ASBOs are imposed disproportionately among certain groups in society, especially young people. In Campbell's (2002) study, almost three-quarters of ASBOs issued between 1999 and 2001 were imposed on young people. Squires and Stephen (2005), meanwhile, show the severe impact of ASBOs on young people day to day, in terms of the wide and vague exclusions which are often part of ASBOs in practice, and which extend the amount of social control over people's lives. They also cite government data which suggest that most anti-social behaviour is in the form of existing criminal offences which could be dealt with using the police's normal investigative powers, and that ASBOs do not reflect public priorities about which criminal behaviour should be dealt with as a priority.

However, Koffman (2006) found that in his study, ASBOs were mostly used for persistent and extreme cases of anti-social behaviour, and he also found that breaches of ASBOs were treated leniently by local courts overall. While acknowledging the range of social, educational and mental health problems suffered by the young people who most commonly received ASBOs in his study, Koffman emphasises the damaging effects of these young people's anti-social behaviour on its victims. These data suggest that there is a great deal of discretion over how ASBOs are used and enforced in practice (see also Home Office 2007), and that criticism of them may have been overstated.

━━━━━━━━━━━━━━ STUDY EXERCISE 5.10 ━━━━━━━━━━━━━━

Using newspaper archive databases on the Internet, find three reports of cases where ASBOs have been imposed. Based on the information given in each report, explain whether or not you would have imposed an ASBO in each case, and why.

Supervisory penalties and probation

Chapter 4 noted that a new generic community order was introduced as part of the Criminal Justice Act 2003. Mair et al.'s (2007) exploratory research indicated that although the new orders have not been overloaded in terms of requirements, they have failed to reduce the number of custodial sentences being passed, and have not been used differently from the previous community sentences, with an emphasis on supervision and unpaid work.

These findings mean that the practice of the National Probation Service, the organisation responsible for managing community punishment, must be examined more closely to find out how supervisory penalties operate in practice. The discussion here focuses on recent developments. Several key trends can be identified in current probation practice. These should be understood in the context of the increasingly harsh sentencing trends discussed in Chapter 4, which have meant that probation has had to deal with more minor offenders than before (Mair and Canton 2007: 283). The first trend is a continuing and increasing level of control of local probation practice by the government in a bureaucratic sense, which has meant that local-level probation workers have less discretion about the types of work they do with offenders. This has meant a series of structural and organisational changes for probation, involving increasing levels of accountability and bureaucracy (see Morgan 2007).

Secondly, probation policy which has been imposed in this way has become more related to risk and control rather than the traditional probation approach of help and treatment for offenders (Kemshall 2003). The moves towards risk-based practice can be seen in two different ways. On the administrative level, the use of standardised electronic databases such as the Offender Assessment System (OASyS) to measure the levels of risk posed by offenders has become a key part of probation practice. However, the ways in which these risk assessment tools are used in practice are still shaped by probation values at a local level (Robinson 2002) and can be affected by poor training in how to use them, and lack of time to complete assessment properly (Mair et al. 2006). All of these factors are capable of reducing the impact of risk assessment in probation practice. On the practice level, the management of high-risk offenders (such as sex offenders) has focused around control, public protection and surveillance techniques, such as tagging. However, there has also been increasing recognition of the value of a more harm reduction-based approach to risk management in probation practice, focusing on public health strategies to reduce the risk from sex offenders, for example.

Thirdly, despite the trend towards risk management discussed above, rehabilitation – the traditional focus of probation work – has continued to have an influence on probation practice (Ward and Maruna 2006). The new approach to rehabilitation focuses on cognitive behavioural techniques which aim to change the way offenders think about the consequences of their offending, and encourage them to think about alternatives to committing crime – an approach of rehabilitation combined with individual responsibility for offending (Raynor 2004). This development has combined with the 'what works' model of probation work, under which different types of probation programme are evaluated and accredited to measure their effectiveness. However, Mair (2004) has pointed out that the evidence supporting 'what works' initiatives is not always reliable, and has questioned the narrow focus of accreditation on cognitive behavioural programmes. Other writers have criticised the focus of 'what works' on the reasons for offending rather than the desistance factors which lead offenders to stop committing crime (Farrall 2002), and the failure of national 'what works' strategies to recognise the needs of ethnic minority and female offenders (Gelsthorpe and McIvor 2007).

This snapshot of current issues affecting probation work has revealed a trend towards more managerialist supervision of probation practice, and the increasing use of technology to aid risk assessment and management. However, there is more to probation practice than risk management, bureaucracy and crime control. Raynor and Robinson (2005), for example, argue that rehabilitation and reform does and should play a continuing role in probation work, particularly in the form of social integration approaches which fuse individual responsibility with the development of responses to social problems – such as poor education and drug abuse – which can create the context for offending. On this view, there is still evidence of discretion in probation practice being used to address social harm issues through rehabilitation and restorative justice.

████████████████████████ STUDY EXERCISE 5.11 ████████████████████████

What would you say should be the main aim of probation practice? Should the main aim be the same for everyone being punished, or should it be different for young people, women and ethnic minorities?

██

Custodial penalties

It was noted in Chapter 4 that suspended sentences – a form of custodial penalty due to their threat of custody if the offender breaches the sentence – were re-launched as part of the Criminal Justice Act 2003, with community order attachments. Mair et al. (2007) found that usage of suspended sentence orders had increased rapidly since the Act's implementation. Mair et al. also found that suspended sentence orders tended to have more requirements attached to them than community orders, despite Sentencing Guidelines Council guidance that this should not occur; and that the breach rate for suspended sentence orders was high. This research suggested that suspended sentence orders, in their new form, were being used in a risk-based way which made the punishments of offenders harsher and more likely to be breached, with custody the probable result.

The discussion now moves on to look at prisons themselves, and how they punish offenders. As with the discussion on community penalties above, the focus here is on current issues. Cavadino and Dignan (2007: chapter 6) argue that the prison system in England and Wales is currently in crisis. Their arguments can be used to examine how prisons punish people in more detail. Cavadino and Dignan identify seven separate areas of crisis, which are linked to each other in terms of their causes. For them, however, the most important crisis facing the prison system is the crisis of legitimacy. Legitimacy is the idea that prisoners feel that they are being treated fairly and with respect (Liebling and Arnold 2004). Cavadino and Dignan (2007: 237) argue that other prison crises, such as overcrowding, security breaches and violence in prisons, play a part in limiting the legitimacy of prison regimes in the view of prisoners. These limits on legitimacy strengthen the argument of critical writers such as Scraton et al. (1991) that the aim of prisons is to exercise power and control, often in a psychologically and physically violent and damaging way, against powerless and socially excluded prisoners, rather than trying to treat them fairly or rehabilitate them. The research on the discrimination which can be faced by young, female and ethnic minority prisoners, discussed in Matthews (1999: chapters 7–9), could also be said to support this view, as could the arguments of Christie (2000) that the powerful have turned prisons into a profit-making industry for controlling and socially excluding the powerless in society through introducing the privatisation of prisons. However, detailed empirical research (e.g. Sparks et al. 1996) has shown that prisons can have other punishment objectives, such as rehabilitation and due process justice for prisoners. The success of these objectives depends on prison staff acknowledging the power that prisoners have in maintaining order and discipline, by treating prisoners with respect and fairness so that prisoners see prisons as being morally legitimate.

A good example of how this has been achieved in practice is the therapeutic regime at HMP Grendon (see Genders and Player 1995), where even violent and sexual offenders have shown reduced reconviction rates compared with those in other prisons, and the reconviction rate was lower the longer a prisoner stayed at Grendon (Marshall 1997).

STUDY EXERCISE 5.12

Read Cavadino and Dignan (2007: chapter 7). Do you think that privatising more prisons will help to solve the prison crisis and treat prisoners more fairly?

Discussion and Conclusions

This chapter started off by examining some forms of criminal liability which go further than just criminalising an individual on the basis that they have committed the right *actus reus* and *mens rea* for a particular offence. First, the discussion looked at strict liability offences, which require *actus reus* but not *mens rea* (for at least one part of the *actus reus*). The liberal view of criminal law and criminal justice presents strict and corporate liability as being an exception to the rules of *mens rea* and individual responsibility where the activity of individuals or groups presents a real danger to public safety or vulnerable victims. But the reality of how strict liability is used in practice shows that it is far from being exceptional in the criminal law. Ashworth and Blake's (1996) research showed that 40% of offences which were triable in the Crown Court were strict liability – and the majority of these offences carried maximum prison sentences of more than six months. This is particularly significant given the expansion of strict liability from offences designed to protect the public from corporate harm (Norrie 2001) to cover a wide range of offences, from gun ownership (*Howells*) through illegally importing endangered animal products (*Matudi*) to sexual assault (*BvDPP*). Norrie argues that these decisions represent an attempt to inject the morality and interests of the powerful in society into the law, in a range of different situations.

The use of strict liability in this way raises questions about whether it is being used fairly, in criminal law and in criminal justice. However, Wells (2001: 73) points out that many offences which do need proof of *mens rea* are not proved fully in court either because of the range of pressures on defendants to plead guilty, such as plea-bargaining and charge-bargaining (see Chapter 3). When viewed in this context, strict liability is no more unfairly enforced in criminal justice than other, non-strict liability offences. The courts have noticeably refused to state that strict liability offences breach Article 6 of the ECHR (the right to a fair trial) (e.g. G [2008] UKHL 37).

Secondly, the chapter looked at corporate liability, and found that liability for businesses in the criminal law was based around the principle of holding an individual responsible for crime. This identification approach cannot reflect the processes of decision-making in an organisation which result in corporate crime (Gobert and Punch 2003). The larger the company is, the less likely it is that there will be one person with enough *actus reus* to satisfy the requirements of a corporate liability offence, even if that offence is strict liability (Wells 2001). But as Nelken (2007: 747–8) points out, corporate crime such as fraud might be in the interests of particular powerful individuals, but it is not in the interests of the powerful generally because it is likely to disrupt the trade which gives economic power to businesses. Although the maintenance of power certainly plays a role in corporate liability law, it is vital to see the law as reflecting a wider variety of interests than just power. Other aspects of the law's response, such as efficiency in terms of saving criminal justice money by trying to prevent harm before it happens, must be considered as well.

Thirdly, the legal discussion looked at the principles of complicity, where people can be criminally liable despite not having committed the *actus reus* and the *mens rea* of the main offence involved. It would seem that the law on complicity is generally based around the management of risk. Secondary offenders do not commit criminal offences 'directly', but they do have knowledge of what the main offender is going to do, and do help the main offender to commit their crime. It could be argued that the secondary offender has made the main crime easier to commit, in terms of helping to factually cause the crime, and so is morally to blame when the main offence occurs.

However, it could be questioned whether secondary offenders should receive the same punishment as main offenders, as they currently can. For most offences, the court has the discretion to reduce the secondary offender's sentence compared with the main offender's, if it wants to do so. In cases of murder, though, only the life imprisonment sentence can be imposed, and so in these cases the secondary offender has to receive the same sentence as the main offender. It is interesting that the cases which have seen the *mens rea* requirements for secondary offenders being reduced – *Bryce*, DPP for Northern Ireland v *Maxwell* and *Powell*; *English* (Ashworth 2005: 440–1) – were all murder cases. These developments point towards the law being concerned with the reduction of risk, rather than with liberal ideas about punishment in line with the level of blameworthiness in terms of *actus reus* and *mens rea*. The new Serious Crime Act 2007 proposals claim to abolish the common law incitement offence rather than changing the law on complicity. The new incitement offences, under which the offence is committed as soon as D's help or encouragement has taken place, differ from complicity liability, under which the full offence must be carried out before D can be held liable. However, there is the potential for overlap between these provisions, which could cause confusion in the criminal law and criminal justice in future. On one hand, if offenders are charged under the 2007 Act, it could be seen as a more liberal approach based on individual responsibility for crime because offenders would be charged with helping or assisting as a separate offence, rather than with the full offence. On the other hand, under the 2007 Act there is no requirement that the full offence actually has to have taken place, and so the law could be seen as moving even further towards risk-based criminality in terms of its substantive requirements. Such confusion also threatens to breach Article 7 of the ECHR (the right to know exactly what the offence someone is accused of involves in terms of criminal behaviour).

Fourthly, the discussion examined inchoate offences in more detail. Like complicity, these offences move away from requiring the full *actus reus* and *mens rea* of an offence to be completed, but still allow the same punishments to be given as for offenders who do complete the full offence. As shown above, the new offence of statutory incitement does not require the full offence to be carried out, and only requires belief that the offence will be committed, rather than intent. The offence of conspiracy is clearly aimed at reducing risk from those who do not become involved in committing the main offence, but have intentionally played a part in agreeing that the full offence is committed. In the law of attempt, the discretion left to courts to decide how far people can go towards committing the full *actus reus* of an offence has led to inconsistent decisions in practice, and the criminalisation of impossible attempts seems to prioritise the risk posed by those who intend to commit crime over the fact that no harm has actually been caused (Duff 1997). Overall, these developments could be seen as another move towards risk-based criminality, or as a legitimate, paternalistic state response to public fear of crime, particularly serious crime such as terrorism. The danger with such approaches is that they can lead to the erosion of rights and due process in the name of reducing risk (Zedner 2005), such as the right to liberty under Article 5 of the ECHR.

Turning to criminal justice issues discussed in this chapter, the aim of the case study was to ask whether different forms of punishment – financial and admonitory penalties community penalties and custodial penalties – punished convicted offenders in a way which respected due process and the extent of their criminal behaviour, or whether they had other punishment aims in mind, such as reform, risk management or the maintenance of social power.

Garland's (1990) work is a particularly useful way of placing explanations of how punishment is carried out in context. Garland examines the work of writers on punishment whose arguments fit in with the major theoretical approaches to criminal justice introduced in Chapter 1. Garland argues that although all of these approaches play a part in explaining the aims of punishment as they are today, they all have weaknesses too, especially in the sense that each approach does not recognise that the others also have a part to play in explaining punishment. In other words, Garland argues that punishment has more than one aim and reflects more than one set of interests. He therefore takes a pluralistic approach to understanding punishment.

The discussion of the different aims of punishment above fits in with Garland's pluralistic view. It is certainly true that there has been a trend towards risk management and crime control across the whole range of punishments available. If ASBOs can be seen as an admonitory penalty, they certainly seem to be driven by social control approaches, extending the net of criminal justice (Cohen 1985) to punish behaviour which is not defined as a crime and threatening those who do not comply with prison. The National Probation Service, the agency mainly responsible for operating community punishment, has moved towards a risk-assessment and surveillance-based approach to punishment, using electronic risk assessment tools such as OASyS to respond to offenders according to how dangerous they are perceived to be. Similarly, the prison network in England and Wales has been argued by radical writers such as Mathiesen (2005) to be concerned with controlling those who are seen to be a threat to the powerful in society, repressing and dehumanising them using harsh prison conditions and physical violence.

However, risk management and punitive approaches cannot explain everything about criminal justice punishment in England and Wales today. The fine, which is not used as a punishment as much as it used to be but is still one of the most common punishments overall, does not involve any supervision or surveillance, and is best understood as a just deserts or due process-based way of punishing (Bottoms 1983). Managerialism and bureaucracy also play a key part in community punishment, with the use of National Standards for the National Probation Service and for Youth Offending Teams. Although managerialism can combine with punitive and social control methods of punishment to produce more centralised and extensive methods of punitive, social control-based punishment across different levels of the punishment network where the government force local-level criminal justice workers to take a tougher approach to their work – what Cavadino and Dignan (2007) call 'punitive managerialism' – it can also lead to less punishment in practice, such as the speeding up of youth justice court cases and the requirements for different criminal justice agencies to work more closely together in administering punishment under New Labour (ibid.).

There is also some evidence that probation staff still have discretion over how they punish people, despite the increase in managerialist control over their practice, and use this discretion to try to rehabilitate offenders rather than just socially controlling them – something which indicates that the medical model of individualised, treatment-based response to crime still plays a part in criminal justice (King 1981: 108–11) – as well as using other approaches to punishment which are capable of recognising offenders' human rights by treating them fairly, such as restorative justice in referral orders and reparation orders for young people and restorative projects for both minor and serious adult offenders (Shapland et al. 2006). Similarly, the evidence of Liebling and Arnold (2004) points not only to the discretion that prison staff have over how they deal with offenders, but also to the fact that prisons are also capable of rehabilitating prisoners and treating them with fairness and respect, recognising their basic human rights. The regime at HMP Grendon is an excellent example of how such an approach can – and does – work in practice.

Overall, then, there seems to have been a trend towards harsher punishments and social control in punishment. But it is important not to fall into the trap of thinking that this trend explains everything about punishment (e.g. Matthews 2005). Individual discretion over how punishment works in practice, including recognition of the role of offenders in how well punishment works, means that only a range of different explanations for punishment (including rehabilitation and just deserts/human rights) can do justice to how it really works. In the same way, a range of different approaches to criminal responsibility can be found in the criminal law, in the shape of complicity, strict liability and inchoate offences, which move beyond liberal ideas about proportionate criminal responsibility based on an individual's voluntary actions.

This chapter concludes the first part of the book, which has explained basic legal principles and how the key stages of the criminal justice process can be explained and understood on the basis of the different theoretical approaches outlined in Chapter 1. The second part of the book builds on the concepts explained in the first part, to look at specific types of criminal offence, how criminal justice responds to them, and why the law and criminal justice respond in the ways in which they do.

FURTHER READING

Allen, M. (2007), *Textbook on Criminal Law* (9th edn): chapters 4, 7 and 8. Oxford: Oxford University Press.

Ashworth, A. (2006), *Principles of Criminal Law* (5th edn): chapters 10 and 11. Oxford: Oxford University Press.

Gelsthorpe, L., and Morgan, R. (eds) (2007), *Handbook on Probation*. Cullompton: Willan.

Jewkes, Y. (ed.) (2007), *Handbook on Prisons*. Cullompton: Willan.

Squires, P., and Stephen, D.E. (2005), *Rougher Justice: Antisocial Behaviour and Young People*. Cullompton: Willan.

Part Two

Specific criminal offences

Non-fatal assaults

Chapter Aims

After reading Chapter 6 you should be able to understand:

- Which non-fatal, non-sexual assault offences there are in the criminal law
- What the *actus reus* and *mens rea* requirements are for each offence
- What the consent defence is in the context of assault, and how it works
- How criminal justice responds to non-fatal assaults
- How criminal justice responds to violence committed on the grounds of gender and race
- How the evidence on non-fatal assaults in the criminal law and criminal justice fits in with the theoretical models introduced in Chapter 1

Introduction

Chapter 6 is the first of the chapters in the book which explain the major types of specific criminal offence. This chapter covers non-fatal, non-sexual assaults against the person.[1] The first part of this chapter explains the law on non-fatal assaults in detail. The second part of the chapter then contextualises the law by examining how it is used in criminal justice practice.

Non-Fatal Assaults: The Law

Making sense of non-fatal assaults

DEFINITION BOX 6.1

NON-FATAL, NON-SEXUAL VIOLENT OFFENCES

Criminal offences which involve some kind of physical or psychological harm being caused to V by D, which does not involve sexual activity.

The law on non-fatal offences against the person deals with situations where the criminal law prohibits contact with, and sometimes injury of, another person's body. The law is based around statutory definitions of different types of assault, contained in the Offences against the Person Act 1861 (hereafter 'OAPA'). The different categories of assault will now be discussed, starting with the least serious offences and moving towards the most serious. A defence to non-fatal assaults – consent – will then be explained.

Common assault

Actus reus

Common assault is now defined as a criminal offence in s. 39 of the Criminal Justice Act 1988, although the common law offence is still in operation (*DPP v Taylor; Little* [1992] 1 All ER 299). The *actus reus* is the same for both the statutory and the common law offences. D must cause V to 'apprehend immediate application of unlawful violence to the body' (*Venna* [1976] QB 421). V must fear that they will suffer unlawful violence in the immediate future, rather than at some other later time (*Tuberville v Savage* (1669) 1 Mod Rep 3). There is no need for the violence to actually occur, as long as V feels that they are about to suffer such violence against them. Under *Logdon v DPP* [1976] Crim LR 121, as long as V is in fear, it does not

---

[1]The discussion in this chapter does not relate to sexual assaults, which are the focus of Chapter 7. This chapter refers to non-fatal non-sexual assaults as 'non-fatal assaults', to save space.

matter if the violence is not actually possible in the circumstances. Conversely, if V does not fear unlawful violence, then the *actus reus* of assault has not been committed, even if V actually does suffer unlawful violence which has been caused by D (*Lamb* [1967] 2 QB 981). *Fagan v Metropolitan Police Commissioner* [1969] 1 QB 438 shows that assault can be committed by D's omissions as well as acts. *Ireland; Burstow* [1998] AC 147 made it clear that assault can be committed by words alone, as well as by D's physical actions.

Although 'immediate unlawful violence' must be feared by V, the threat of violence does not actually have to be capable of being carried out immediately, in the sense of the next few seconds. In *Smith v Chief Superintendent of Woking Police Station* (1983) 76 Cr App Rep 234, V saw D through a closed and locked window. D was guilty of assault even though it would have taken him some time to get through the window and cause unlawful violence to V. This principle was taken further by *Ireland; Burstow*, where the House of Lords stated that V fearing the possibility of immediate violence was enough to meet the *actus reus* requirements for assault. This principle covers the situation where, for example, D makes threatening phone calls to V, and V does not know exactly where D is, but fears that D might be close enough to carry out the threat of unlawful violence immediately.

Mens rea

Under *Venna*, common assault can be committed either intentionally or recklessly. *Savage; Parmenter* [1991] 1 AC 699 decided that only subjective recklessness is enough, so that D must see the risk of V apprehending immediate unlawful violence and continue with their actions anyway.

STUDY EXERCISE 6.1

Is the extension of the 'immediacy' principle in *Ireland; Burstow* justified in terms of preventing social harm?

Battery

Actus reus

The *actus reus* of battery is defined as causing the application of unlawful force to V's body (*DPP v Taylor; Little*). As with common assault, the *actus reus* of battery is defined in s. 39 of the Criminal Justice Act 1988, but is also a common law offence. Any force applied to someone else's body can be enough for the *actus reus* of battery – at least in theory. The *actus reus* of battery can be committed directly (*Fagan v MPC*) or indirectly, where D does not directly apply force to V's body but still *causes* unlawful force to be applied, as in *Martin* (1881) 8 QBD 54, *DPP v K* [1990] 1 WLR 1067, and *Haystead v Chief Constable of Derbyshire* [2000] 3 All ER 890.

Mens rea

The *mens rea* requirements for battery are exactly the same as the *mens rea* requirements for common assault (see above).

▬▬▬▬▬▬▬▬▬▬▬▬ STUDY EXERCISE 6.2 ▬▬▬▬▬▬▬▬▬▬▬▬

Hirst (1999) argues that battery should not be able to be committed indirectly. Do you agree? Explain your answer.

Racially and religiously aggravated assault

▬▬▬▬▬▬▬▬▬▬▬▬ DEFINITION BOX 6.2 ▬▬▬▬▬▬▬▬▬▬▬▬

RACIALLY AND RELIGIOUSLY AGGRAVATED ASSAULTS

Assault which is at least partially motivated by hostility shown by D to V on the grounds of V's racial or religious background, or by hostility to the members of a racial or religious group based on their membership of that group.

Section 29 of the Crime and Disorder Act 1998 created a new offence of racially aggravated assault. This is proved where D, at the time of committing the offence, or immediately before or after committing it, showed V hostility based on V's membership (or presumed membership) of a racial group, or where D's offence is wholly or partly motivated by hostility towards members of a racial group based on their membership of that group. Section 39 of the Anti-Terrorism, Crime and Security Act 2001 set up a parallel offence of religiously aggravated assault, where D, at the time of committing the offence, or immediately before or after committing it, showed V hostility based on V's membership (or presumed membership) of a religious group, or where D's offence is wholly or partly motivated by hostility towards members of a religious group based on their membership of that group.

Although *DPP v Pal* [2000] Crim LR 756 decided that D calling V 'a white man's arse licker' was not a racial insult because it did not refer to V being Asian, later cases have taken a wider view of the law. *DPP v Woods* [2002] EWHC Admin 85 decided that racist language was enough aggravation in itself. *White* [2001] WLR 1352 decided that a racially aggravated offence could be committed against another person from the same racial group as D. Finally, in *Attorney-General's Reference (No. 4 of 2004)* [2005] 1 WLR 2810, the phrase 'immigrant doctor' was held to amount to racial aggravation, even though the phrases covered a range of racial groups, not just one.

████████████████ STUDY EXERCISE 6.3 ████████████████

In *Rogers* [2006] 1 Cr App Rep 14, D used the phrase 'bloody foreigners' and this was enough to convict him of a racially aggravated offence. Was this the right outcome?

Harassment

████████████████ DEFINITION BOX 6.3 ████████████████

HARASSMENT OFFENCES

Offences involving D causing harassment or fear of violence to V through a course of conduct, where D knows or should know that this will be the effect of their behaviour.

The 1997 Protection from Harassment Act created two new offences of harassment. The prohibited conduct must be a 'course of conduct' amounting to 'harassment', so that D knows or should know that their conduct amounts to harassment, and a reasonable person would agree that the conduct amounted to harassment, even if D did not (s. 1 of the 1997 Act). *Lau v DPP* [2000] Crim LR 580 shows that there needs to be at least two incidents to count as a 'course of conduct' with a link between them. In *Kelly v DPP* [2003] Crim LR 45, D made three phone calls in five minutes to V, leaving an answer phone message each time. V listened to the messages one after the other and this was held to be enough to be a 'course of conduct'. But *Lau* showed that the incidents do not have to be close together like this. They could even be up to a year apart. However, as there has to be a link between them, the longer the gap in time is between the incidents, the less likely it will be that they will amount to a course of conduct. *Hills* [2001] Crim LR 318 shows that a s. 2 course of conduct does not have to be same kind of incident each time, although repetition of behaviour is a factor to be taken into account.

The more serious harassment offence is causing fear of violence on at least two occasions (s. 4 of the 1997 Act). There has to be a course of conduct involving at least two occasions where V is put in fear of violence, where D knows or ought to know that it will cause V to fear that violence will be used against them. D ought to know this if, on any occasion, a reasonable person in possession of the same information would think that the course of conduct would cause V to fear violence on that occasion. *Henley* [2000] Crim LR 582 confirms that for the s. 4 offence, the fear of violence must occur on at least two occasions, and be caused by a course of conduct which must also involve at least two incidents. This case also shows that the *mens rea* for the s. 4 offence is that D knew or ought to have known that the course of conduct would cause fear to V on each occasion.

In terms of the fear of violence required, *Henley* shows that the s. 4 fear of violence does not have the same requirements as common assault because for s. 4 there is no need for the violence to be immediate. *Caurti v DPP* [2002] Crim LR 131 shows that all of the incidents must be targeted at the same person for the s. 4 offence, and that V must fear violence against themselves, not just violence against someone else. Under *Patel* [2005] Crim LR 649, there must be a link between the two incidents, in terms of their type, context and proximity, to prove that there was a course of conduct. This requirement is the same as the one for the s. 2 offence.

STUDY EXERCISE 6.4

Do we need the Protection from Harassment Act offences now that *Ireland; Burstow* has confirmed that causing psychiatric harm counts as assault under the Offences against the Person Act 1861?

Assault occasioning actual bodily harm

Actus reus

This offence (hereafter 'ABH') is defined in s. 47 of OAPA. There are three *actus reus* requirements for ABH. The first is that the *actus reus* of either common assault or battery has occurred. Secondly, D must cause the ABH to occur – both factual and legal causation must be proved in this context (*Lewis* [1970] Crim LR 647). Thirdly, 'actual bodily harm' itself has to be 'occasioned' to V. *Miller* [1954] 2 QB 282 defines ABH as 'any hurt or injury calculated to interfere with health and comfort of V', and *T v DPP* [2003] Crim LR 622 again gives ABH a broad and loosely defined scope in stating that it includes any harm that is more than 'transient or trifling'. *Chan-Fook* [1994] 2 All ER 552 and *Ireland; Burstow* show that psychiatric injury can count as ABH as long as it is in the form of a medically recognised psychiatric condition, rather than simply nervousness, fear or anxiety; and *Constanza* [1997] 2 Cr App Rep 492 states that ABH can be committed by words alone as well as actions.

Mens rea

The only *mens rea* required for proof of ABH is the *mens rea* for either common assault or battery, that is either intention or subjective recklessness (*Roberts* (1971) 56 Cr App Rep 95).

STUDY EXERCISE 6.5

Why do you think the legal definition of ABH overlaps so much with the legal definitions of common assault and battery?

Wounding or inflicting grievous bodily harm

Actus reus

The definition of these offences is contained in OAPA s. 20. There are two separate offences under s. 20. The *actus reus* for wounding is any break in the continuity of V's skin (*Moriarty v Brookes* (1834) 6 C & P 684). Even a minor external cut which draws blood can be enough to meet the *actus reus* requirements, although internal bleeding does not count as a wound (*JCC v Eisenhower* (1984) 78 Cr App Rep 48), and neither do broken bones, where the skin is not broken (e.g. *Wood* (1830) 1 Mood CC 278).

Broken bones would instead be classed as grievous bodily harm (hereafter 'GBH'), the other offence under s. 20. GBH, like ABH, is widely defined. The *actus reus* of GBH is inflicting 'really serious harm', under *DPP v Smith* [1961] AC 290, and the jury has to decide whether V's injuries are serious enough to be classed as GBH on the facts. In making this decision, the jury has to take into account the overall extent of V's injuries rather than individual injuries one by one (*Birmingham* [2002] EWCA Crim 2608) and must also consider the impact of the injuries on V in particular, taking into account V's age and state of health (*Bollom* [2004] 2 Cr App Rep 6). GBH can also include really serious psychiatric injury (*Ireland; Burstow*).

The other key issue regarding the *actus reus* of GBH and wounding is what 'inflict' really means in this context – in other words, what D actually has to do to commit GBH or wounding. In *Wilson* [1984] AC 242, the House of Lords decided that 'inflicting' GBH did not have to mean that a common assault or a battery had been committed – it had a wider meaning than this. *Ireland; Burstow* provided more detail on the scope of 'infliction' by stating that there was no difference between 'inflicting' and 'causing', and that, for both GBH and wounding under s. 20, there was no need for violence to be directly applied to V's body in the form of an assault or battery. As with the other assault offences, causation of GBH or wounding must be proved in terms of factual and legal causation, and where V is injured trying to escape from D, the chain of causation will be broken where V's escape is not foreseeable by a reasonable person – V's personal characteristics, such as age, are not taken into account (*Marjoram* [2000] Crim LR 372).

Mens rea

The *mens rea* requirements are the same for both s. 20 offences. The word used for *mens rea* in s. 20 itself is 'maliciously', which means that D must have intention or subjective recklessness (*Savage; Parmenter*). However, D only has to intend or foresee the risk of *some* bodily harm, not necessarily GBH or wounding. D also only has to foresee the risk that some harm *might* happen (*Mowatt* [1968] 1 QB 421), not an obvious and significant risk of harm (*Brady* [2007] Crim LR 564).

The maximum sentences for s. 20 GBH and s. 47 ABH are the same (five years' imprisonment). Is this fair?

Wounding with intent or inflicting grievous bodily harm with intent

Actus reus

These offences are covered by s. 18 of OAPA. The meanings of 'wounding' and 'GBH' are the same as they are for s. 20 GBH. As with the other non-fatal assaults, factual and legal causation must be proved.

Mens rea

It is the *mens rea* requirements which make the s. 18 offences different from the s. 20 offences. There are two stages to the *mens rea* for s. 18. First, unlike s. 20 GBH, s. 18 GBH cannot be committed recklessly (*Belfon* [1976] 3 All ER 46). D must intend to inflict GBH, having either direct or oblique intent. Secondly, D must also have what is known as an ulterior intent. In other words, D must not only inflict the GBH or wounding itself intentionally, but must also have a pre-existing, ulterior direct or oblique intent to do this. As a result, for offences of causing GBH or wounding with intent to do GBH, intention means the same as it does for murder (*Bryson* [1985] Crim LR 699). There is also a subsidiary s. 18 offence of inflicting GBH with intent to resist arrest. Here, although the *actus reus* is the same, the *mens rea* requirements are slightly different from the other s. 18 offences. The ulterior intent to resist arrest must be present, but D does not have to have intent to inflict GBH – subjective recklessness as to whether GBH would be inflicted on V is enough for a conviction (*Morrison* [1989] 89 Cr App Rep 17).

STUDY EXERCISE 6.7

How easy do you think the *actus reus* and *mens rea* requirements for s. 18 GBH are to prove in court? Why?

Consent as a defence to non-fatal assaults

DEFINITION BOX 6.4

THE CONSENT DEFENCE TO ASSAULTS

A defence to D's assault-related offence against V, on the grounds of V's consent to being assaulted by D in one of a range of circumstances allowed by the criminal law.

Introduction

In some circumstances, V can consent to the assault committed against them. In this situation, consent acts as a defence to the assault charge for D. In effect, there is a two-stage test to find out whether the defence of consent can be used. The first stage asks whether there is express or implied consent. The second stage asks whether the law will allow someone to consent to physical harm in a particular situation. Both of these stages will now be discussed in turn.

Express or implied consent?

The starting point for the criminal law is to ask whether or not there actually has been express or implied consent to an assault by V. Although any non-consensual contact with someone else's body is technically enough *actus reus* for a battery, the law recognises that there has to be implied consent from 'victims' for every-day contact with others – for example, contact with other people while brushing past someone in a busy street – so in situations like this the law will not take action (*Collins v Wilcock* [1984] 3 All ER 374). In some cases the law will not allow people to consent to bodily contact because, for example, of their age (e.g. *Burrell v Harmer* [1967] Crim LR 169).

Another issue is what happens when V gives consent to an assault against them, but only does so because of fraud by D. The general rule here is that D's fraud can remove consent if the fraud relates to whom D is, or what D is doing to V, but not if the fraud relates to the circumstances surrounding what D is doing. In *Richardson* [1999] QB 444, there was implied consent by Vs to ABH (in the form of dental treatment) where they knew that D was a dentist, but did not know that she had been disqualified from practice. On the other hand, in *Tabassum* [2000] 2 Cr App Rep 328, the female victims did not impliedly consent to indecent assault where they knew what D was doing to them (touching their breasts), but did not know that he had lied to them about who he was because he was not a qualified doctor as he claimed. In *Dica* [2004] QB 1257, it was decided that V did not impliedly consent to the risk of GBH through being infected with HIV/AIDS where she had sex with D, not knowing that D was infected with the disease. In *Konzani* [2005] 2 Cr App Rep 14, another case of HIV/AIDS infection, the Court of Appeal emphasised that only informed consent to contracting a potentially fatal disease could be a defence. Taking the risk of potential harm from unprotected sex was not implied consent to the risk of contracting HIV/AIDS. Therefore, D was guilty of s. 20 GBH where he knew that he had HIV/AIDS, did not tell V, and recklessly infected V with the disease.

What legal limits are there on consent?

Attorney-General's Reference (No. 6 of 1980) [1981] QB 715 decided that the limit of the consent defence is ABH. D is guilty, even though V has consented, if ABH or any worse level of harm is intended and/or caused. The exception to this rule is where the law decides that consent to the harm is in the 'public interest'. There have been a wide range of cases, before and after *Attorney-General's Reference (No. 6 of 1980)*, which have decided the situations in which the law will and will not allow people to consent to harm committed against them. Two general categories of case involving this decision will be considered here – cases involving sexual activity or violence (or both), and cases involving sports.

Sex and violence cases

The criminal law has tended to disallow the consent defence where consensual harm is caused during sexual activity. In *Donovan* [1934] 2 KB 498, V was not allowed to consent to D caning her, and causing injury to the level of ABH as a result, for sexual pleasure. Similarly, in *Boyea* [1992] Crim LR 574, where D's behaviour during consensual sex caused injury to V's vagina, V could not consent to the ABH which resulted because D's act was 'likely' to cause harm. The most famous case in this category is *Brown* [1994] 1 AC 212, where a group of Ds engaged in consensual but violent homosexual sadomasochism in private, causing injury to one another as a result. The House of Lords decided that Vs could not consent to the intentional infliction of serious harm, and therefore the Ds were guilty of ABH and GBH as a result. However, this decision was only made by a majority of three to two. The majority thought that violence for sexual pleasure was not in the public interest, and that the risk to participants' health could not be justified, although none of the participants needed hospital treatment. The minority argued that there was no permanent injury or damage to health, and that everyone involved had consented fully to what was done to them. Therefore, the law should not get involved by criminalising their behaviour. The two Law Lords in the minority prioritised the Ds' individual rights to freedom of expression over the public interest in not having to witness the behaviour involved. *Brown* was later applied to heterosexual sadomasochism in *Emmett* (1999) *The Times*, 15 October, where D was convicted of ABH after causing consensual injury to V, his girlfriend, during sex. In contrast, the D in *Slingsby* [1995] Crim LR 570 was not guilty of unlawful act manslaughter where the assault he caused to V (which she consented to lawfully during sex) unintentionally caused V's death.

Cases such as *Brown* can be contrasted with other cases which involve non-sexual violence. Here, the criminal law is more reluctant to criminalise people's behaviour. In *Jones* (1986) 83 Cr App Rep 375, the Court of Appeal decided that V impliedly consented to reckless 'horseplay' which caused GBH, and therefore the Ds were not guilty of any offence. Similarly, in *Aitken* [1992] 4 All ER 541, the Court of Appeal stated that the Ds were not guilty of GBH where they had poured flammable white spirit over V and set it alight, causing severe burns, because V had impliedly consented to 'horseplay'. There was no express consent from either of the Vs in these two cases. The courts found implied consent from Vs' behaviour before and during the causing of their injuries. Another interesting example of the courts deciding not to get involved in consensual violence is *Wilson* [1997] QB 47, where D was not guilty of ABH where he branded his wife's bottom after she had asked him to. The Court of Appeal decided that this was allowed because it was similar to tattooing, another physical injury allowed under the public interest.

Sports cases

A series of cases has addressed the issues of liability and consent where D injures V while they are both playing sport. *Billinghurst* [1978] Crim LR 553 shows that V impliedly consents to contact or injury caused within the rules of the sport being played, and also impliedly consents to illegitimate contacts which are an 'inevitable part' of the game being played – a late tackle in a game of football which causes pain or injury, for example. However, there are limits to this principle, as shown by *Birkin* [1988] Crim LR 855, where the court decided that V could not and did not consent to being punched while playing football because punching is clearly not allowed under the rules of this game. *Barnes* [2005] 1 WLR 910 clarified the criteria by which courts had to decide whether a victim had consented to sporting injuries. Lord Woolf CJ stated that a range of issues had to be considered in making this decision, such as the type of sport played (i.e. whether it was a contact or a non-contact sport), the level at which the game was being played (amateur or professional), the nature of the act committed by D, and the level of force used by D in assaulting V.

The second part of the chapter considers the law on non-fatal assaults in their criminal justice context.

STUDY EXERCISE 6.8

In *Laskey, Jaggard and Brown v UK* [1997] 2 EHRR 39, the European Court of Human Rights decided that the decision in *Brown* did not breach Article 8 of the European Convention on Human Rights (the right to privacy and respect for private life under the criminal law). Do you agree with this decision? Why?

Non-Fatal Assaults and Criminal Justice

Example I: non-fatal assaults – police, courts and punishment

The police in England and Wales recorded a total of 1,046,437 incidents of violence in 2006/07, a decrease of 1% compared with 2005/06, while the British Crime Survey (BCS) estimated that there were 2,471,000 incidents of violence against adults in England and Wales in 2006/07 (Jansson et al. 2007: 54–7). Of violent offences recorded by the police in 2006/07, 47% did not involve any physical injury to anyone (ibid.: 57), and violent crime reported to the BCS has decreased by 41% comparing 2006/07 figures to the peak figure in 1995 (ibid.: 54). These data portray violence as being an issue which may be a persistent problem in society, but which does not cause serious harm in most cases.

However, the statistics only give a limited picture of non-fatal violence in England and Wales, for a number of reasons. First, violence itself does not have a fixed meaning, and its meanings in a particular time and place can depend on a number of social and legal factors (Stanko 2003). For example, common assaults were only counted in police crime statistics from 1998 onwards. Secondly, there is the problem of the public not reporting the majority of violent crimes which occur to the police – a factor which BCS data highlight – and the additional incidents which are reported to the police but not recorded by them, as shown in Chapter 2 (Mayhew 2007). Sivarajasingam et al. (2007), who studied 33 hospitals' Accident and Emergency records on admissions for violent injuries, and found that even though on these data serious violence declined by 2% between 2005 and 2006, rates of violence discovered were twice as high as BCS figures, and around three times higher than police records. Thirdly, offences which do not cause physical injury can still have a serious impact upon victims. Pathé and Mullen (1997), for example, found that 83% of the people in their study had experienced increased levels of anxiety as a result of stalking, 55% had experienced intrusive flashbacks and recollections of the stalking, and 24% had had suicidal thoughts.

STUDY EXERCISE 6.9

List three reasons why you think the recorded rate of non-fatal violent crime has increased in England and Wales since the mid-1990s.

Cretney and Davis (1995) argue that unless a victim makes a complaint, and so shows commitment to making a statement and providing evidence in court, the police are reluctant to take any further action. Factors such as victims seeing themselves as being socially marginalised, or not wanting to have their conduct examined by the police, were also important in victims deciding not to report incidents as well as fear of reprisals (Clarkson et al. 1994: 11–13). However, Cretney and Davis go on to argue that a victim's effectiveness and commitment to the prosecution process are more important than the police's view of how 'deserving' the victim is of help. The police can either test the victim's effectiveness and willingness to help in the criminal justice process – by asking victims to gather further evidence or deliberately delaying investigation of the case, for example – or try to encourage a complaint to be made, by seeking out witnesses following arrests in a public order incident, or by charging for assault in an attempt to secure a plea-bargain for an alternative public order offence, such as affray or violent disorder, which represented a public challenge to police authority on the streets (McConville et al. 1991).

In terms of CPS attitudes to violence, Cretney and Davis found that the CPS's guidelines, policies and discretion were able to limit police decision-making power to prosecute. In their study, the police were reliant upon the CPS, as well as victims and witnesses, to bring a case to court. Cretney and Davis found that the CPS routinely reduced the initial charge, but blamed this on the outdated structure of the assault offences and difficulties of proving the elements of each offence. As a result, for example, s. 18 GBH charges were almost always reduced to s. 20 GBH, to make the process of securing a conviction easier. This process does, of course, distort the link between the seriousness of harm caused and the punishment received. Clarkson et al. (1994) found extensive levels of plea-bargaining to lesser offences, with as many as a third of cases being 'defined down' through agreement between the prosecution and defence before the start of a trial.

Turning to how the courts deal with offences of violence, in 2006, 29.5% of those convicted of violence against the person were sentenced to immediate custody (Ministry of Justice 2007c: 10), compared with 22% in 1994 (Levi et al. 2007: 719), and although the average custodial sentence length for violent offences in the Crown Court has decreased slightly since 2002, to 23.2 months in 2006, the average sentence length in the magistrates' court has increased since 1996, to 4.0 months in 2006 (Ministry of Justice 2007c: 12, 14). This is the case even though violent offences made up only 19% of the police-recorded crime and 22% of the BCS-recorded crime in 2006/07 (Thorpe et al. 2007: 17). Genders (1999) found confusion between the different offences in the courts. Only 19% of cases in her study that were charged as s. 18 GBH were convicted of the same offence. Genders found that the main reason for this was not police or CPS action, but 're-labelling' in the courts, which accounted for 60% of the changes. This suggested over-optimistic charging by police and CPS staff, based on moral judgements about the blameworthiness of different defendants, which did not reflect the difficulties of proving intent for the s. 18 offence. Fielding's (2006) study did not find evidence that the overlaps between the legal categories of assault in terms of *actus reus* and *mens rea* (see above) were seen as problematic for defendants, victims and witnesses. However, defendants, witnesses and victims were frustrated by legal language used in court (which many found difficult to understand) as well as legal procedures on evidence which they felt did not allow them to tell their story and put their views across effectively in court. A lack of resources – such as prison vans not delivering defendants to the court on time – often affected the efficiency and fairness of the violent offence hearings, to the point where miscarriages of justice were made very likely.

Finally, turning to methods of punishing violent offenders, Jones (2000: chapter 10) provides an overview of the literature on the effectiveness of different approaches. Jones shows that most offenders do not have the opportunity to address and change their offending behaviour until they have been convicted in the criminal justice process. Jones argues that cognitive-behavioural approaches to treating violent offenders have largely replaced psycho-analytical approaches, which are based around psychiatrists counselling individual offenders. He claims that the two main reasons for this change were that psycho-analytical programmes could not be evaluated exactly enough to produce the clear evidence on re-offending rates which politicians want, and that cognitive-behavioural programmes were based around the idea of blaming offenders for their voluntary conduct, rather than implying that offenders were not fully responsible for their actions, as psychoanalytical work tended to do. Jones goes on to say that cognitive-behavioural programmes have been shown to work best for minor offenders rather than serious ones (ibid.: 165–6), and points to alternative forms of treatment, such as the intensive group therapy used in HMP Grendon, which has been shown to reduce re-offending even with serious violent offenders.

▓▓▓▓▓▓▓▓▓▓▓▓▓▓▓▓▓▓▓▓▓▓ STUDY EXERCISE 6.10 ▓▓▓▓▓▓▓▓▓▓▓▓▓▓▓▓▓▓▓▓▓▓

Observe a trial of non-fatal violence in either a magistrates' or a Crown Court near you. Was the process of justice slowed down by delays and witnesses and victims struggling to understand what was going on, as Fielding (2006) found in his research?

Example II: domestic violence and criminal justice[2]

The Home Office currently defines domestic violence as any violent behaviour targeting a current or former partner. The extensive social harm caused by domestic violence is well documented (e.g. Stanko 1985). Walby and Allen (2004), for example, found that 4% of women (12.9m incidents) and 2% of men (2.5m incidents) questioned by the BCS had experienced non-sexual domestic violence in the previous year, and that women were not only more likely to be the victim of domestic violence overall, but were also far more likely than men to suffer serious and multiple attacks. They also found (ibid.: 112) that when self-completion techniques were used by the BCS for questions about domestic violence, the number of incidents reported was five times higher than the usual BCS levels, showing that even the BCS figures are a significant underestimate of how much domestic violence really occurs in England and Wales. Stanko (2001) counted all the telephone calls made to the police in the UK about domestic violence on one day, and found that even in this short period of time, injuries reported included stabbings and severe psychological trauma.

As shown by the explanation of the law on non-fatal assaults earlier, there is no specific offence of domestic violence in the criminal law. Therefore, criminal justice has to respond to this type of violence within the framework of non-fatal assaults in the Offences against the Person Act 1861, as well as the more recent harassment offences introduced by the Protection from Harassment Act 1997. There are also powers of police arrest for breaches of civil law injunctions aimed at preventing further domestic violence from occurring.

Looking at police responses first, early research showed that police were very reluctant to intervene in cases of domestic violence (Dobash and Dobash 1979). Over time, however, public opinion began to recognise how serious a problem domestic violence was, and began to demand that criminal justice did more to respond to it effectively (Dobash and Dobash 1992). The government responded by directing the police to develop new proactive policing to tackle domestic violence, and to form multi-agency partnerships with other agencies in doing this.

---

[2]A distinction is made in this subsection between non-sexual violence suffered in and around the home and sexual violence in the same context, which is discussed in more detail in Chapter 7. However, as Lacey et al. (2003: 629) point out, this distinction is artificial, and there is considerable overlap between non-sexual and sexual domestic violence in practice.

However, Kelly's (1999) study, which evaluated a project involving a police and civilian response team to tackle domestic violence in London, showed no significant improvement in arrest and charge rates for domestic violence, and inconsistent and unsystematic police record-keeping, even after the project had been implemented. Over time, though, multi-agency co-operation between the police and other agencies increased, as did victims' level of confidence in the police, while the number of repeat calls to police about domestic violence decreased. In relation to the Protection from Harassment Act powers, there is evidence that their impact on domestic violence has been limited. In Harris's (2000) study, victims were not always made aware of the powers available, the police did not record evidence consistently and rarely asked for CPS advice before charging, and the police did not keep most victims well informed about the progress of their case after charge.

Hoyle (1998) gave some indications as to why the improvement in the police response has been limited. She found that although victims sometimes withdrew their statements to the police, and that there was some evidence of the police not wanting to get involved with domestic disputes, a more significant reason why arrest rates did not improve was that only a third of victims of domestic violence in her study actually wanted the police to arrest their attackers, mainly because they did not want to end their relationship with the attacker, or feared more violence if the attacker was arrested. As a result, Hoyle argued that the police response to domestic violence was about negotiating a satisfactory outcome for the people involved, rather than sexist denial of risk to victims or power-based assertion of control. Overall, then, although the police's response to domestic violence has undoubtedly improved over the past 20 years, significant problems remain, and more projects are needed which use multi-agency, holistic and individually-tailored support for domestic violence victims alongside the formal response of the police (Hester and Westmarland 2005).

Turning to the response of the CPS and the courts to domestic violence, the research evidence has again been mixed. Barnish (2004) found that only between 2% and 4% of domestic violence cases reported to the police result in a conviction. Barnish also found that the majority of cases reaching court were prosecuted as common assault, despite 90% of cases resulting in physical injury, which would qualify as ABH on the current legal definition. One-third of the cases starting out as ABH were reduced to common assault.

In Cretney and Davis's (1997) research, 94% of domestic violence assaults were retained in the magistrates' court rather than being sent to the Crown Court (compared with 79% of non-domestic violence cases) and 18% of domestic violence cases were prosecuted as ABH or GBH (compared with 40% of non-domestic violence cases). Cretney and Davis also found that victims were shocked and distressed by the level of plea-bargaining and court tolerance of intimidatory questioning by the defence. As with the police, therefore, there are question marks over how effectively the CPS and the courts deal with domestic violence cases in terms of taking them seriously, and in terms of listening to victims and what they want from criminal justice.

Tadros (2005) argued that domestic violence is unlike other forms of violence because (a) the violence happens within an intimate relationship and (b) the violence is more systematic than street violence. Do you agree? If so, do you think a special aggravated domestic violence offence would make the criminal justice response to domestic violence more effective than it is now?

Example III: racial violence and criminal justice

Although the BCS has consistently shown that the risk of racial victimisation is no more than 2% for any ethnic group (Ministry of Justice 2007d: 11), the recording of racially violent offences has increased in recent years. From a starting point of 2,687 incidents of recorded racially aggravated 'less serious wounding' in 1999/00, the police recording rate rose to 6,107 in 2005/06, before dropping to 5,609 in 2006/07. The number of recorded racially aggravated harassment offences has risen every year since the offence was introduced, from 10,758 in 1999/00 to 28,485 in 2006/07, while the number of racially aggravated assaults without injury has remained stable, from 4,275 in 1999/00 to 4,350 in 2006/07 (Thorpe et al. 2007: 36).

In 2005, 51% of racially aggravated cases coming before the magistrates' courts, and 63% of cases coming before the Crown Court, resulted in conviction (Ministry of Justice 2007d: 12). These data suggest that criminal justice is taking racial violence more seriously than it did in the 1990s. However, the clear-up rate for racially and religiously aggravated violent offences has remained consistently lower than for non-racially and religiously aggravated violent offences of the same type – 40% for harassment compared with 68%, 42% for less serious wounding compared with 49%, and 35% for common assaults compared with 42% (Ministry of Justice 2007d: 11).

Evidence on the reality of criminal justice's responses to racist violence may help to explain why the attrition rate between the occurrence of racist violence and convictions for it remains high (Burney 2003). Bowling (1999) conducted research into the police's response to violent racist incidents in an area of high victimisation (East London). The research was conducted in the context of the publication of the Macpherson Report (Macpherson 1999) into police failures in the investigation of the racially motivated murder of Stephen Lawrence in 1993, in which the Metropolitan Police had been heavily criticised and labelled as 'institutionally racist' (see McLaughlin 2007: chapter 6) for further discussion). Bowling found that there was a low rate of satisfaction with police response to racial incidents, with only 5% feeling very satisfied with the way in which the police handled racial harassment in the local area, and less than a third of respondents feeling satisfied at all. Bowling also heard frequent complaints that the police did not do enough to respond to violent racism, showed lack of interest, and failed to keep victims informed about progress made in their case. In addition, Bowling's interviews with police officers revealed some evidence of racial prejudice on their part. His observation of the police at work found that these attitudes were reflected in their behaviour towards ethnic minorities, both as victims and suspects of crime. Bowling (1999: chapter 9) concluded that whatever changes there had been to levels of violent racism had very little to do with changes in police policy and practice, and that there were significant limits on the extent to which the police's attitudes could be changed due to the features of 'cop culture' (Reiner 2000).

Burney (2003: 31) cites data from the Home Office which suggested that the CPS downgrade racially aggravated offences to 'ordinary' offences of the same type in a significant minority of cases, and accepted guilty pleas to the lesser offences too often. On the other hand, the vagueness of the legislation meant that other offences were wrongly prosecuted as 'racial' when the motivation behind the offence was some other factor. This was partly due to the legislation itself, and the difficulty of proving motivation of offenders by hostility, as the 1998 Crime and Disorder Act requires.

Burney argues that punishing offenders harshly has a very limited effect – not only in the sense of the mixed evidence on how well deterrence works (von Hirsch et al. 1999), but also in the sense that so few perpetrators of racial violence are actually convicted for their behaviour. Hall (2005: chapter 12) supports this view. He argues strongly that it is unrealistic to expect the police to tackle violent racism on their own. While not arguing that any method is guaranteed to change the community-based attitudes that express themselves in racist violence (Sibbitt 1997), Hall reviews the evidence on community-based approaches to changing behaviour, and concludes that they are capable of making more of a difference than changes in police or sentencing policy. Hall emphasises the role of education in changing racist attitudes at a young age. This is a powerful message that there should be more to tackling racist violence than criminal justice alone.

STUDY EXERCISE 6.12

Which do you think is the best way of tackling racially aggravated crime effectively: (a) more powers for police; (b) tougher maximum sentences for these crimes in courts; or (c) better education on anti-racism in schools? Give reasons for your answer.

Discussion and Conclusions

The framework of criminal offences regulating non-fatal violence in England and Wales dates back to 1861. Horder (1994) is heavily critical of the different offences in the non-fatal assault framework, in terms of how the law splits them up from one another, and the uneven relationship between the blame attached to each offence, the harm caused by each offence, and the punishments available. For example, ABH has the same maximum penalty as s. 20 GBH when they are arguably not only different in terms of seriousness of harm, but also different types of offence. Such overlaps have human rights implications in terms of lack of certainty in the criminal law.

In some respects the law on assaults can be seen as reflecting liberal principles of protecting people from harm by others, or even risk-based principles of managing the danger caused to society by harassment, which can lead to more physical violence later – for example, *Ireland; Burstow* criminalising psychiatric assault, the s. 2 offence in the Protection from Harassment Act 1997, which is very wide in terms of the behaviour it can criminalise (Finch 2002), and the wide interpretation given to what counts as racial aggravation by the courts in *Rogers*. However, the criminal law has been reluctant to change the overall legal framework on assaults. On the other hand, it has been far more proactive in deciding how the defence of consent should work. There is no clear definition of consent in relation to non-fatal non-sexual offences, and the law has maximised its own power by reserving the discretion to decide when consent can and cannot be used for itself, even stating in recent cases that the defence cannot apply unless the law says it can, rather than the opposite (Bronitt 1994) – effectively reversing the burden of proof and placing it on the defendant. This has caused widespread confusion in the law.

On the one hand, a moral paternalistic approach, interfering with a person's freedom to do what they want to with their bodies on the basis of moral interests which that person themselves does not care about (Roberts 1997: 393–4), has been taken in cases where violence has been caused during consensual sex, such as *Brown, Boyea* and *Emmett* – decisions which challenge Articles 8 (the right to respect for private life) and 10 (the right to freedom of expression) of the ECHR. This moral paternalistic approach can also be seen where D has obtained consent to harm through fraud by passing on a sexually transmitted disease to V without telling V they have the disease, after the decisions in *Dica* and *Konzani*, where the law has moved towards risk-based criminality in this area, spreading fear of HIV/AIDS while failing to acknowledge the social reality of people who are aware of the risk of contracting sexually transmitted diseases but choose not to protect themselves against this risk (Weait 2007).

On the other hand, the law has taken a much more liberal approach to the issue of consent to injury while playing sports such as boxing (Bix 1993). Perhaps one explanation for the law's approach here is that the playing of sport has stereotypically been seen as something which is done by men in society (e.g. Williams and Taylor 1994: 215–16), and that it is therefore not appropriate for the law to become involved with 'natural' masculine activities. However, Gunn and Ormerod (1995) reviewed the evidence for and against boxing being legal, and concluded that, given the extensive medical evidence on increased chances of serious brain damage and other injuries for boxers (ibid.: 193–6), boxing could not be said to be in the 'public interest'. *Barnes* gives the courts maximum discretion to decide whether consent to the risk of sport-related injury has been breached, while making it clear that criminalisation will be the exception rather than the rule. Again, this represents a liberal approach to applying the criminal law, which is very different from the approach taken to violence caused during consensual sex. Another example of the more liberal approach is the so-called 'horseplay' cases such as *Aitken* and *Jones*, where consent was implied on very little evidence. The approach taken in these cases could also be argued to reinforce societal views on how men should behave. Connell (1987) has claimed that there is a 'hegemonic masculinity' in society which expects men to behave in a macho and violent way, and that this culture can be linked to the fact that men currently commit the vast majority of violent crime, at least on the basis on available statistics.

Given the chaotic and outdated nature of the criminal law on non-fatal, non-sexual assaults, criminal justice agencies have had to make sense of the response to violent behaviour largely for themselves. CPS charging standards, for example, have tried to differentiate between the offences by giving more details on which charge should be used in which circumstances, but these guidelines do not have the same influence as the law itself. More importantly, clear priorities have been made by the criminal justice agencies in terms of which types of violence they focus upon, and how different types of violence are dealt with. Cretney and Davis (1995) provide evidence of managerialist concerns influencing the police's response to different types of violence, in terms of the police taking into account how likely a victim is to assist criminal justice throughout the police and court process when deciding whether or not to investigate a case. Elsewhere, a mixture of crime control, managerialist and risk-based values have been found in the CPS approach to prosecuting violence, with Genders (1999) finding evidence of police and CPS over-charging, which had to be put right in the courts, and Cretney and Davis (1995) finding that the CPS routinely reduced initial police assault charges to lesser offences, but only did so to make the process of proving legal guilt easier, and the chances of conviction higher. This could be read as an attempt to make the court process as efficient as possible, a risk-based attitude which considered prosecution and punishment for something to be better than allowing a defendant to go free on the original charge, or a mixture of both. In this context, it is interesting that Fielding (2006) found that the processes which professional court agencies use to make their work more efficient – such as the privatisation of prison escort services bringing defendants to court and the specialised processes of giving evidence in court – actually made things less efficient in reality because they led to delays in court resolution of cases, which in turn made victims and witnesses less likely to understand and take part in the process effectively, which in turn made cases more likely to collapse.

These studies provide valuable evidence on the aims of criminal justice when it comes to dealing with violence. But equally valuable evidence can be found in terms of how and why criminal justice does *not* respond to some types of violence as effectively as others. Stanko (1994) argues that criminal justice's understanding of violence is heavily influenced by the idea of individuals committing violent acts in public spaces, such as alcohol-related street violence. In a risk-based approach, violence which does not fit in with this stereotype is seen as being 'low risk' and is responded to leniently; violence which is public and seen as a threat to public order is responded to more harshly.

Stanko's approach might explain why the rate of custodial sentences given for violence generally has increased rapidly in recent years, as the public fear of violence increases. But it might also explain the problems experienced by criminal justice in dealing effectively with violence against vulnerable victims. It was seen in the case studies in this chapter that although criminal justice policy has recently tried to compensate for its traditional ignorance of the impact of violence against women and ethnic minorities, and although public reporting of these offences has increased, changes to police and CPS practice in this area have been slow to take effect. It has been difficult to change cultural criminal justice attitudes about how different types of violence should be prioritised. This suggests that risk-based perceptions blend together with power-based, socially-excluding ideas about who is most likely to need, and most in need of, help as a victim of assault – ideas which stereotype and devalue those who are not always seen as deserving victims, such as women and ethnic minorities.

Such ideas give a distorted picture of the true social harm caused by violence, not only in the contexts of gender-based and racial violence, but also in other contexts. These might include the stereotyping of young people as criminals, which ignores their frequent violent victimisation (Brown 2005: chapter 5), and criminology's traditional ignorance of the impact of violence, which is caused by governments, both during and outside war, around the world (Cohen 2001). Between them, criminal law and criminal justice seem to offer the worst of both worlds in responding to the social harm caused by racist and sexist violence. The new laws introduced to combat these harms have been designed and interpreted too widely, so as to punish those who do not deserve to be punished, but the criminal justice response has remained too narrow in practice.

The next chapter switches focus to a particular type of non-fatal assault, namely sexual assault.

FURTHER READING

Bowling, B. (1999), *Violent Racism: Victimisation, Policing and Social Context*. Oxford: Clarendon Press.

Cretney, A., and Davis, G. (1995), *Punishing Violence*. London: Routledge.

Hoyle, C. (1998), *Negotiating Domestic Violence: Police, Criminal Justice, and Victims*. Oxford: Oxford University Press.

Ormerod, D. (2008), *Smith and Hogan's Criminal Law* (12th edn): chapter 17. Oxford: Oxford University Press.

Padfield, N. (2008), *Criminal Law* (6th edn): chapter 9. Oxford: Oxford University Press.

7

Sexual offences

Chapter Aims

After reading Chapter 7 you should be able to understand:

- The sexual offences introduced in the Sexual Offences Act 2003
- The *actus reus* and *mens rea* required for these offences
- The special offences used to regulate sexual behaviour involving children
- How different types of sexual offence and victim are responded to in criminal justice practice
- How the evidence on the response to sexual offences in the criminal law and criminal justice fits in with the theoretical models introduced in Chapter 1

Introduction

Chapter 7 covers the area of sexual offences in the criminal law. This chapter explains the key provisions in the new law introduced by the Sexual Offences Act

2003 as well as placing them in the wider social and criminal justice context of attitudes towards sexual behaviour. The focus will be on the key adult and child sexual offences. For a full consideration of all of the offences created or amended by the 2003 Act, see Card et al. (2008).

Sexual Offences: The Law

DEFINITION BOX 7.1

SEXUAL CRIMINAL OFFENCES

Offences which involve some kind of sexual activity between or involving D and V which is prohibited by the criminal law, either on the grounds of lack of consent (where the offence involves adults) or on the grounds of V being a child who is prohibited by the criminal law from consenting to sexual activity because of their age.

Rape

DEFINITION BOX 7.2

RAPE

A sexual offence involving the penetration of V's body with D's penis, without V's consent (i.e. where V has not made a free and informed decision to consent to this activity).

Actus reus

The *actus reus* of rape is the penetration of V's vagina, anus or mouth by D's penis, without V's consent. Section 79(3) of the 2003 Sexual Offences Act includes body parts created by surgical reconstruction within the offence of rape, so that transsexuals can be both offenders and victims for the purposes of rape. Section 79(2) defines penetration in such a way that even the slightest degree of penetration is enough (Allen 2007: 391), and states that penetration is a 'continuing act' from the time of entry to the time of withdrawal. This means that if V withdraws consent and D continues the penetration, the penetration has to be without consent (*Cooper and Schaub* [1994] Crim LR 531) and D can be convicted of rape as a 'continuing act' if the penetration continues beyond the point where consent is withdrawn (*Kaitamaki* [1985] AC 147).

Mens rea

D has to intentionally penetrate V's vagina, anus or mouth with his penis. Intention means the same as it normally does in the criminal law. *Watson* [1992] Crim LR 434 suggests that if D has consent to penetrate one of the other person's orifices with his penis, but accidentally penetrates another orifice instead, he will not be guilty of rape.

The second element of *mens rea* is that D must not reasonably believe that V is consenting. Section 1(2) of the 2003 Act says that the reasonableness of D's belief is an objective test, to be decided having regard to all the circumstances, including any steps D has taken to find out whether V is consenting. This means that the jury has to take into account what has happened before the rape as well as during it (*McFall* [1994] Crim LR 226) as well as any characteristics D has which might reasonably affect his understanding of whether V is consenting.

Proving lack of consent and the unreasonableness of D's belief is assisted by ss. 74, 75 and 76 of the Act. Section 74 defines consent as agreeing by choice, and having the freedom and capacity to make that choice (cf. *Olugboja* [1981] 3 All ER 443). However, s. 75 sets up evidential presumptions about the complainant's consent, to make the decision on consent easier for the jury. If it is proved that D did the act (i.e. penetration as above), and any one of six specified circumstances are proved to exist, and D knew they existed, then V is presumed not to have consented unless enough evidence to leave the jury in reasonable doubt is raised to show that V did consent; and D is presumed not to have reasonably believed that V consented unless enough evidence is raised to show that D reasonably believed it. In *Bree* [2007] 2 All ER 676, however, the Court of Appeal was critical of over-generalising in terms of evidential presumptions. Sir Igor Judge P stated that whether or not V had the capacity to consent to sex while voluntarily intoxicated depended on the facts of each individual case and the states of mind of the individuals involved. He added that, while the meaning of consent in s. 74 was clear, the evidential presumptions in s. 75 should not lead to short-cuts in terms of not considering all of the evidence or not giving the jury enough guidance (see also *Zhang* [2007] EWCA Crim 2018).

Section 76 introduces conclusive evidential presumptions regarding lack of consent and the unreasonableness of D's belief in consent. If it is proved that D did the relevant act, and D intentionally deceived V as to the nature or purpose of the relevant act (as in *Flattery* (1877) 2 QBD 410 and *Williams* [1923] 1 KB 340), or intentionally induced V to consent to the relevant act by impersonating a person known personally to the complainant (as in *Elbekkay* [1995] Crim LR 163), then it has to be presumed that V did not consent, and that D did not believe in the complainant's consent. The Court of Appeal has, however, interpreted the scope of the s. 76 provisions narrowly in *Jheeta* [2008] Crim LR 144, stating that they apply only where D deceives the complainant about the nature or purpose of a particular type of sexual intercourse, and not where D deceives the complainant about the circumstances surrounding sex, even where those circumstances may lead V to consent to having sex with D more often that they would have done otherwise – in other words, only deception relating to issues like consent on the basis of D claiming that he is doing research or a clinical examination (cf. *Linekar* [1995] 3 All ER 69). Similarly, in *EB* [2007] 1 Cr App Rep 29, the Court of Appeal decided that D not telling V that he had HIV/AIDS before they had sex did not count as a conclusive presumption that V did not consent to sex – s. 76 did not say anything about 'implied deception' like this.

The third element of *mens rea* in relation to rape, therefore, is required where the prosecution use the presumptions in ss. 75 and 76. For s. 76, the prosecution have to prove that D intentionally deceived the complainant as to the nature or purpose of the relevant act. For s. 75, they have to prove D's knowledge of whichever of the circumstances listed in s. 75 applies in the circumstances.

STUDY EXERCISE 7.1

Read Box's (1983: 120–31) discussion of the legal definition of rape. Taking into account how rape is defined by the Sexual Offences Act 2003 now, do you agree with him that the legal definition of rape should be considerably wider than it currently is?

Sexual assault offences

Actus reus

There are three elements to the *actus reus* for the three sexual assault offences in the 2003 Act. The first element is the act itself – sexual penetration of V's vagina or anus with a part of D's body or anything else for s. 2, sexual touching[1] for s. 3, and sexual activity[2] for s. 4. The second element, for all three offences, is that the conduct is 'sexual', which is defined by s. 78 as something which a reasonable person would consider that (a) whatever its circumstances or any person's purpose in relation to it, it is because of its nature sexual, or (b) because of its nature it may be sexual and because of its circumstances or the purpose of any person in relation to it (or both) it is sexual. In *H* [2005] 1 WLR 2005, the Court of Appeal said that the test in s. 78(b) is a two-stage test on the facts. First, would a reasonable person consider that because of its nature the act could be sexual, where the circumstances before or after the act took place and D's purpose are irrelevant? If the answer is 'yes', the second part of the test is whether, because of the circumstances of the act and the purpose of any person in relation to it, the act actually is sexual. The third element is absence of consent, as defined under s. 74 of the Act – the presumptions in ss. 75 and 76 apply for all three offences.

Mens rea

The *mens rea* for these offences is intention to either penetrate V, touch V in a sexual way, or cause V to engage in sexual activity (as appropriate), and an

---

[1]Defined in s. 79(8) of the Act as 'touching (a) with any part of the body, (b) with anything else, (c) through anything, and in particular includes touching amounting to penetration'. In *H* [2005] 1WLR 2005, touching was held to include touching a person's clothing without applying any form of pressure to the person's body.

[2]Defined in s. 4(4) of the Act as (a) penetration of V's anus or vagina, (b) penetration of V's mouth with another person's penis, (c) penetration of a person's anus or vagina with a part of V's body or by V with anything else, or (d) the penetration of a person's mouth with V's penis.

absence of a reasonable belief that V is consenting, as with rape (see above). It should be noted that, for all three offences, whether a belief is reasonable is to be determined having regards to all the circumstances, including any steps D has taken to ascertain whether the complainant is consenting; and that ss. 75 and 76 apply to all three offences. The latter two provisions are the same as in the statutory definition of rape in the 2003 Sexual Offences Act.

STUDY EXERCISE 7.2

Do you think that *H* defines sexual assault, in terms of the meanings of 'sexual' and 'touching', too widely?

Sexual offences against children

DEFINITION BOX 7.3

SEXUAL OFFENCES AGAINST CHILDREN

Sexual offences where V is a child who is not allowed to consent to sexual activity by law.

The Sexual Offences Act maintains the age of sexual consent as being 16 (s. 9). In addition, as Allen (2007: 407) points out, the Act assumes that children aged less than 13 are incapable of giving sexual consent, although the Act itself does not actually say this. None of the sexual offences against children need proof that V did not consent, which makes them different from the adult sexual offences (see above). However, the categories of sexual offences against children are the same as for adults. The child offences can be split into two categories: offences where V is under 13 years old and offences where V is over 13 but under 16.

Offences against children under 13 years old

Section 5 creates the offence of rape of a child under age 13, where the *actus reus* is D's penetration of V's vagina, anus or mouth where V is under the age of 13, and the *mens rea* is intentional penetration. For this offence consent is irrelevant – G [2008] UKHL 37 emphasised that as long as penetration is proved, D is guilty of rape, even though D has a reasonable belief that V is over 13, s. 5 itself does not actually say that the offence is strict liability, and liability could overlap with the offence under s. 13 (see below). As a result, there was no breach of either Article 6 (the right to a fair trial) or Article 8 (the right to privacy) in G. Section 6 creates an offence of assault of a child under 13 by penetration, where the *actus reus* is D's sexual penetration of V who is under 13, with a part of the body or anything else, of V's vagina or anus, and the *mens rea* is that the penetration is intentional. Absence of consent does not have to be proved for this offence, so D's belief in consent is irrelevant. Section 7 creates an offence of sexual assault of a child under 13, where the *actus reus* is D's sexual touching of V who is under 13, and the *mens rea* is that the touching is intentional. Absence of consent again does not have to be proved for this offence, so D's belief in consent is irrelevant. Section 8 creates an offence of causing or inciting a child under 13 to engage in sexual activity. Here, the *actus reus* is causing or inciting a child under 13 to engage in sexual activity. D's belief in V's consent is once again irrelevant.

Offences against children under 16 years old

The offences of sexual activity with a child (s. 9) and causing or inciting a child to engage in sexual activity (s. 10) have the same *actus reus* and *mens rea* requirements as the offences against children under 13 in ss. 7 and 8, discussed in the previous subsection. The only difference in the ss. 9 and 10 offences is that in *mens rea* terms, the prosecution has to prove that either D did not believe that V was over 16, or that D did believe this, but the belief was not a reasonable one.

Section 11 creates an offence of engaging in a sexual activity in the presence of a child, where the *actus reus* is D (an adult aged 18 or over) engaging in a sexual activity, which they undertake for the purposes of sexual gratification where V (a child under the age of 16) is present or is in a place from which D can be observed. The *mens rea* is that D intentionally engages in a sexual activity; D knows or believes that V is aware, or intends that V should be aware, that D is engaging in the sexual activity; and that D did not believe that V was over 16, or that D did believe this but the belief was not a reasonable one, or that V is under 13 (in which case D's belief is irrelevant anyway).

Section 12 creates an offence of causing a child to watch a sexual act, where the *actus reus* is D (an adult aged 18 or over) causes V (a child under the age of 16) to watch a third person engaging in sexual activity, or to look at an image of any person engaging in a sexual activity, for the purposes of obtaining sexual gratification. The *mens rea* is that D intentionally causes V to watch the sexual activity; and that D did not believe that V was over 16, or that D did believe this but the belief was not a reasonable one, or that V is under 13 (in which case D's belief is irrelevant anyway). In *Abdullahi* [2007] 1 WLR 225, the Court of Appeal confirmed that the sexual gratification did not have to happen at or soon after the same time as causing V to view the sexual activity – the offence could cover a more long-term plan to obtain gratification later.

Section 13 states that it is an offence for D (a child under the age of 18) to do anything which would be an offence under ss. 9–12 if D was an adult. Section 14 creates an offence of arranging or facilitating the commission of a child sex offence under ss. 9–13. The *actus reus* is D arranging or facilitating something that amounts to an offence under these subsections. The *mens rea* is that D intentionally arranges or facilitates the thing that is an offence, and that D intends to commit the offence, intends someone else to commit the offence, or believes that someone else will commit the offence, in any part of the world. Under s. 14(2), D has a defence to this offence if they arrange or facilitate something that they believe another person will do, but that D does not intend to do or intend another person to do, and an offence under ss. 9–13 would be an offence against a child, whom D is protecting by acting. Section 14(3) lists a range of circumstances under which D is taken to be protecting a child by acting as they do, as long as they are not also acting for the purpose of sexual gratification, or for the purpose of causing or encouraging the activity which constitutes the offence under ss. 9–13, or the child's participation in that offence. As Allen (2007: 414) points out, this defence covers police officers using a child as a decoy to trap a child sex offender, and health workers providing contraception advice, contraception and advice on sexually transmitted diseases to children.

Finally in this subsection, s. 15 creates an offence of meeting with a child following sexual grooming. The *actus reus* is D (an adult over 18) meeting or communicating with V on at least two previous occasions, and then meeting V or travelling to meet V in any part of the world, where V is under 16. The *mens rea* is D intentionally meeting V, or having the intention to meet V by travelling; plus intention to do anything in respect of V, during or after the meeting in any part of the world, which if done will involve D committing an offence under Part 1 of the 2003 Act; plus a lack of a reasonable belief on D's part that V is 16 or over.

STUDY EXERCISE 7.3

'The decision in *G* breached Article 6(2) of the ECHR (the presumption of innocence until proven guilty) because it punished D where he was not morally at fault'. Read Tadros and Tierney's (2004) article and discuss this statement.

Offences abolished by the Sexual Offences Act 2003

Finally in this section, it should be noted that the Sexual Offences Act 2003 not only created new sexual offences and amended existing ones. It also abolished several pre-existing sexual offences under Schedule 7 of the 2003 Act. The most important were the offences of buggery, or anal sexual intercourse, gross indecency between men, and solicitation by men for immoral purposes.

STUDY EXERCISE 7.4

Why do you think these offences were abolished? Why do you think they were part of the criminal law in the first place?

The second section of this chapter considers sexual offences in their criminal justice context.

Sexual Offences and Criminal Justice

Example I: sexual offences and criminal justice – overview

The number of sexual offences reported by the public has increased steadily over the last 10 years, as has the number recorded by the police. There were a total of 13,780 recorded rapes in England and Wales in 2006/07, 92% of which were against women, and 24,166 recorded sexual assaults, 89% of which were against women (Jansson et al. 2007: 58). Although recorded rapes and sexual assaults against women decreased in 2006/07 by 5% and 7% respectively compared with 2005/06 figures (ibid.), the rate of recorded rape has risen consistently over time, from just 240 in 1947, to 2,471 in 1987, to 8,593 in 2000/01 (Temkin 2002: 12), to the current figures quoted above.

Despite these increases in recorded crime rates, non-police data reveal the extent to which serious sexual offences, especially rapes, are unreported to the police. The most recent BCS data, from 2005/06,[3] suggested that the police found out about only 13% of rapes reported as happening to victims since the age of 16 (Hoare and Jansson 2008: 74). Feminist writers would argue, however, that what the law and criminal justice exclude from the category of rape is just as important as what they include in it (e.g. Kelly 1988). Other data provide convincing evidence that for a large number of women, rape and sexual assault are such a common occurrence in their lives that they become 'institutionalised'. Myhill and Allen (2002) found that only 70% of women in their sample who self-classified the most recent attack against them saw it as being a 'crime'. This suggests that some rape victims experience rape so often that they can no longer equate rape and criminality – it is just 'something that happens'. Myhill and Allen also found that 32% of women in their study had been raped by their partner, 22% had been raped by an acquaintance, current partners had committed 45% of reported rapes, and 55% of victims had been raped in their own homes. If these estimates are in any way accurate, the common occurrence of rape at home, and at the hands of someone whom the victim trusts, must be a key reason why rape is still an extremely under-reported offence.

STUDY EXERCISE 7.5

Mackinnon (1983) argues that it is difficult for women to tell the difference between rape and 'normal' sex because society is systematically controlled by men and biased against women. Do you agree with this view? How well do you think Mackinnon's arguments explain (a) recent developments in the definition of rape in England and Wales and (b) what is known about how much rape is reported to police?

---

[3] The BCS does not normally include sexual offences in its surveys because the numbers reported are too low to analyse reliably. The 2005/06 survey was the last time that specialist questions were asked about victims' experiences of serious sexual assault throughout their adult lives.

Example II: sexual offences, the police and the CPS

A variety of evidence points to the fact that the police traditionally failed to take the reporting of rape to them seriously. The police regularly ignored and failed to record reports of rape, embarrassed and traumatised victims through intrusive questioning and physical examinations, and alleged that the victim was making false accusations (e.g. Chambers and Millar 1983). Jordan (2001) found a clash of cultures between police and rape victims in terms of their aims. Police culture in her study was about crime-fighting, not making things better for victims. This had the effect of alienating victims and sidelining their needs in practice. However, Gregory and Lees (1999) reported improvements in the police's response to rape victims, such as use of female rather than male officers to examine victims physically for evidence after an attack, specialist rape suites where victims can be questioned by police in as much comfort and privacy as possible, and female 'chaperone' officers who can stay with victims to make them feel safer in the first few days after the rape has occurred. The question is to what extent these improvements have continued since their study was carried out.

An important recent report evaluating the progress of police and the CPS in dealing with rape cases was published by the police and CPS inspectorates recently (HM Inspectorate of the Constabulary and HM Crown Prosecution Service Inspectorate 2007). The report studied a sample of 752 reported rape cases. The police only recorded 573 (76.2%) of the 752 offences. Further attrition was found in the number of victims who withdrew charges (102 cases). The CPS charged 160 of the 752 cases (21.3%). In a smaller sub-sample of 75 cases which did reach court, the CPS offered no evidence in 17 of the 75. The report also found that the police and CPS tended to over-estimate the number of false allegations of rape made to them (around 3% in reality), and also found evidence of subjective judgements being made about the credibility of victims based on their background and character as well as a lack of specialist training for frontline police officers in dealing with reports and victims of rape. Overall, it seems that while improvements have undoubtedly been made in the police's response to rape victims, there is still the scope for unfairness and inefficiency in the investigation of rape, which could lead to victims' human rights being breached.

--- STUDY EXERCISE 7.6 ---

List three possible explanations for the low recording rate of rape offences by police in the HMIC and HMCPSI report (2007).

Example III: sexual offences and the court process

The nature of rape as a criminal offence means that there is often a heavy reliance upon the evidence of the victim as a witness to the offence in court. This is particularly true given the importance of proving lack of consent in rape cases – since consent is really about the victim's state of mind, it will normally be one person's word against another's in court (Harris and Grace 1999). However, a range of studies have shown that rape victims giving evidence in court have often felt as if they were the ones on trial. A major factor in this 'secondary victimisation' is the reliance upon oral evidence, which was mentioned in Chapter 3. Research has shown that the cross-examination of rape victims by defence barristers was regularly experienced by victims as upsetting and traumatic, involving continual questioning on the details of the rape, the victim's sexual history with the defendant and others, and the 'respectability' of the victim's behaviour (e.g. Chambers and Millar 1987). Temkin (2000) revealed extensive hostility and prejudice towards rape victims from barristers who had conducted rape cases for both the prosecution and the defence, sometimes blaming them for the rape they had suffered. Lees (1997) argued that the rape trial acted as a social control on women, by warning them about the consequences of being sexually active, and punishing women who broke sexist stereotypes of female respectability and passiveness by giving evidence against those who had sexually attacked them in court.

The New Labour government responded to these criticisms by introducing a range of measures in the Youth Justice and Criminal Evidence Act 1999 that were designed to make the experience of giving evidence in court easier for the victims of sexual assault. For example, it banned defendants in rape cases from defending themselves, and therefore cross-examining their victim themselves, in court, and also introduced a presumption in favour of special measures being used in court in rape cases, such as victims giving evidence from behind screens so that the public in court could not see them, giving evidence from another room via video link, or the use of pre-recorded video evidence. Most importantly in this context, s. 41 of the 1999 Act prohibits the use of evidence about a victim's sexual behaviour in court, except where one or more of four exceptions applies (Temkin 2003). The House of Lords in *A* [2001] 3 All ER 1 decided that not allowing sexual history evidence generally where it was directly relevant to the current offence was a breach of Article 6 of the ECHR (the right to a fair trial), and added this exception to the four listed in s. 41 wherever not allowing the evidence would endanger the fairness of the trial.

However, the effectiveness of s. 41 in reducing the use of unnecessary sexual history evidence is questionable. Kelly et al. (2006) studied a sample of over 400 rape cases that reached court. They found that an application was made to the judge to allow sexual history evidence in a third of cases, and that two-thirds of applications were allowed. References to sexual history evidence outside the s. 41 exceptions were made without application – something which is now illegal – in three-quarters of cases, there was a significant relationship between reference to it and acquittals, and the rules about making applications to allow sexual history evidence before the trial and in writing were almost always broken. Kelly et al. found that judges and barristers were mainly in favour of legislation to control sexual history evidence in theory, but most thought that the s. 41 rules were too restrictive and did not give judges enough discretion on whether to allow evidence in each case (cf. Kibble 2005).

Should sexual history evidence ever be allowed in a rape trial? Explain your answer with reference to the current rules under s. 41 of the Youth Justice and Criminal Evidence Act 1999.

Example IV: sexual offences, sentencing and punishment

Rape carries a maximum sentence of life imprisonment. However, sentences can vary widely in practice. The Court of Appeal issued new sentencing guidelines for rape in *Millberry* [2003] 2 All ER 939. These new guidelines, designed with help from the Sentencing Advisory Panel, have a starting point of five years' imprisonment. There are then seven named aggravating factors. If at least one of these applies, the starting point goes up to eight years' imprisonment. For serial rapists, the starting point is 15 years' imprisonment and, as Ashworth (2005: 128) points out, if they are considered to be a danger to the public, they could also receive indeterminate sentences under the Criminal Justice Act 2003. *Millberry* made it clear that the starting point for sentencing should be the same whether it was stranger rape, acquaintance rape or marital rape, whether the victim is male or female, and whether the rape is vaginal or anal. However, the court in *Millberry* also stated that an offender's culpability in sentencing terms would be 'somewhat less' where the victim had consented to 'sexual familiarity' with the offender on the occasion when the rape occurred, and this principle has been included in the Sentencing Guidelines Council's guidance document on sentencing rape (Sentencing Guidelines Council 2007: 21). The average sentence for rape was seven and a half years' imprisonment in 2006 (Travis 2006). Ashworth (2005: 129) argues that the starting point and average for rape sentencing are too low, when sentences are compared to those for crimes such as robbery and persistent theft, which do not necessarily involve personal harm being caused to the victim.

Despite these criticisms, the number of sexual offenders receiving custody generally has increased since 1996, as has the average custodial sentence length for sexual offences (Ministry of Justice 2007c: 10). Also, as was noted in Chapter 4, the number of offenders receiving indeterminate sentences has increased significantly since 2004. The trend towards increasing punishment and risk assessment has meant that although Sex Offender Treatment Programmes are in place throughout the prison estate, and have achieved moderately encouraging results (Hedderman and Sugg 1996), doubts over whether sex offenders can ever be completely cured mean that some sex offenders, especially more minor sex offenders, receive little or no treatment in prison (Henham 1998).

▬▬▬▬▬▬▬▬▬▬▬▬▬ STUDY EXERCISE 7.8 ▬▬▬▬▬▬▬▬▬▬▬▬▬

Design a framework of sentencing guidelines for rape, including a minimum sentence, a maximum sentence and starting points for different types of rape in between. Should 'date rape' and marital rape be given harsher sentences than stranger rape, or the other way round?

Example V: male-victim rape and criminal justice

It could be argued that if female-victim rape is still a 'hidden' offence, male-victim rape is even more concealed from criminal justice's view, despite the fact that it has been recognised as a form of rape since the Criminal Justice and Public Order Act 1994. Only a small amount of criminological research has been done into this form of rape. What is known, however, indicates that although male-victim rape is less common than female-victim rape, the social harm that results from it can be just as severe, and that male victims receive even less support from criminal justice than female victims receive. In King et al.'s (2000) survey, almost 3% of men reported that they had experienced non-consensual sex at some time in their adult lives and just over 5% reported sexual abuse before the age of 16. They also found significant links between being abused as a child and being abused as an adult, and between increasingly serious abuse and reported psychological problems (ibid.: 9–10). Although rates of reporting to the police are increasing (Rumney 2001), partly due to some improvements in police responses to this offence (Gregory and Lees 1999: chapter 5), they remain low, at between 2% and 20% on the basis of the studies reported by Rumney and Morgan-Taylor (2004: 145).

Rumney (2001) conducted a study into how male rape is handled by the court process. He found evidence that male victims of rape were stereotyped in very similar ways to female victims when giving evidence in court. The defence's accounts of 'normal' behaviour for victims during and after the rape did not match research evidence on how victims actually did tend to behave. For example, male victims who had not tried to fight off their attacker or run away after the attack were characterised as having consenting to sex, even where they had in reality 'frozen' due to fear; and male victims were sometimes accused of falsely reporting rape or being unreliable witnesses, in the same way that research suggests that female victims tend to be.

▬▬▬▬▬▬▬▬▬▬▬▬▬ STUDY EXERCISE 7.9 ▬▬▬▬▬▬▬▬▬▬▬▬▬

Read Seaton's article in *The Guardian* (Seaton 2002) on male rape at www.guardian. co.uk/world/2002/nov/18/gender.uk. If you could make three changes to society and/or criminal justice to improve the effectiveness of the response to male rape, what would those changes be in the light of this article?

Example VI: child sexual abuse and criminal justice

The true extent of child sex abuse remains unknown. Silverman and Wilson (2002: 21) found estimates in various studies, ranging from 3,500 to 72,600 cases per year in England and Wales. Although reporting rates have increased following the rediscovery of child abuse as a high-profile, emotive issue by the public and media (Soothill and Walby 1991), since 2004, rates of recorded sexual offences against children have remained generally stable, apart from slight increases in the numbers of recorded rapes of male and female children under age 13 (Thorpe et al. 2007: 37). Evidence also suggests that conviction rates for offences of sexual activity with a child under 13, sexual activity with a child under 16, and incest have all increased since the 2003 Act was implemented, but only to 298, 1,009 and 153 cases respectively in 2006 (Ministry of Justice 2007b: 70). As with other offences discussed in this book, it seems likely that only a tiny percentage of the amount of child sex abuse which occurs ever reaches the criminal justice process.

The context of police responses to child sexual abuse is the shame and fear of reprisals which can prevent victims from reporting the offences against them. Although the police response to child sexual abuse has undoubtedly become more effective and thorough since the 1980s, Thomas (2005: 72–3) has also pointed to high-profile failures to share police intelligence with other forces, which was named as a factor in the failure to prevent Ian Huntley, a convicted sex offender, from killing Holly Wells and Jessica Chapman in Soham in 2002.

The court response to child sex offenders in England and Wales has been extended significantly in recent years, in line with the greater public and media focus on such behaviour. This process has culminated in the introduction of indeterminate custodial sentences for sexual offenders whom a court thinks pose a serious risk of harm to the public, under s. 225 of the Criminal Justice Act 2003 (the same Act also introduced two civil orders: Sexual Offences Prevention Orders for either convicted or unconvicted people posing a risk of sexual harm, and Risk of Sexual Harm Orders for convicted offenders, specifically aimed at child sex offenders). Although sentencing trends for child sex offences cannot be analysed exactly through Ministry of Justice sentencing data, it seems likely that sentences for child sex offenders have become tougher overall, given the increasing trend towards longer custodial sentences for sexual offences generally, which was discussed above.

The increasing number of civil measures aimed at child sexual offenders has been an equally important trend in recent years. The most high-profile development in this context has been the introduction of the Sex Offenders' Register in 1997. Under the Sexual Offences Act 2003 s. 83, convicted sex offenders are required to give their name, National Insurance number and address to police within three days of being convicted in court, and also required to notify the police of any changes to these details within three days of changes occurring (s. 84) and submit an annual report to police confirming these details for as long as they are on the Register (s. 85).

A key issue in relation to the Register is what access (if any) the public should be allowed to have to the details contained in it. The Criminal Justice and Court Services Act 2000 introduced Multi-Agency Public Protection Panels (MAPPPs), whose job it would be to assess the level of risk posed by sex offenders in the community, and to decide whether a sex offender's name and address could be disclosed to certain individuals in the interests of the public. The MAPPPs include representation from the police, the National Probation Service, social services and the public. Kemshall et al. (2005) found that the MAPPPs' division of supervision of offenders into three levels according to the level of risk was effective, and that supervision was more effective with a trained co-ordinator (which only two-thirds of MAPPPs had). However, they also found that training for MAPPP members and the keeping of administrative records were inconsistent, and that some over-allocation of offenders into a higher risk category than was necessary was occurring.

Some writers have been highly critical of the concept of the Sex Offenders' Register itself, and of attempts to increase public access to its contents. Soothill and Francis (1997) pointed out that the Register includes not just non-consensual child sex offenders, but also anyone convicted of a wide variety of sexual offences, even convicted by caution at the police station rather than in court. They conclude that the Register is 'criminal apartheid', designed to socially exclude sex offenders. Ironically, such exclusion can make offenders go 'underground', out of the reach of supervision. This, in turn, can make them more likely to offend as well as making vigilante-style violence against sex offenders – or even people who are only wrongly suspected of being sex offenders – more likely (Silverman and Wilson 2002).

Compliance rates with the Register's requirements have consistently run at around 95%, indicating effectiveness on its own terms, but no conclusive proof could be found by Plotnikoff and Woolfson (2000) that it has actually made communities any safer from the perceived dangerousness of child sex offenders. It is arguable that the focus on 'stranger danger' that the Register implies ignores the fact that around 80% of child sex offences are committed by someone whom the child knows, rather than a stranger, according to estimates (Grubin 1998). Finally, there is the danger that the Register has become so punitive, in terms of making notification increasingly difficult, increased police powers to track down those who have not complied, and the denial of early release from prison to those on it, that it is now a punishment in its own right, rather than the administrative measure to improve community safety that it is supposed to be (Thomas 2008).

STUDY EXERCISE 7.10

Should we have a 'Sarah's Law' allowing unrestricted access to sex offenders' personal details by the public, as the *News of the World* newspaper campaigned for following the murder of Sarah Payne by a paedophile in 2000? What measures could be enacted to deal with the risks that passing such legislation might create?

Discussion and Conclusions

Both the criminal law which regulates sexual offences, and the criminal justice enforcement of that law, have undergone radical change in recent years. The Sexual Offences Act 2003 redefined a range of major sexual offences, including rape, sexual assault, and most of the sexual offences against children. It could be argued that the 2003 Act reflected liberal ideas about what role the criminal law should play in society. As Selfe and Burke (2001: chapter 2) point out, previous sexual offences, such as buggery and gross indecency, were heavily linked with the criminalisation of, and discrimination against, male homosexuality. The Act abolished these, moving towards the liberal approach of treating all consensual sexual behaviour between adults in the same way, whether it is heterosexual or homosexual – an approach which is in line with the right to respect for private life included under Article 8 of the ECHR. The Act also extended the offence of rape to include non-consensual oral penetration as well as the anal and vaginal types. Equally significantly, consent, the element which if absent turns lawful sex into rape, was defined for the first time. Again, the definition was liberal, framing consent in terms of being able to make a free and informed choice about whether or not to have sex.

However, the new law is not really about liberal concerns. The definition of consent may be liberal on the surface, but it is vague, and as a result juries will be able to include their own ideas about what 'freedom' and 'choice' mean (Temkin and Ashworth 2004: 336) – ideas which may reflect risk-based criminality (by being too harsh on defendants) or patriarchal values (by being too lenient on defendants) rather than liberalism. The need for a reasonable belief in consent also moves the law away from liberal ideas about punishing only on the basis of what the defendant actually thought or saw themselves. There is also room for sexist stereotyping in asking the jury to assess the reasonableness of belief in consent in 'all the circumstances' without defining which circumstances should be considered (ibid.: 342). The 2003 Act also includes situations where there is a conclusive presumption, or a rebuttable presumption, that consent was not given. These provisions move beyond liberalism and due process to reflect the risks or immorality of certain types of conduct (McEwan 2005: 18), and it is interesting that the courts have already tried to claw back some due process by limiting the presumptions in *EB* and *Jheeta*, perhaps showing their awareness of the threat to Article 6 of the ECHR (the right to a fair trial) posed by evidential presumptions.

If the presumptions are supposed to reflect morality or risk, their ordering does not really make sense. Deceit as to identity carries a conclusive presumption of non-consent, which may not reflect what actually happened in the sense that the victim might still have consented despite the deceit (McEwan 2005: 21), but consent through threats or involuntarily intoxicating the victim only carry a rebuttable presumption even though they look morally 'worse' than some forms of deceit (Temkin and Ashworth 2004: 337), and consent where the victim has voluntarily become drunk does not carry any presumption at all. These provisions are clearly aimed at reflecting morality, the defendant's blameworthiness and risk rather than liberal independence (McEwan 2005: 19), but they are so confusing and discretionary that they are unlikely to end the sexist stereotyping of rape victims and low conviction rates that they were designed to tackle. When this evidence is combined with new offences which do not require any physical contact, such as voyeurism, the extensive interpretation of terms such as 'sexual' and 'touching' in sexual assault cases such as *H*, and the imposition of strict liability on rape offences involving children of a similar age where the defendant has a reasonable belief that the victim is over 13 years old in *G*, the conclusion must be that, in trying to respond to the social harm caused by sexual abuse generally, the law has gone too far in imposing risk-based criminality in cases where the harm was minimal.

Criminal justice has traditionally faced accusations that it has failed to take the harm caused by sexual offences seriously. However, policies have been put in place in the last 10 years which seem to have improved victims' treatment by police (Gregory and Lees 1999). On the other hand, recent evidence from HM Inspectorate of the Constabulary and HM Crown Prosecution Service Inspectorate (2007) would suggest that although progress has been made in police responses, crime control and efficiency remain more important than victims' welfare, as Jordan (2001) argued.

A similar story can be told with developments in the courts' handling of sex offence cases. Legislation such as s. 41 of the Youth Justice and Criminal Evidence Act 1999 is aimed at making things easier for victims giving evidence in court, by excluding intrusive cross-examination about their sexual behaviour in the past under certain circumstances. But the legislation is not well defined, and the result is that it threatened to prejudice defendants' right to a fair trial, at least before the House of Lords' decision in *A*. On the other hand, it has not improved the court experience for victims either. Temkin and Krahe (2008) found that despite s. 41, myths and stereotypes about what is and is not 'real rape' persist in the criminal justice process. The study uncovered evidence that six of the 17 senior judges interviewed found the legislation to be weak and easy to get round, so as to preserve judges' traditional discretion over whether or not to allow sexual history evidence to be used in court. The judges were also reluctant to prohibit sexual history evidence in most cases. In this situation, the power of courts to exercise discretion and impose their own views on what is and is not acceptable sexual behaviour still takes priority over efficiency and the interests of victims.

The sentencing and punishment of sex offenders has seen several moves towards risk-based punitiveness. Sentencing has become harsher despite guidelines in *Millberry* which tried to retain proportionality. The new civil orders which are backed up with criminal punishment if they are breached, such as the Sexual Offences Prevention Order, which does not require any criminal conviction for a sexual offence before it can be imposed, extend the reach of criminal punishment (Matravers 2003). The Sex Offenders' Register, marketed as an administrative tool to make the public safer from sex offenders in the community, has become so difficult to comply with that it is effectively a punishment in itself (Thomas 2008), and its effectiveness in preventing sex offending is questionable (Plotnikoff and Woolfson 2000). The emphasis on risk has also limited the amount of treatment available to sex offenders in prison (Henham 1998), despite evidence that the risk posed by offenders would be more effectively managed by a reintegrative and restorative approach than by the current retributive focus (McAlinden 2007). At the same time, while child sex abuse is a focus for public and media attention (sometimes over-attention), the problem of male-victim rape and sexual assault remains largely hidden from public and criminological discussion (Rumney 2001).

The next chapter switches the focus from non-fatal offences against the person to crimes involving the victim's death, in the form of homicide.

FURTHER READING

Card, R. (2008), *Card, Cross and Jones' Criminal Law* (18th edn): chapter 9. Oxford: Oxford University Press.

Matravers, A. (ed.) (2003), *Sex Offenders in the Community: Managing and Reducing the Risks.* Cullompton: Willan.

Silverman, J., and Wilson, D. (2002), *Innocence Betrayed: Paedophilia, the Media and Society.* Cambridge: Polity Press.

Simester, A.P., and Sullivan, R. (2007), *Criminal Law: Theory and Doctrine* (3rd edn): chapter 12. Oxford: Hart.

Temkin, J. (2002), *Rape and the Legal Process* (2nd edn). Oxford: Oxford University Press.

8

Homicide

Chapter Aims

After reading Chapter 8 you should be able to understand:

- The *actus reus* and *mens rea* required for murder
- The *actus reus* and *mens rea* required for voluntary manslaughter, and what defences to murder there are in the criminal law
- The *actus reus* and *mens rea* required for the different forms of involuntary manslaughter
- What other forms of homicide there are in the criminal law
- How homicide law is enforced in criminal justice practice
- How the evidence on the response to homicide in the criminal law and criminal justice fits in with the theoretical models introduced in Chapter 1

Introduction

Chapter 8 discusses the range of offences which involve unlawful killing, or homicide, in the criminal law in England and Wales. The law will then be considered within the specific framework of its application in criminal justice practice. The chapter will examine the unlawful killing offences, starting with murder, moving on to voluntary manslaughter, then the different types of involuntary manslaughter, and finally other forms of homicide created and defined by statute law.

Homicide: The Law

> **DEFINITION BOX 8.1**
>
> HOMICIDE
>
> One of a range of offences involving D's unlawful killing of V, another person, in peacetime (i.e. not during a war), with the right *mens rea*.

Homicide: overview

Homicide has a common law definition in the criminal law in England and Wales that dates back several hundred years. This definition is the unlawful killing of a human being, caused by another human being, under the Queen's peace (Ormerod 2008: 473). All of the homicide offences listed above have these *actus reus* requirements. It is the *mens rea* requirements which separate the individual offences from one another. 'Unlawful killing' simply means any death which the law considers to be unlawful; 'human being' has been taken to mean any person who is alive, although *Attorney-General's Reference (No. 3 of 1994)* [1997] 3 WLR 421 decided that foetuses who are still in their mothers' wombs are not 'human beings' until after they are born; 'causation' shows that both factual and legal causation must be proved; and 'under the Queen's (or King's) peace' means killings which do not take place during wartime. The broad definition of common law homicide means that 'borderline' cases, where the courts have to decide whether or not homicide has actually occurred, sometimes occur. The more specific legal requirements separating the different homicide offences will now be considered in turn.

> **STUDY EXERCISE 8.1**
>
> Imagine you are designing a new Criminal Code for England and Wales. How would you define the *actus reus* of homicide in the criminal law?

Murder

> **DEFINITION BOX 8.2**
>
> MURDER
>
> One of a range of offences involving D's unlawful killing of V, another person, in peacetime (i.e. not during a war), with the *mens rea* of 'malice aforethought'.

The *actus reus* for murder was discussed in the previous section. *Mens rea* for murder was defined in common law as 'malice aforethought'. This is the intention to either kill or do grievous bodily harm, a principle shown by *Vickers* [1957] 2 QB 664 and *Cunningham* [1982] AC 566. Intention here means the same as it does generally in the criminal law.

Voluntary manslaughter

DEFINITION BOX 8.3

VOLUNTRY MANSLAUGHTER

The offence of murder, including all the *actus reus* and *mens rea* requirements, where one of four defences applies which reduces the offence of murder to one of manslaughter.

Both the *actus reus* and *mens rea* of voluntary manslaughter are exactly the same as those for murder (see above). This is because voluntary manslaughter is an offence of murder plus one of four defences which can only be used for murder: diminished responsibility, provocation, infanticide and suicide pact. If successfully used, these defences reduce a charge of murder to a charge of voluntary manslaughter. The legal requirements for each of these defences will now be discussed in turn.

Voluntary manslaughter I: diminished responsibility

The basic definition of the diminished responsibility defence can be found in s. 2 of the Homicide Act 1957. There are three requirements for the defence in s. 2(1) of the Act. The defence must prove, on the balance of probabilities (*Dunbar* [1958] 1 QB 1), that all three requirements applied to D at the time when D committed the homicide (under s. 2(2)).

The first requirement is that D must have an abnormality of the mind. *Byrne* [1960] 2 QB 396 shows that the phrase 'abnormality of mind' can cover uncontrollable impulses which D suffers, or all other aspects of the 'mind'. *Byrne* also shows that the abnormality of mind must make D's mind so different that a reasonable person would say it was abnormal; and that whether or not there is an abnormality is a question of fact for the jury to decide. *Lloyd* [1967] 1 QB 175 shows that in cases where D is suffering from impulses to commit violence, there is no need for the defence to prove that D was *totally* unable to resist the impulses, as long as the impulses caused substantial mental impairment and were more than trivial or minimal.

The second requirement is that D's abnormality of the mind must be caused by arrested or retarded development, any inherent causes, or induced by disease or injury. *Sanderson* [1993] Crim LR 857 gave guidance on the meanings of the terms used here. 'Induced by disease or injury' covered organic or physical injury, or any disease of the body, including the brain. 'Inherent causes', on the other hand, covered 'functional mental illness', that is psychological conditions causing an abnormality.

The third requirement is that the abnormality of the mind, caused by one of the diseases, injuries or conditions discussed above, must have caused substantial impairment to D's mental responsibility for their acts or omissions at the time of the homicide. Whether there has been a 'substantial impairment' is, like the question of whether there is an abnormality, a question of fact for the jury to decide (*Byrne*).

An important question is whether D can still use the diminished responsibility defence if intoxication, due to alcohol or drugs, caused their substantially impairing abnormality. The House of Lords decided in *Dietschmann* [2003] 1 AC 1209 that as long as there was a 'substantial impairment' caused by a condition which is recognised under s. 2 of the Homicide Act, it does not matter that D was also intoxicated at the time of the killing. In other words, intoxication can be one cause of the killing as long as there is another cause which is allowed for the purposes of diminished responsibility.

STUDY EXERCISE 8.2

Should anyone who has become voluntarily intoxicated be banned from using the diminished responsibility defence, even if they have a recognised mental abnormality?

Voluntary manslaughter II: provocation

The legal test for the provocation defence is contained in s. 3 of the Homicide Act 1957. There are two parts to the test, which is a mixture of subjective and objective elements. If there is evidence that the provocation defence could apply, whether that evidence comes from either the defence or the prosecution case, the trial judge must leave the issue of whether it does apply for the jury to decide (*Baillie* [1995] Crim LR 739). There must be evidence of a specific act or word of provocation raising a reasonable possibility of a loss of self-control, however, and not just a speculative possibility of provocation, before the judge has to leave the issue to the jury (*Serrano* [2007] Crim LR 569). Provocation does not have to be in the form of an unlawful act. It can be in the form of any words or actions, whether they are lawful or unlawful (*Doughty* (1986) 83 Cr App Rep 319).

The first (subjective) part of the test asks whether D suffered a sudden and temporary loss of self-control at the time of the killing. This means that if D regained their self-control between the provocation and the killing, or showed signs of planning the killing in a premeditated way, then the provocation defence cannot be used (*Ibrams* (1981) 74 Cr App Rep 154). The subjective test has caused problems in cases involving battered women, who had been the victims of domestic violence at the hands of their partners for years before killing their abusers. As was decided in *Thornton* [1992] 1 All ER 306, the gap in time between the most recent provocation suffered and the killing meant that women in this situation could not use the provocation defence. However, in *Ahluwalia* [1992] 4

All ER 889, the Court of Appeal recognised that victims of domestic violence could be suffering from a psychological condition, 'battered woman syndrome', which meant that D could suffer a sudden and temporary loss of self-control even if there was a gap in time between the most recent provocation and the killing, and even if the final act of provocation was minor (*Thornton (No. 2)* [1996] 1 WLR 1174). However, the decision on whether there was a sudden and temporary loss of self-control is still one which the judge and jury have discretion over. For example, in *Pearson* [1992] Crim LR 193, there was a gap in time between the last provocation and the killing, and there was also evidence that the Ds had planned the killing, yet the Ds were allowed to use the provocation defence. Finally, loss of self-control is different from loss of self-restraint. *Cocker* [1989] Crim LR 740 shows that if D has only lost self-restraint in killing V, they cannot use the provocation defence.

The second (objective) part of the provocation test asks whether a reasonable person would have acted in the same way that D did in the circumstances. This means that the jury has to answer two questions: would a reasonable person have lost control like D did, and would a reasonable person have killed as a result of losing self-control like D did? To decide whether or not a reasonable person would have responded in the same way, the jury needs to know which of D's characteristics can be taken into account as part of the reasonable person test. A crucial distinction has to be made between things that D is provoked about, that is which affect the gravity of the provocation, and characteristics which affect D's ability to stay in control. In terms of characteristics which affect the gravity of the provocation, the jury can take anything into account as long as there is a clear link between the provocation and D's characteristic (*Newell* (1980) 71 Cr App Rep 331). So, for example, in *Morhall* [1996] AC 90, D was provoked about his glue-sniffing habit and killed the provoker as a result. The House of Lords decided that the jury should have been told to ask themselves how a reasonable glue-sniffer would have reacted to the provocation.

On the other hand, the issue of which characteristics that affect D's ability to stay in control can be taken into account by the jury has been much more controversial in the criminal law. The most recent key case on this issue has been *Attorney-General for Jersey v Holley* [2005] 3 WLR 29, followed in *James; Karimi* [2006] 1 All ER 759, where the Privy Council decided that only D's age and gender could be taken into account, and nothing else about D could be considered, such as, for example, any mental characteristics which D had. This decision followed the earlier cases of *DPP v Camplin* [1978] AC 705 and *Luc Thiet Thuan v R* [1997] AC 131, which had taken the same approach. It rejected a line of cases, especially *Smith* [2001] 1 AC 146 and *Weller* [2004] 1 Cr App Rep 1, which had successively taken more and more of D's mental characteristics into account for the purposes of the objective test, so that almost any of D's characteristics could be taken into account, including depression and jealousy. The decisions in *Attorney-General for Jersey v Holley* and *James; Karimi* therefore limit the scope of the provocation defence, and separate it clearly from the usage of the diminished responsibility defence, which deals specifically with mental conditions affecting D's behaviour (see above).

Using books and journal articles which discuss provocation, make a list of advantages and disadvantages of the approach to the objective test for provocation which was taken in *Attorney-General for Jersey v Holley*.

Voluntary manslaughter III: infanticide

Infanticide is defined by the Infanticide Act 1938 (s. 1(1)) as follows. Where a mother causes the death of her child which is under 1 year old, by act or omission (i.e. has the *actus reus* and *mens rea* for murder), but, at the time of the killing, the balance of her mind is disturbed due to not having recovered from the birth, or because of the effects of lactation after birth, and this defence is accepted by the jury, the offence is punished as voluntary manslaughter, not murder. Section 1(2) allows infanticide to be used as a defence to murder where the prosecution charge D with murder in these circumstances. It can be used as an offence in its own right or as a defence to murder.

STUDY EXERCISE 8.4

Should infanticide be a separate defence to murder, or should it become part of diminished responsibility instead? Give reasons for your answer.

Voluntary manslaughter IV: suicide pact

This defence is defined in s. 4 of the Homicide Act 1957. It covers cases where D and V have agreed a suicide pact, that is an agreement that both of them will kill themselves while intending to do so, and D kills V with the *actus reus* and *mens rea* for murder under that agreement. Where this has happened, D is guilty of voluntary manslaughter, not murder. However, if D aids, abets, counsels or procures V to commit suicide themselves, D is guilty under the Suicide Act 1961 s. 2 because there is no defence of euthanasia in the criminal law in England and Wales.

Involuntary manslaughter

DEFINITION BOX 8.4

INVOLUNTARY MANSLAUGHTER

One of a range of offences which involve the *actus reus* of homicide, without the *mens rea* of malice aforethought, but with one of a range of other *mens rea* which are prohibited by the criminal law in relation to unlawful killing.

Involuntary manslaughter has the same basic features as murder and voluntary manslaughter in terms of the unlawful killing of another person in peacetime (see above), but does not have the same *mens rea*. It is one general offence, but includes three different types of manslaughter, each with its own *actus reus* and *mens rea*. Each of these will now be discussed in turn.

Subjectively reckless manslaughter

This type of involuntary manslaughter is most easily thought of as covering cases which are 'not quite murder', that is cases where D has foresight of causing death or GBH to the victim, but not enough foresight to meet the *mens rea* test for murder as set out in *Woollin* [1998] 3 WLR 382 and *Matthews and Alleyne* [2003] 2 Cr App Rep 30, that is foresight of death or GBH as a virtually certain result of D's actions (see Chapter 3). To be guilty of subjectively reckless involuntary manslaughter, D must foresee the risk of V's serious injury or death as highly probable, and go on to run that risk unreasonably (*Lidar* (2000) 4 *Archbold News* 3). D must therefore be subjectively (*Cunningham* [1957]) reckless, although normally in the criminal law subjective recklessness only needs foresight of the prohibited outcome as possible, rather than as highly probable.

Unlawful act manslaughter

There are four basic requirements which must be met to prove unlawful act manslaughter has occurred, as shown in *Goodfellow* (1986) 83 Cr App Rep 23. First, D must have committed a crime. It should be noted that any crime is enough here – the crime does not have to be a violent one. However, the offence cannot be committed by omission (*Lowe* [1973] QB 702). There is some uncertainty in the law about whether any voluntary unlawful act is enough, as stated in *DPP v Newbury* [1977] AC 500 and *Mitchell* [1983] QB 741, or whether D has to have the full *mens rea* for the crime as well as the *actus reus*, as stated in *Lamb* [1967] 2 QB 981 and *Arobieke* [1988] Crim LR 314. However, if D has a defence to the basic crime, they cannot be guilty of unlawful act manslaughter because there is no unlawful act (*Jennings* [1990] Crim LR 588). In *Dhaliwal* [2006] 2 Cr App Rep 348, the Court of Appeal held that where D inflicts physical and/or psychological abuse on V, and thereby causes them some kind of recognised psychiatric illness, D can be liable for unlawful manslaughter if the illness causes V to commit suicide.

Secondly, D's unlawful act must cause V's death. The normal rules about proving factual and legal causation apply here. Examples of these causation principles being applied in relation to unlawful act manslaughter include *Mitchell*, which involved indirect factual causation, and *Kennedy (No. 2)* [2007] 3 WLR 612, which decided (after previous uncertainty in the law) that where D supplies the victim with drugs, and the victim then voluntarily takes those drugs and dies as a result, legal causation is not proved, and D is not guilty of unlawful act manslaughter.

Thirdly, D's unlawful act does not have to be 'directed at' the victim. As long as causation has been proved, D is still guilty. This principle is illustrated by *Mitchell* (see above) and *Goodfellow*.

Fourthly, D's unlawful act must be objectively dangerous. This means that the act must be likely to injure someone physically (*Larkin* [1943] KB 174), so that all reasonable people would recognise the risk of some physical harm, although not necessarily serious physical harm (*Church* [1966] 1 QB 59). Whether or not D's act is dangerous is an objective test, for the jury to decide. Therefore, D's act can still be dangerous even if D does not see the risk themselves, as shown by *Ball* [1989] Crim LR 730. However, the dangerousness of what D does is judged according to the facts and circumstances which D would have reasonably known about at the time of the offence. So, in *Watson* [1989] 1 WLR 684, D's act was objectively dangerous and resulted in his conviction for unlawful act manslaughter (because D could see that V, whose house he was burgling, was old and frail), whereas in *Dawson* (1985) 81 Cr App Rep 150, D's act was not objectively dangerous, and his conviction for unlawful act manslaughter was quashed (where D could not reasonably have known that V had a heart condition). The dangerousness of the act cannot be proved by adding together the behaviour of a group of Ds towards V, during the group public order offence of affray, for example (*Carey* [2006] Crim LR 842).

All of the four factors discussed above must be proved before D can be convicted of unlawful act manslaughter. The requirements that D commits an unlawful act which is dangerous in the sense that it is recognised by sober and reasonable persons as subjecting V to the risk of some physical harm, which in turn causes V's death, are not the same as saying that if D commits an unlawful act without which V would not have died, D is liable for V's manslaughter. Objective dangerousness and causation have to be proved in each case (*Carey*).

STUDY EXERCISE 8.5

Read the case of *Carey*. Is it fair to have unlawful act manslaughter as part of the criminal law? Would you have convicted the Ds of unlawful act manslaughter in this case?

Gross negligence manslaughter
The three legal requirements for proving gross negligence manslaughter, which can either be done by act or by omission, are set out in *Adomako* [1995] 1 AC 171. First, there must be a duty of care between D and V. Whether or not there is a duty of care has to be decided by the jury on the facts of the case (*Willoughby* [2005] 1 WLR 1880). To decide this issue, the jury has to use the basic principles of negligence, which come from the civil law rather than the criminal law – looking at the foreseeability that D's negligence would put V at risk, and the fairness of punishing D for what has happened (*Adomako*). If the gross negligence manslaughter charge comes from D's omission, rather than an act, D must have had a legal responsibility to do what they failed to do, such as a landlord failing to check the safety of the gas fire in a tenant's property, resulting in the tenant's death from carbon monoxide poisoning, as happened in *Singh* [1999] Crim LR 582.

Wacker [2003] QB 1207 shows that there can still be a duty of care between D and V even where they are involved in a joint unlawful enterprise together.

Secondly, there must be a gross breach of the duty of care between D and V. Again, as *Adomako* shows, this is a question of fact for the jury to decide – the breach must be so bad, or fall so far below what could reasonably be expected of D in the circumstances, taking into account any specialist knowledge or skills that D has, that it deserves to be punished as a criminal offence. As this is an objective test, it does not matter that D did not foresee the grossness of the breach in duty of care in what they did, as long as a reasonable person at the scene would have. *Misra* [2005] Crim LR 234 states that the grossness of the breach is proved if a reasonable person present at the scene of the offence would have foreseen an obvious and serious risk of death – only a risk of death is enough to prove the offence. *Misra* also decided that the gross negligence manslaughter offence did not breach Article 7 of the ECHR (the right to legal certainty). Thirdly, the gross breach of the duty of care must have caused V's death. The normal principles of proving factual and legal causation apply again here.

STUDY EXERCISE 8.6

Read the article on the BBC website about the case of Dr Feda Mulhem (BBC News 2001, available online at: news.bbc.co.uk/1/hi/health/1284244.stm). Based on the facts of the case, if you had been on the jury at Feda Mulhem's trial for gross negligence manslaughter, would you have convicted him? Give reasons for your answer.

Other types of homicide

There are a few other types of homicide which have been created by statute law. They are discussed in this section. The first type – infanticide – has already been discussed because it is both a defence to murder under the Infanticide Act 1938 s. 1(2), and a specific offence under s. 1(1) of the same Act.

The next three types of homicide to be discussed all involve unlawful killing caused while driving a vehicle. The Road Traffic Act 1988 ss. 2 and 2A define the offence of causing death by dangerous driving, which is committed where D drives in a way which falls far below what would be expected of a competent and careful driver, and it would be obvious to a competent and careful driver that driving in that way would be dangerous (s. 2A(1)), or it would be obvious to a competent and careful driver that driving the vehicle in its current state would be dangerous (s. 2A(2)). Section 2(A)(3) defines 'dangerous' as a danger of injury or serious damage to property. It should be noted that this is an objective offence because it depends on the objective standard of D's driving (or the condition of D's vehicle), rather than D's own *mens rea*. The Road Traffic Act 1991 s. 3 also creates an offence of causing death by careless driving while under the influence of drink or drugs, so that D's alcohol level is over the legal limit for driving or D is unfit to drive due to intake of drugs, and D's driving is objectively careless on the facts. Finally, s. 20(1) of the Road Safety Act 2006 creates new offences of causing death by careless driving and causing death while driving without insurance. As with the previous two offences, D's standard of driving is judged objectively by the jury on the facts – no *mens rea* is required from D. All of these offences also require causation to be proved, in factual and legal terms, in the same way as the other forms of homicide, such as murder and manslaughter.

Finally, the Domestic Violence, Crime and Victims Act 2004 s. 5(1) creates the new offence of causing or allowing the death of a child or vulnerable adult, where V dies because of an unlawful act or omission of someone who was a member of the same household as V, or who had frequent contact with V; D was such a person at the time of that act; at that time there was a significant risk of serious physical harm being caused to V by the unlawful act of such a person; and either D's act caused V's death, or (i) D was, or should have been, aware of the significant risk of harm, (ii) D failed to take such steps as were reasonable to protect the victim from the risk, or (iii) the act occurred in circumstances of the kind that D foresaw or should have foreseen.

STUDY EXERCISE 8.7

Should all cases involving the causes of death where someone is to blame be treated as either murder or manslaughter rather than as one of a range of separate offences?

The next section of this chapter places the law on homicide in its criminal justice context.

Homicide and Criminal Justice

Example I: homicide and criminal justice – overview

In 2006/07 in England and Wales, the police recorded 755 homicides, including murder, manslaughter and infanticide offences, a decrease of 11 (1%) compared with 2005/06, and a significant decrease from the 1,047 offences recorded in 2002/03 (Thorpe et al. 2007: 36). However, the 2002/03 figures included the 173 murders confirmed as having been committed by Harold Shipman over a number of previous years – only a proportion of the number of patients he was suspected to have killed (Newburn 2007: 445–6) – and the 2005/06 figures included the 52 people murdered in the bomb attacks in London on 7 July 2005 (ibid.: 40), which shows how incidents of mass murder such as these can distort the homicide statistics. The British Crime Survey (BCS) relies on victims reporting the crimes committed against them, and so it cannot collect data on homicide.

It is crucial to think not just about what the homicide statistics include, but also about what they leave out in terms of killing. There are, in fact, several categories of killing that are not included in the homicide statistics. First, there is the category covering work-related killings. This includes such incidents as deaths in industrial incidents which happened due to breaches of health and safety legislation which aims to maintain safe working conditions, among various other types. Tombs and Whyte (2007: 47) show that while the Health and Safety Executive recorded 223 deaths due to work-related incidents in 2004/05, the total number of these, including deaths to members of the public, deaths while driving for work purposes, and other work-related deaths, would have been between 1,600 and 1,700. Secondly, although driving offences causing death are recognised as forms of criminal killing (and are discussed further below), it should be noted here that killings caused while driving are not included in the homicide statistics either. Newburn (2007: 465) notes that in 2005, 3,201 people were killed in traffic incidents in Britain. Thirdly, deaths in custody and during the course of arrest by the police are not counted in the homicide statistics. INQUEST, an organisation which monitors deaths in custody, state that in 2008, there were 100 deaths in prison which were not self-inflicted, and 65 deaths involving the police (INQUEST 2009). It is unclear how many of these deaths were caused by unlawful behaviour from police and prison officers, although INQUEST suspects that many of them were due to gross negligence or excessive institutional violence by these agencies. Finally, there are various other deaths which cannot be proved to be homicide, and which are not counted in the homicide statistics because of this uncertainty. These include bodies of homicide victims which are hidden or buried by their killers, missing persons who might have been the victims of homicide, those who have died and been the subject of an inquest where the jury returned an open verdict, and cases where people have died while under medical care, but where the exact cause of death cannot be established (Brookman 2005: 20–2).

STUDY EXERCISE 8.8

Which of the above categories of killing would you include in the annual homicide statistics, and why?

The discussion will now look at the individual homicide offences in their criminal justice context, starting with murder.

Example II: murder and criminal justice

Murder, at least in terms of how it is defined by the criminal law and criminal justice, is a rare offence. But it poses particular problems for criminal justice. As Innes (2003) argues, the police investigating murder often have the problem of filtering out inaccurate or misleading information which has been received from the public due to intensive media coverage of murder cases. Innes has also shown that the police investigate murder cases by 'socially constructing' the events surrounding the crime, and then presenting their construction of events as 'facts', hiding the process of subjective interpretation which has produced their version of what has happened. The police investigation is organised in line with a standard 'process structure'. This structure has been shaped not only by the criminal law governing the legal requirements of the offence of murder and the circumstances and evidence in each particular case, but also by the organisation and values of the police itself, under the influence of 'cop culture' (Reiner 2000).

Despite the restrictions on the use of bail in murder cases under s. 56 of the Crime and Disorder Act 1998 (Ashworth and Redmayne 2005: 217), following the case of *Caballero v UK* (2000) 30 EHRR 43, which declared the previous total ban on granting bail (under the 1994 Criminal Justice and Public Order Act) incompatible with the ECHR, 13% of the defendants facing a murder charge in England and Wales on 31 January 2008 had been released on bail (Ministry of Justice 2008b). There were 372 people convicted of murder in 2006, a decrease from 394 in 2005, but an increase from 257 in 1996 (Ministry of Justice 2007b: 69). The 2006 figure comprises 80.3% of the total number of people tried for murder in that year (463), with only 19% of the total number pleading guilty, but 76% of those pleading not guilty being found guilty (ibid.: 35). In other words, nearly 20% of people tried for murder in 2006 were acquitted. Turning to sentencing, the mandatory life sentence for murder is misleading. As Clarkson (2005: 214–15) points out, very few murderers spend the rest of their lives in prison. Only 36 prisoners are currently on 'whole life' orders in England and Wales (Ford and Strange 2008). The number of life prisoners serving sentences for murder in England and Wales has increased significantly over time in England and Wales, from 58 in 1965 to 310 in 2002 (Shute 2004: 894).

In all murder cases, a minimum tariff has to be set by the judge hearing the case, under s. 269 of the Criminal Justice Act 2003, and in line with the principles set out in Schedule 21 of the 2003 Act. As Ashworth (2005: 117) shows, this sets out three starting points for the sentencing of murder:

- 'Exceptionally serious cases', e.g. the premeditated killing of two or more people – whole life order;
- 'Particularly serious cases', e.g. killing a police officer on duty – 30 years;
- All other cases – 15 years if the offender is aged 18 or more, 12 years if the offender is under 18.

However, Schedule 21 also states that these starting points are only guidelines, and that aggravating or mitigating factors can move the sentence up or down from the starting point which is closest to the circumstances of the case. Therefore, judges have a great deal more discretion over the sentencing of murder cases than the phrase 'mandatory life sentence' suggests.

STUDY EXERCISE 8.9

Using the Internet, find out about the facts of the case of the murder of Sophie Lancaster in Bacup on 11 August 2007. How long a minimum term would you have sentenced the two offenders to if you had been the judge in this case? What reasons and principles would you base your decision on? Was the minimum sentence you decided on higher or lower than the minimum terms imposed by the trial judge in the actual case?

Example III: voluntary manslaughter and criminal justice

Diminished responsibility and criminal justice

Mackay (2000) identifies three key problems with how the diminished responsibility defence works in practice. First, the criterion 'abnormality of mind', as it is defined in *Byrne*, has included a wide range of defendants – even 'mercy killers' who have no real evidence of any mental illness – due to the vagueness of the term's meaning. As a result, this aspect of diminished responsibility operates in an inconsistent way, based more on confusion about what the law is (Horder 1999) and how sympathetic the court feels towards a defendant than solid psychological evidence. Secondly, because after *Cox* (1968) 52 Cr App Rep 130 the prosecution can accept a plea to manslaughter due to diminished responsibility where all the medical evidence supports this conclusion, juries only make decisions in around 15% of all diminished responsibility cases, and around 10% of successful ones. This is a particular problem given the previous point about the inconsistency of medical evidence in some cases. Thirdly, psychiatrists tend to measure 'mental responsibility' using their own psychiatric knowledge, rather than assessing the defendant's moral or legal responsibility as they should do, and have to give evidence on whether a defendant's responsibility has been substantially impaired in most cases when this is really a job for the jury (see also Dell 1984).

Occasionally the courts will add to the confusion about diminished responsibility by rejecting psychiatric evidence from doctors and not allowing the defence to be used. This has happened where they feel that the doctors have been too sympathetic, as happened in *Vinaigre* (1979) 69 Cr App Rep 104. More controversially, it has also happened where they feel that public opinion is strongly against 'letting off' a particular defendant by allowing them to plead guilty to manslaughter instead of murder, as happened in *Sutcliffe* (1981) *The Times*, 30 April.

Provocation and criminal justice

There is evidence to suggest that provocation, like diminished responsibility, is applied very inconsistently by judges and juries (McColgan 1993). The main focus of criticism has been the apparent gender bias in the usage of the defence, particular in relation to murders where the offender and victim are partners or ex-partners and the idea that provocation can only be used where D suffered a sudden and temporary loss of self-control at the time of killing. Women such as the defendants in *Thornton* [1992] and *Ahluwalia* [1992], who have been the victims of domestic abuse – sometimes for many years – seem to have a lot of difficulty in persuading the courts to allow them to use the provocation defence. It has also been argued that women who are allowed to use provocation can only do so if the court sees them as being 'mad' rather than 'bad'. Nicolson (1995) contrasts the ways in which the *Thornton* and *Ahluwalia* provocation cases were seen by the courts to show how this approach works in practice. Both cases involved women who had killed their husbands after suffering years of systematic and violent abuse. But Sara Thornton was portrayed by the Court of Appeal as being an aggressive and evil woman who killed to get revenge, whereas Kiranjit Ahluwalia was portrayed as being a passive and caring woman who only killed because she was mentally ill at the time.

There is also evidence that men who kill their wives and use the defence of provocation receive lighter sentences (less than five years' imprisonment on average) than men who kill in a non-domestic setting (where sentences normally start at five years) (Gibb 2005). Burton's (2003) research shows that the average sentence where D kills his wife is between five and seven years' imprisonment. There have been a few notorious cases where a man who has used provocation has not been sent to prison by the courts. For example, Joseph McGrail was given a two-year suspended sentence in 1991 for kicking his alcoholic wife to death, with the trial judge commenting that McGrail's wife's nagging would have 'tried the patience of a saint'.

Overall, the usage of provocation in criminal justice is inconsistent and contradictory. The discussion here has focused on the subjective part of the test, which requires a sudden and temporary loss of self-control. But many writers have criticised the objective part of the test as well, which now (after *Attorney-General for Jersey v Holley*) only allows age and gender to be taken into account when assessing D's ability to stay in control. Wells (2000) and Power (2006) have argued that criminal justice needs to reflect cultural differences between individuals, in terms of their environment and place in society, to a far greater extent than this to ensure that justice is done. On the other hand, Macklem and Gardner (2001) argued that there was no need to take any more human characteristics into account in the provocation test, and that extending the test would effectively be accepting that violence against women was inevitable in society.

━━━━━━━━━━━━━━━━━━━━━ STUDY EXERCISE 8.10 ━━━━━━━━━━━━━━━━━━━━━

Design a new Act of Parliament with the aim of ending provocation's discrimination against women. What provisions would the Act include, and why?

Infanticide and criminal justice

Infanticide is, as shown above, a defence to murder with a much narrower scope than either provocation or diminished responsibility. As a result, criminal justice rarely has to deal with cases where infanticide is used, either as an offence or as a defence. Mackay's (1993) research found that women who killed their children were often dealt with leniently, either by being allowed to use infanticide as a defence and being given a community sentence, or by not being prosecuted at all. Men who killed their children, however, received an average custodial sentence of 4.5 years, were not allowed to use the infanticide defence at all by the law, and have been stereotyped by the courts as being evil and calculated killers (Wilczynski 1997). Wilczynski and Morris (1993) argue that about half of the women convicted of infanticide are not suffering from any mental illness at all, and therefore claim that infanticide is being used to introduce socio-economic factors which may have contributed to the child's death (ibid.: 35). They conclude that women who kill very young children are treated more leniently through the usage of infanticide, but conclude that this is the result of sexist stereotyping of women who kill as being 'mad' by criminal justice, due to assumptions that 'normal' women are passive and caring and would never kill a young child.

Suicide pact and criminal justice

The suicide pact defence is like diminished responsibility in that D has to raise evidence of the defence. However, unlike diminished responsibility, the defence does not need proof of mental abnormality. It is interesting to contrast the suicide pact defence, which reduces murder to manslaughter, with the approach of the Suicide Act 1961, which legalised suicide, but introduced the offence of assisting the suicide of another, which carries a maximum penalty of 14 years' imprisonment. Where a mentally competent but physically paralysed patient wants to die, but needs help from someone else to do so, criminal justice will not guarantee that it will not investigate and prosecute the helper for the offence of assisting a suicide under the Suicide Act 1961. There is no right to die under Article 2 of the ECHR, which guarantees a right to life (*Pretty v DPP* [2002] 1 FCR 1 – the decision was upheld by the European Court of Human Rights in *Pretty v UK* [2002] 2 FCR 97). Tur (2003) argues that the response in *Pretty* should have been centred on allowing the individual freedom to die, and making it clear in what situations the DPP would prosecute cases of assisting a suicide. In *R (Purdy) v DPP* [2009] UKHL 45 the House of Lords held that the Director of Public Prosecutions should make clear the factors to be considered when deciding whether or not to prosecute for assisting a suicide.

Example IV: involuntary manslaughter and criminal justice

The explanation of the law on the three different forms of involuntary manslaughter earlier in this chapter showed how wide this type of homicide is in the criminal law. It is for this reason that Clarkson (2005: 216) has called involuntary manslaughter a 'dustbin offence', with only the fact that someone's death has been caused linking the different types of the offence together. The boundaries between involuntary manslaughter and other offences are not clear as a result of the width of the offence. At the 'top end', there is considerable overlap between involuntary manslaughter and murder in terms of what defendants are convicted and punished for, an overlap which can be difficult to understand, especially for the relatives of victims of homicide (Blom-Cooper and Morris 2004). Povey (2004), for example, found that 55% of people who were charged with murder in 2002/03 were eventually convicted of involuntary manslaughter. A key explanation for these results is the difficulty of proving intent to kill or do GBH, especially oblique intent as it is defined under *Woollin*, for juries in practice. Brookman (2005: 12) argues that the decision to charge and convict of murder or manslaughter may reflect judgements about defendants' and victims' moral worth, tactical CPS judgements about the chances of securing a conviction, and the success of defences, rather than a clear-cut distinction between different classes of behaviour.

The problems surrounding the offence of gross negligence manslaughter epitomise criminal justice's problems in addressing involuntary manslaughter generally. Quick's (2006) study found that the CPS had wide-ranging power and discretion over the prosecution of gross negligence manslaughter cases involving medical misconduct, and that prosecutions (and convictions) for this offence have increased since the mid-1990s. However, Quick also found extensive inconsistency between individual prosecutors in terms of when they felt that a defendant's negligence was 'gross' enough to be punished, and uncovered evidence suggesting racial and geographic bias in prosecutions. Herring (2006: 311) has pointed out that under *Adomako*, juries are being told to convict if they believe that the defendant's behaviour was so grossly negligent that it deserves to be punished as a crime. This approach makes inconsistency in jury decisions very likely, with juries of different social backgrounds having different views about the blameworthiness of defendants' conduct and whether defendants who did something socially useful, but did it negligently, should be convicted of manslaughter.

Further problems for gross negligence manslaughter have occurred in relation to corporate manslaughter – in other words, gross negligence manslaughter which is caused by organisations or companies rather than individuals. The use of corporate liability offences in criminal justice has attracted criticism from writers who think that these offences are not enforced and punished effectively (e.g. Tombs and Whyte 2007; cf. Hawkins 2002). As of 10 December 2007, only 22 incidents in England and Wales involving work-related death had ever resulted in a conviction for corporate manslaughter. This has meant that only seven companies, 16 company directors, and eight business owners have ever been convicted of corporate manslaughter, and the longest sentence given has been 14 years' imprisonment (Centre for Corporate Accountability 2007). The low conviction rate has been blamed by many writers (e.g. Blom-Cooper and Morris 2004) on the so-called 'identification principle' which required there to be one individual who had the necessary *actus reus* and *mens rea* for gross negligence manslaughter, a principle which in practice meant that only small companies with one person in overall charge had any chance of being prosecuted or convicted (Wells 2001). After promising new legislation to address this issue for 10 years, the government finally introduced the Corporate Manslaughter and Corporate Homicide Act 2007. This Act introduces a new offence of corporate killing, which requires a gross breach of a duty of care at senior management level to have been the substantial cause of death. Gobert (2008) sees the Act as being a more effective response to corporate killing than the previous law. However, he also points out that it is harder to prove causation for this offence than it normally is under the criminal law, that the offence does not include individual liability for assisting corporate homicide, that limiting liability to senior management wrongdoing still focuses too much on individual fault and not enough on systemic or cultural causes of corporate killing, and that the requirement for the DPP's consent to all prosecutions will probably restrict the number of prosecutions.

Using a newspaper archive website, read an account of what happened in the Southall train crash of 19 September 1997. Could either the train driver or the train company have been convicted of corporate killing under the Corporate Manslaughter and Corporate Homicide Act 2007? Give reasons for your answer.

Overall, the incoherence of the criminal law on involuntary manslaughter is matched by the discretion and inconsistency of criminal justice approaches to responding to the offence, in terms of prosecution, conviction and sentencing decisions.

Example V: other forms of homicide and criminal justice

The various driving-related homicide offences were originally introduced because juries were very reluctant to convict motorists of manslaughter (Ashworth 2006: 299). Legislative attitudes to causing death on the roads have become harsher in recent years, with the maximum penalties for causing death by dangerous driving and causing death by careless driving while under the influence of alcohol or drugs both being increased from 10 years' imprisonment to 14 years' imprisonment by the Criminal Justice Act 2003, and the Road Safety Act 2006 introducing the new offences of causing death by careless driving and causing death by driving while unlicensed, disqualified or uninsured, with maximum penalties of five years' and two years' imprisonment respectively.

However, prosecutions for vehicle-related homicide are rare. In 2006, for example, 3,172 people were killed in vehicle-related incidents in England and Wales (Department for Transport 2007: 7), but only 252 people were prosecuted for causing death by dangerous driving, and only 66 people were prosecuted for causing death by careless driving while 'under the influence', in England and Wales. The dangerous driving offence had an 88.5% conviction rate and a 94.2% rate of immediate custodial sentencing for those convicted, while the 'under the influence' offence had a 98.5% conviction rate and a 98.5% rate of immediate custodial sentencing for those convicted (Ministry of Justice 2007b: supplementary table S2.1A). Evidence suggests that while the CPS has significant power and discretion over the prosecution of offenders for these offences (Cunningham 2005), criminal justice is reluctant to take action against those who cause death on the roads, despite the toughening-up of maximum penalties recently and the introduction of offences which only require negligence as *mens rea*. Corbett (2003) argues that the lenient criminal justice treatment of vehicle-related killing compared to other types of homicide is due to the central role which cars and car ownership play in society, and the level of identification of the people who make decisions in criminal justice with the situations of offenders.

▰▰▰▰▰▰▰▰▰▰▰▰▰▰ STUDY EXERCISE 8.12 ▰▰▰▰▰▰▰▰▰▰▰▰▰▰

Draw up a list of three reasons why all driving-related homicides should be treated as either murder or manslaughter, and three reasons why we should have specialist offences instead.

Discussion and Conclusions

This chapter has shown that the legal and criminal justice responses to homicide, the 'ultimate crime' of taking someone else's right to life under Article 2 of the ECHR, are more complicated than they first appear. The criminal law presents murder, manslaughter and other homicide offences as being based on individual responsibility for the lethal harm caused. The requirements for murder in terms of *mens rea*, for example, are clearly labelled by the law – only intent to do GBH or kill will be enough to prove guilt – and this suggests that the law on homicide is based around liberal and due process values. Yet the inclusion of oblique intent as *mens rea* for murder, as well as the intention to do GBH rather than kill, indicates that the law wants to leave itself the room to make moral choices about who and who not to blame for murder, based on paternalistic or even power-based assumptions (Norrie 2005).

This trend is particular noticeable in terms of the types of killing which the law does not label as unlawful homicide. For example, the law will not intervene to make the killing of a foetus murder or manslaughter, except while the foetus is actually being born (Wells and Morgan 1991), but gives doctors extensive discretion over whether to continue to treat seriously ill or disabled patients while only intervening to regulate this discretion in very rare cases (Wells 1989). The law also makes decisions, based on patients' quality of life rather than individuals' wishes, to allow certain death in cases like *A* [2001] 3 All ER1 (Huxtable 2002), but will not allow competent but incapacitated adults to enlist help to kill themselves, even on human rights grounds, in cases like *Pretty*. The law on murder is therefore more moralistic and paternalistic than it appears to be. The discretion allowed to doctors to end life is also based on social assumptions about the expertise and good motives of the medical profession, and contrasts sharply with the activities of Harold Shipman, the doctor and mass murderer who arguably was only allowed to carry on killing vulnerable people for as long as he did because the legal and medical regulatory authorities refused to believe that any doctor was capable of doing what he did.

In terms of the criminal justice response to murder, again it is presented as being based on liberal choice and crime control, with a mandatory sentence of life imprisonment. But this view hides the discretion criminal justice agencies have in investigating murder, allowing bail for murder cases, and setting the minimum sentence tariff. The evidence above suggests that criminal justice takes a individualistic, risk-based approach to investigating, prosecuting, sentencing and punishing murder, even though there is more discretion in this process than there appears to be. D'Cruze et al. (2006) argue that one reason for this individualistic response is that media and political responses to murder makes notorious murder cases, such as the Moors Murders, seem pathologically 'bad', set apart from the rest of society, and therefore more evil. The reality of the social context of murder, however, is very different from the individualist approach taken by criminal justice. Brookman and Maguire (2005) found that 50% of male-on-female homicides involve a woman being killed by her current or former partner, and that alcohol is a factor in around half of male-on-male murders. Dorling (2004: 185), meanwhile, shows that in the 1990s, the poorest people in society were 182% more likely to be murdered than the richest. Even more disturbingly, he shows that the murder rate for those born after 1965 in England and Wales is increasing as they get older, in a way which is not occurring for those men born in 1964 or before (ibid.: 189). Dorling explains this effect by pointing to the economic policies of the Thatcher government in the 1980s, which had the effect of creating recession and mass unemployment among the very poorest in society. This analysis shows how criminal justice's individualist, risk-based approach to responding to murder ignores the social harm done by economic policies at government level.

Similarly, the legal and criminal justice response to manslaughter (both voluntary and involuntary) is presented as 'black and white', but is based on a series of moral assumptions. The defence of diminished responsibility is defined in vague terms to allow both legal and psychiatric views of mental illness to be considered. It operates in practice to allow criminal justice's sexist stereotyping of women as being predisposed to mental illness, based on the medical model of criminal justice, as well as extending it to allow morally 'good' killers, such as mercy killers, to escape a murder conviction. Before its scope was narrowed again in *Attorney-General for Jersey V Holley*, provocation's objective test widened in the past to reflect the law's concern with the moral stigma of being labelled as mentally ill in court by misguidedly trying to help those who could have claimed diminished responsibility to use provocation instead (Macklem and Gardner 2001). In criminal justice practice, provocation's definition again discriminates against women and in favour of men, in terms of when the defence is used and what sentences are given when it is used. The scope of involuntary manslaughter is so wide, and so based around the idea of morally punishing the outcome of death rather than the individual's blameworthiness in causing that death, that it clearly goes against the liberal idea of the law punishing based on individual responsibility and chosen outcomes, as well as arguably breaching the right to a fair trial under Article 6 of the ECHR. It is based more around the idea of risk assessment. Yet in the one area of social harm where this approach could more easily be justified – that of corporate killing – the law and criminal justice refuse to label a great deal of blameworthy corporate activity as homicide, and prosecute and convict companies very rarely. As such, breaches of the right to life of the victims of corporate killing are rarely enforced.

Finally, the attitude towards other types of homicide, such as that caused by vehicles, seems to be more lenient than the attitude towards most forms of murder and manslaughter (apart from corporate killing, as discussed above). The law has gone out of its way to create special offences of vehicle killing because of a traditional reluctance to convict drivers of manslaughter or murder. Criminal justice has given more power to the CPS to prosecute these offences, and more power to the courts to sentence them harshly. But although conviction rates for these offences are high, prosecution rates are low, and average sentences are far below the maximum allowed. Again, the liberal and risk-assessment approach presented by the law hides the reality of criminal justice's enforcement. And again, this softer response is based around the social respectability and importance of car ownership and the greater moral sympathy with vehicle offenders that this cultural factor creates.

The next chapter of the book switches the focus of the discussion to property offences.

FURTHER READING

Allen, M.J. (2007), *Textbook on Criminal Law* (9th edn): chapter 9. Oxford: Oxford University Press.

Blom-Cooper, L., and Morris, T. (2004), *With Malice Aforethought: A Study of the Crime and Punishment for Homicide.* Oxford: Hart.

Brookman, F. (2005), *Understanding Homicide.* London: Sage.

Ormerod, D. (2008), *Smith and Hogan's Criminal Law* (12th edn): chapters 14–16. Oxford: Oxford University Press.

Tombs, S., and Whyte, D. (2007), *Safety Crimes.* Cullompton: Willan.

9

Property offences

Chapter Aims

After reading Chapter 9 you should be able to understand:

- The *actus reus* and *mens rea* requirements for theft in criminal law
- The *actus reus* and *mens rea* requirements for fraud in criminal law
- The *actus reus* and *mens rea* requirements for burglary in criminal law
- The *actus reus* and *mens rea* requirements and available defences for criminal damage in criminal law
- The *actus reus* and *mens rea* requirements for robbery in criminal law
- How criminal justice responds to these offences
- How the evidence on these property offences in the criminal law and criminal justice fits in with the theoretical models introduced in Chapter 1

Introduction

Chapter 9 discusses criminal offences against property, before placing them in their criminal justice contexts. The chapter cannot cover the whole extensive range of property offences, and so focuses on the major types of crime in this area.

Property Offences: The Law

DEFINITION BOX 9.1

PROPERTY OFFENCES

A range of offences which prohibit various types of interference with property rights.

Theft

DEFINITION BOX 9.2

THEFT

The dishonest appropriation of someone else's property with the intention of permanently depriving them of it.

Statutory definition
Theft is defined by the Theft Act 1968 s. 1(1) as the dishonest appropriation of property belonging to another person, with the intention to permanently depriving that other person of it. There are therefore several elements to both the *actus reus* and the *mens rea* of theft, which will now be explained in more detail.

Actus reus
There are three elements of the *actus reus* which must be proved. The first is an 'appropriation'. 'Appropriation' is defined by s. 3(1) of the Theft Act as an assumption of the rights of the owner of the property. Someone who owns a piece of property has various rights in terms of what they can do with it. For example, they can sell it to someone else, rent it to someone else, or give it away to someone else. A key question which the criminal law has had to answer is how much a D has to do before an appropriation of someone else's property can be said to have taken place. Can D still appropriate property if V has consented to them

doing so? This situation might occur because D has lied about what they are going to do with V's property, leading V to voluntarily hand the property over (e.g. *Lawrence* [1972] AC 626). *DPP v Gomez* [1993] AC 442 decided that there can be an appropriation even where the victim consents to D taking their property, following *Lawrence* and *Dobson v General Accident* [1990] 1 QB 274.

DPP v Gomez also decided, following *Morris* [1984] AC 320, that an assumption of any (not all) of the property owner's rights was enough to count as an appropriation. So an appropriation is more than just taking someone's property without their consent. Ashworth (2006: 366–7) gives a good example of what can count as an appropriation: if D, a supermarket customer, touches a tin of beans on the shelf, they have appropriated the beans and are guilty of theft as long as they have the right *mens rea* for theft (see below) because they have assumed the supermarket owner's right to possess the beans. *Hinks* [2001] 2 AC 241 extends the meaning of appropriation further, by stating that it can occur even where the victim has made a valid gift of the property to D, as long as D has the right *mens rea*. This means that even though the civil law would not see D's conduct as illegal, the criminal law could still convict D of theft.

The second element of the *actus reus* is property, so the question here is what the law counts as being property for the purposes of theft. Section 4(1) of the 1968 Theft Act includes money, all personal property, all real property (i.e. land) and all things in action (i.e. intangible property which people can sue one another in respect of, e.g. copyright in music or books). But land cannot be stolen (s. 4(2)), except in three particular circumstances. Also, wild flowers, fruit or foliage growing on land cannot be stolen, unless they are taken for reward or commercial sale (s. 4(3)); and wild animals cannot be stolen, unless they have been tamed or are in captivity (s. 4(4)). The courts have also decided that confidential information, such as the questions on a future exam paper, is not property (*Oxford v Moss* (1978) 68 Cr App Rep 183), and that corpses are not property unless they have been treated or prepared, for example for medical teaching (*Kelly* [1998] 3 All ER 741).

The third element of the *actus reus* of theft is that the property 'belongs to another'. Under s. 5(1) of the 1968 Act, this does not only include the property's owner, but also whoever is in possession of it at the time of the theft, whoever is in control of it at the time of the theft, a trustee of the property, or anyone with a 'proprietary interest' in the property. The phrase 'belonging to another' is therefore widely defined by the criminal law and can cover property which is owned by the thief, as shown by *Turner (No. 2)* (1971) 55 Cr App Rep 336 (where D took back his own car from the garage where it was being repaired to avoid paying for those repairs) and property which its owner did not know about, as shown by *Woodman* [1974] QB 354 (where D took materials from a derelict factory owned by V, who had never visited the site and so did not know they owned the material inside). In *Goodwin* [1996] Crim LR 262, D did not 'own' money which he had dishonestly won from a slot machine using foreign coins. The money still belonged to the owner of the machine.

━━━━━━━━━━━━━━━ STUDY EXERCISE 9.1 ━━━━━━━━━━━━━━━

Should it be theft to touch a tin of beans in a supermarket, without taking them off the shelf, as long as you have the right *mens rea*?

Mens rea

There are two elements to the *mens rea* of theft. First, under s. 1 of the Theft Act 1968, D must commit the *actus reus* dishonestly. Section 2 of the Act gives three scenarios where conduct cannot be dishonest, but does not explain exactly what is or is not dishonest behaviour. In *Feely* [1973] QB 530, it was stated that whether D is dishonest or not is to be decided by the magistrates or jury in each case as a question of fact, using community values relating to what is thought of as dishonest behaviour. *Ghosh* [1982] QB 1053 added to *Feely* by using a mixed subjective/objective test for dishonesty. Under *Ghosh*, D must be dishonest according to standards of reasonable honest people (the objective part), and D must realise that what they did was dishonest according to those standards (the subjective part).

The second element of the *mens rea* for theft is that D must have 'an intention to permanently deprive' V (the person to whom the property belongs) of that property. 'Intention' here means the same as it normally does in the criminal law. However, only intention to *permanently* deprive is normally enough *mens rea*. If D intends to return the property, even after having it for a long time, there cannot be an intention to permanently deprive, that is keep the property forever.

But even if this is the case, D can still be guilty of theft under s. 6 of the Theft Act 1968. This section states that where D intends to treat the property as their own regardless of V's rights, or where D borrows or lends the property but the borrowing or lending is for a period and in circumstances making it equivalent to an outright taking or disposal, D still has the intention to permanently deprive which is needed. *Lloyd* [1985] QB 829 states that borrowing property can only count as an intention to permanently deprive under s. 6 where D only returns the property after all the 'goodness and virtue' has been taken out of it – for example, where D takes V's bus ticket, which only allows travel for one day, and does not return it until the following day (see also *Fernandes* [1996] 1 Cr App Rep 175). Section 6 can also apply where D treats the property as their own – as happened in *Velumyl* [1989] Crim LR 299 and *DPP v Lavender* [1994] Crim LR 297. 'Conditional intent' can also be enough to be intention to permanently deprive – so that if D opens a door or bag, and the jury or magistrates believe that D was about to steal whatever was inside if they thought it was valuable, D would still be guilty of attempted theft (*Attorney-General's References (Nos. 1 & 2 of 1979)* [1980] QB 180).

━━━━━━━━━━━━━━━━ **STUDY EXERCISE 9.2** ━━━━━━━━━━━━━━━━

Make a list of types of behaviour you would consider to be dishonest. Then ask someone else to make a list of what they see as dishonest behaviour. Are the two lists the same or different? What implications do you think this has for juries and magistrates who have to decide whether or not behaviour is dishonest in practice?

Fraud

━━━━━━━━━━━━━━━━ **DEFINITION BOX 9.3** ━━━━━━━━━━━━━━━━

FRAUD

The dishonest making of a false representation, failure to disclose information or abuse of a position of trust, done with the intention of making a gain at V's expense, causing loss to V, or exposing V to the risk of loss; or the obtaining of V's services by deception.

Statutory definition

The offence of fraud is now defined by s. 1 of the Fraud Act 2006. Under s. 1, the general offence of fraud can be committed in one of three ways. These are: dishonestly making a false representation (under s. 2 of the 2006 Act); dishonestly failing to disclose information which D has a legal duty to disclose (s. 3); and dishonestly abusing a position of trust (s. 4). The 2006 Act also introduces a new general offence of obtaining services by deception in s. 11, again to replace the previous range of specific offences covering this type of behaviour, where D persuades V through fraud to do something for them without paying for it.

Fraud by making a false representation – actus reus *and* mens rea

The *actus reus* of this offence is making any representation as to fact or law, or anyone's state of mind, which is untrue or misleading. The representation can be expressly made in terms of what D says or does. But it can also be implied from what D says or does, as shown in the pre-Fraud Act cases of *DPP v Ray* [1974] AC 370 and *Lambie* [1982] AC 449, which shows that a false representation can be made where D uses a credit card to buy goods in a shop, knowing that their card account is overdrawn. The representation can be made to a computer or any other machine as well as to a person. The *mens rea* is that D must dishonestly make the false representation, and must also intend to make a gain through the representation (either to D themselves or to a third party), to cause a loss to V, or to expose V to the risk of loss. 'Dishonesty' and 'intention' mean the same here as they do for the offence of theft. The gain and loss only apply to money or other property, either real or personal.

Fraud by failing to disclose information – actus reus *and* mens rea

The *actus reus* of this type of fraud is failure to disclose information to V which D has a legal duty to disclose, for example because of a contractual obligation, a fiduciary relationship (see *Bristol & West Building Society v Mothew* [1998] Ch 1 for the legal definition of this term), or their status as V's employer. The *mens rea* for the offence is that D must fail to disclose the information dishonestly, and must also intend to make a gain at V's expense, cause loss to V, or expose V to the risk of loss as a result of failing to disclose the information. The *mens rea* is therefore the same as for the s. 2 offence discussed above.

Fraud by abuse of a position of trust – actus reus *and* mens rea

For this offence, the *actus reus* is an abuse by D, either by act or by omission, of a position where they are expected to protect someone else's (V's) financial interests, or are expected not to act against them. The *mens rea* for the offence, similarly to the offences in ss. 2 and 3 of the Fraud Act 2006, is that D must dishonestly abuse their position of trust, and must also intend to make a gain at V's expense, cause a loss to V, or expose V to a risk of loss, by doing so.

Obtaining services by deception – actus reus *and* mens rea

For this offence, the services can be obtained by D either for themselves or for someone else, and can be obtained either from another person or a machine. There are four elements to the *actus reus*. First, D has to obtain services by an act. Secondly, D's act must cause the services to be provided. Thirdly, the services must be made available on the basis that they have been paid for, are being paid for or will be paid for. Fourthly, D must obtain the services without any payment having been made, or without paying for them in full.

There are two elements to the offence's *mens rea*. First, when D obtains the services, they must know that the services are being made available on the basis that they have to be paid for, or might have to be paid for. Secondly, D must have the intention not to pay for the services, or not to pay for them in full.

Burglary

DEFINITION BOX 9.4

BURGLARY

The entry of a building as a trespasser with intent to commit one of a range of criminal offences, or the committing of one of a range of criminal offences following entry into a building as a trespasser.

Statutory definition

The 1968 Theft Act defines several types of burglary. Under s. 9(1)(a), D is guilty of burglary if they enter a building or part of building as a trespasser and with intent to commit theft, GBH or criminal damage. Under s. 9(1)(b), D is guilty of burglary if, after entering a building or a part of a building as a trespasser, they commit theft, attempted theft, GBH, or attempted GBH while inside. Section 26 of the Criminal Justice Act 1991 amended s. 9 to distinguish between domestic burglary, committed in buildings where people live, and nondomestic burglary. Section 10 of the Theft Act 1968 defines a more serious form of burglary, aggravated burglary, as a burglary committed while D has a firearm, imitation firearm, any offensive weapon, or any explosive with him at the time. Both the s. 9(1)(a) and the s. 9(1)(b) forms of burglary can be committed in this aggravated form.

Entry – actus reus

In both forms of burglary, the prosecution has to prove that D entered the building as a trespasser. The question here is how far D has to go before they have committed an 'entry' into the building. *Collins* [1973] QB 100 stated that D had to have made an 'effective and substantial entry' into building as a trespasser, and that this was a question for magistrates or juries to decide on the facts of each case. However, *Brown* [1985] Crim LR 212 decided that D's entry only had to be effective, not effective *and* substantial. *Ryan* [1996] Crim LR 320 again stated that D's entry only has to be effective, and could be effective even if not all of D's body had actually entered the building.

Trespass – actus reus

Trespassing, in civil law terms, means being on someone else's property or land without their permission. *Jones and Smith* [1976] 3 All ER 54 shows that where D enters a building where they have general permission to be, but enters knowing that they are going further than they are allowed to in the building, or entered being subjectively reckless about whether they were doing this, then D is trespassing. *Walkington* [1979] 2 All ER 716 states that it is possible to trespass in a *part* of a building, which does not have to be a separate room from the part of the building where D has permission to be.

Building or part of a building – actus reus

What D enters as a trespasser must be a building or part of a building. In most cases it is obvious that a structure counts as a building. However, the issue is not always clear. Section 9(4) of the 1968 Theft Act states that inhabited vehicles or vessels can count as buildings for the purposes of burglary, but in other cases, the courts have decided whether or not a structure counts as a building on a case-by-case basis, taking into account, for example, how permanent a structure is. This can mean differing outcomes on similar sets of facts (cf. *B & S v Leathley* [1979] Crim LR 314 and *Seekings and Gould* [1986] Crim LR 167, for example).

Entry, trespass and other requirements – mens rea

Collins sets out the *mens rea* requirements for both types of burglary. Under s. 9(1)(a), the prosecution must prove that at the time of D's entry into the building, they knew that they had entered as a trespasser, or were subjectively reckless about whether they had entered as a trespasser or not, and also that they had an intention to commit theft, GBH or criminal damage while inside. Under s. 9(1)(b), the prosecution must prove that at the time when D committed the offence of theft, attempted theft, GBH, or attempted GBH, they knew that they had entered as a trespasser, or were subjectively reckless about whether they had entered as a trespasser or not, and had the right *actus reus* and *mens rea* requirements for the offence which they committed. As with theft, a conditional intent is enough *mens rea* for burglary, under *Walkington* and *Attorney-General's References (Nos. 1 & 2 of 1979)*.

Aggravated burglary – actus reus and mens rea

Aggravated burglary has to be either the s. 9(1)(a) or s. 9(1)(b) type, with the *actus reus* and *mens rea* requirements that each type has. In addition, D must have a firearm or imitation firearm, offensive weapon or explosive with them. All of these terms are legally defined in s. 10(1). For the s. 9(1)(a) type of burglary, D has to have had the aggravating item with them at the time when they entered the property as a trespasser (*Francis* [1982] Crim LR 363). For the s. 9(1)(b) type of burglary, D has to have had the aggravating item with them at the time when they committed the offence of theft, attempted theft, GBH, or attempted GBH inside the property (*O'Leary* (1986) 82 Cr App Rep 341).

STUDY EXERCISE 9.3

'Any entry into another person's property should count as burglary with the right *mens rea*, even if someone only puts their arm inside the property.' Discuss this statement.

Criminal damage

DEFINITION BOX 9.5

CRIMINAL DAMAGE

The intentional or reckless destruction or damage of someone else's property (or of D's own property in certain circumstances), by fire or in any other way, without lawful excuse.

Statutory definition

Criminal damage is defined by s. 1(1) of the Criminal Damage Act 1971 as where D without lawful excuse, destroys or damages any property belonging to another, and does so either intending to destroy or damage any such property, or being reckless as to destroying or damaging it. Under s. 30 of the Crime and Disorder Act 1998, this offence can be committed in a racially aggravated way, and following Part 5 of the Anti-Terrorism, Crime and Security Act 2001 (which amends ss. 28–32 of the Crime and Disorder Act 1998), also in a religiously aggravated way. Section 1(3) creates a separate offence where D without lawful excuse, destroys or damages any property belonging to another *by fire*, and does so either intending to destroy or damage any such property, or being reckless as to destroying or damaging it (commonly known as arson). Either of these offences can also be committed in aggravated form under s. 1(2), where D commits criminal damage either intentionally or recklessly endangering life. In addition, under s. 2, D commits an offence if they make threats to destroy or damage property with a known likelihood of endangering life by doing so, and under s. 3, D commits an offence if they have an article intending without lawful excuse to use it to destroy or damage property belonging to another. The offences under ss. 1(2) and 2 can be committed against property belonging to D themselves as well as property belonging to someone else.

Under s. 5(2) of the Act, two categories of behaviour which provide a 'lawful excuse', and so act as defences to a criminal damage charge, are given, although they do not apply to the s. 1(2) and s. 2 offences. First, D has a defence where they believe that the owner of the property would consent to its damage or destruction (*Jaggard v Dickinson* [1981] QB 527). Secondly, D has a defence where they take reasonable action because they believe that there is an immediate need to protect either their own or someone else's property. Under s. 5(3), D's belief must be subjective and honest in both cases.

Finally, s. 10 of the 1971 Act defines what counts as 'property belonging to another' for the purposes of criminal damage. The definition of property is similar to the one in the definition of theft (see above), except that it includes land where the theft definition of property does not. However, it does not include intangible property (since amended in s. 3 of the Computer Misuse Act 1990 and ss. 35–38 of the Police and Justice Act 2006; see also Wasik 1991) or things in action. 'Belonging to another' includes anyone who has custody or control of the property, who has a proprietary right or interest in it, who has a charge on it, or who has the right to enforce a trust to which the property is subject.

Actus reus

As the definition discussed above shows, the 1971 Act defines s. 1(1) criminal damage's *actus reus* as being the destruction or damage of property, and the Act also defines what 'property' means and what 'belonging to another' means. But it does not define 'damage'. *Hardman v Chief Constable of Avon and Somerset* [1986] Crim LR 330 shows that temporary damage to property can still count as damage, especially if the damage costs money to repair, and *Morphitis v Salmon* [1990] Crim LR 48 also shows that either permanent or temporary physical damage can count, and so can either permanent or temporary damage to usefulness or value of the property. Whether damage has occurred is a question of fact for the magistrates or jury, and partially depends on the nature and value of the property which has been damaged. For the offence of aggravated criminal damage under s. 1(2), the property does not have to belong to someone else (*Merrick* [1995] Crim LR 802). For the offence of threatening to destroy or damage property under s. 2, the test is whether a reasonable person would regard D's words or actions as a threat to damage property (*Cakmak* [2002] Crim LR 581).

Mens rea

Section 1(1) states that for the basic form of criminal damage under ss. 1(1) and 1(3), D must have intended or been reckless as to the destruction or damage of property. For aggravated criminal damage under s. 1(2), as well as intention or recklessness as to destroying or damaging property, the prosecution also needs to prove that D intended or was reckless as to the endangerment of someone's life as a result of the criminal damage. G [2003] 3 WLR 1060 decided that for criminal damage offences, subjective recklessness was needed. *Steer* [1988] AC 111 shows that the endangerment to life must be proved to have resulted from the criminal damage itself, not from D's actions which caused the criminal damage. Under *Dudley* [1989] Crim LR 57, the prosecution does not have to prove that anyone's life actually was endangered by D's criminal damage, as long as D had the right *mens rea* for the offence. Also, the property that endangers V's life does not have to be the same property which D damages (*Attorney-General's Reference (No. 3 of 1992)* [1994] 1 WLR 409).

Defences

The defences to the basic form of criminal damage are defined in s. 5 of the 1971 Act (see above). *Hunt* (1978) 66 Cr App Rep 105 and *Hill and Hall* (1989) 89 Cr App Rep 74 state that whether the damage was done 'in order to protect property' is an objective test based on whether D's actions could reasonably be said to protect the property, although the test is based on D's subjective belief in the reasonableness of their actions. *Blake v DPP* [1993] Crim LR 586 states that D's actions must not be too remote from the property to be reasonably capable of protecting it. This case also shows that D must honestly and subjectively believe that a living person had consented or would consent to the damage to the property in order to use the defence under s. 5(2)(a) of the 1971 Act. In *Jones and Milling* [2007] 1 AC 136, the Ds criminally damaged an RAF base as a protest against the Second Iraq war and an attempt to prevent the aircraft at the base from taking part in the war. The Ds claimed the general defence of prevention of crime because they argued that the war was illegal under the international law crime of aggression. The House of Lords decided that even if the war was illegal in this way, a crime against international law was not a crime which could act as a defence to a charge of criminal damage in English and Welsh law.

━━━━━━━━━━━━━━ STUDY EXERCISE 9.4 ━━━━━━━━━━━━━━

Which defences to criminal damage should be allowed in the law, if any? Give reasons for your answer.

Robbery

━━━━━━━━━━━━━━ DEFINITION BOX 9.6 ━━━━━━━━━━━━━━

ROBBERY

Theft where D uses force against V immediately before or during the theft, or tries to put V in fear of being subjected to unlawful force at this time, in order to steal.

Statutory definition

Under s. 8(1) of the Theft Act 1968, robbery is defined as theft where D, immediately before or at the time of the theft, uses force on V or seeks to put V in fear of being subjected to unlawful force then and there, in order to steal.

Actus reus and mens rea

Robinson [1977] Crim LR 173 shows that all of the *actus reus* and *mens rea* requirements of theft have to be proved before robbery itself can be proved because robbery requires an offence of theft to be taking place. In addition, D needs to use unlawful force, or put V in fear of immediate unlawful force, immediately before or at the time of theft. This means that the *actus reus* and *mens rea* of an offence against the person – common assault or any more serious violent offence – also need to be to proved in terms of occurring immediately before or at the time of the theft.

Dawson [1976] Crim LR 692 shows that whether or not force has been used immediately before or during the theft is a question of fact for the jury to decide. Even very slight force will be enough for the *actus reus* here, however, as *Corcoran v Anderton* (1980) 71 Cr App Rep 104 shows. It must also be proved that the force or threat of force was used in order to steal, so that causation must be established between the use of or threat of force and the theft itself – although as Ormerod (2008: 801) points out, the force or threat do not have to be carried out against V. They also can be carried out against someone else in order to steal from V. This still meets the *actus reus* requirements for robbery. *Hale* (1979) 68 Cr App Rep 415 and *Lockley* [1995] 2 Cr App Rep 554 explain that whether or not the theft has finished is also a question of fact for the jury to decide. If the force or threat are carried out after the theft has been committed, then robbery has not been committed. However, as *Hale* and *Lockley* show, the time of the theft will be judged to last for as long as the theft is continuing 'in practical terms'. Finally, where D has a right to claim the property which they take by force, no robbery offence is committed, even though they realise that they have no right to use force in order to reclaim the property that is theirs (*Robinson*).

The second part of the chapter places the property offences discussed above in their criminal justice contexts.

━━━━━━━━━━━━━━━━ STUDY EXERCISE 9.5 ━━━━━━━━━━━━━━━━

Should robbery be limited to cases where D uses violence of actual bodily harm or worse?

━━━

Property Offences and Criminal Justice

Example I: theft and criminal justice

In 2006/07, non-vehicular theft was jointly the most commonly recorded property crime by the police (30% of all property crime) and the most commonly recorded property crime by the British Crime Survey (BCS) (39% of all property crime) (Taylor et al. 2007: 73). The high percentage of 'other theft' in these figures points to the incidence of theft from shops, or 'shoplifting' as it is commonly known. Shoplifting has increasingly been the focus of criminal justice-related research into theft. Although the BCS does not cover theft from businesses, Shury et al. (2005: 5) show that in the 2002 Commercial Victimisation Survey, 70% of respondents had suffered some form of property crime in the previous year, and 43% had been the victim of shoplifting by customers. The British Retail Consortium (BRC) estimated in 2006 that in 2005, shoplifters stole £767m worth of goods, costing retailers £2.1bn, and that retail crime had increased by 70% since 2000. On the basis of this data, the BRC has argued that criminal justice takes a lenient approach to shoplifting.

However, in 2006, theft from shops constituted 60.4% of all theft convictions – a far higher clear-up rate than for any other form of theft (Ministry of Justice 2007b: 71). Also, in 2006, more custodial sentences were given for shoplifting in magistrates' courts than for any other offence (around 10,600) (Ministry of Justice 2007c: 31). In addition, the average percentage of all theft cases given a custodial sentence in England and Wales was 17.1% in magistrates' courts (ibid.: 116) and 46.2% in Crown Courts (ibid.: 124), with an average custodial sentence of 2 months in the magistrates' courts and 7.2 months in Crown Courts (ibid.). This has occurred despite the clear sentencing guidelines on shoplifting set out by the Court of Appeal in *Page* [2004] EWCA Crim 3358, which stated that custody should only be used for shoplifting offences as a last resort, encouraged community penalties where the shoplifting was motivated by drug use, and suggested that even persistent but minor offenders could be given community sentences, and should be given a maximum of one to two months' custody. These statistics suggest that criminal justice takes a much more punitive approach to shoplifting than the business community claim. In addition, 38,800 people were given a £80 fixed penalty notice for shoplifting in 2006, an increase of 76% compared with 2005 (ibid.: 41). The role of discretion in reporting shoplifting is also significant. Speed and Burrows (2006: 7) found that only 10 individual retail companies accounted for 40% of the shoplifting offences in their study – a sign that different companies have different discretionary policies about whether or not to contact the police following detection of a shoplifting offence.

STUDY EXERCISE 9.6

In what circumstances (if any) do you think that shoplifters should be jailed?

Example II: fraud and criminal justice

Fraud and forgery comprised 5% of crimes recorded by the police in England and Wales in 2006/07 (Taylor et al. 2007: 74). However, the police recording rate is misleading because the reporting rate of fraud to the police is very low. Taking just one type of fraud – cheque and plastic credit card fraud – as an example, the police recorded 59,035 offences in 2006/07 (ibid.), but other data show 2.3 million recorded offences during 2006, costing £428m (APACS 2007). Levi and Burrows (2008) estimated that fraud cost the UK at least £13.9bn in 2005 (not including the criminal justice costs of responding to it), including fraud against the public sector, businesses and private individuals. They also indicated that this figure was an underestimate of the true extent of fraud because it did not include income tax or EU fraud or the fraud which is not classed as a criminal offence.

Cybercrime, that is crime which is committed via the Internet, has also provided new opportunities to commit fraud. Yar (2006: 15) cites data which claims that a credit card fraud is committed on the Internet every 20 seconds. Yar goes on to discuss the wide range of types of Internet fraud, such as advanced fee frauds and phishing scams, which seem to be both extremely common and rarely reported to criminal justice agencies due to such factors as victims' embarrassment at being conned and victims not knowing who to report the matter to (ibid.: chapter 5). The costs of fraud to its victims and the pubic generally are huge, and seemingly outweigh the costs of shoplifting, the most common form of recorded theft (see above). Also fraud appears to be committed across a wider social spectrum than theft, from working-class credit card fraudsters to extremely wealthy 'elite' offenders who engage in insider dealing (Levi 2002a: 149).

Given the extensive social harm caused by fraud (Levi and Pithouse 1992), criminal justice might be expected to treat offenders harshly. Indeed, a greater proportion of fraud cases received a custodial sentence in magistrates' and Crown Courts combined in 2006 (24%) than theft and handling stolen goods cases (19.9%). The average custodial sentence for fraud (10.9 months) was also longer than the average custodial sentence for theft and handling (4.3 months) in 2006 (Ministry of Justice 2007c: 10).

However, the reality of the response to fraud is more complex. Levi (2002b) notes that the police, who investigate most frauds, often have difficulties in gathering the documentary evidence needed to investigate fraud thoroughly. He also notes that even though there is a specialist investigation and prosecution agency which deals with large-scale fraud, the Serious Fraud Office (SFO), which has the power to require information from suspects and others and compel them to answer its questions, has very limited staff and financial resources compared with the losses it is investigating and the funds available to some of the corporations and individuals it is investigating (ibid.: 430).

There have also been high-profile, lengthy and very expensive court cases involving fraud which have collapsed due to problems with the juries involved (e.g. Leigh 2005). These cases have been used as justification for attempts by the government to introduce legislation allowing some fraud trials to be heard without a jury, claiming that juries find complex financial evidence difficult to understand. Other criminologists have pointed to the higher cautioning rate for corporate fraud offences compared with more 'traditional' forms of crime such as theft, and lighter sentences for corporate offenders who commit fraud than others (Croall 2001). Finally, Cook (1989) has pointed out that although benefit fraud costs the UK far less than tax fraud in economic terms, it is punished more harshly by criminal justice. For example, Cook found that many of those convicted of benefit fraud in her study had to pay a fine as well as paying back the stolen money, whereas those accused of tax fraud were often not prosecuted by the Inland Revenue in exchange for paying back the money they owed. Incapacitation can also be used as a response to fraud, in the shape of disqualifying offenders from owning a business for example, although Gobert and Punch (2003) point out how easy it is to re-launch a business under a different name even after being disqualified.

STUDY EXERCISE 9.7

On the basis of what you have read, do you think that there is class-based bias in criminal justice's response to different types of fraud? Give reasons for your answer.

Example III: burglary and criminal justice

Between 1995 and 2006/07, the number of domestic burglaries recorded by the BCS had fallen by 59% in England and Wales, and the number of domestic and non-domestic burglaries recorded by the police fell by around 20% over the same period, so that burglary made up 15% of the crime recorded by the police in 2006/07 (Taylor et al. 2007: 74–5). The 1992 BCS found that one-fifth of burglaries involved an initial loss of property worth less than £100, and due to some property owners having insurance, a majority of burglaries involved net losses of less than £50 (Lacey et al. 2003: 345). Between 1996 and 2006, the number of people sentenced for burglary in magistrates' and Crown Courts has declined by around a third. However, the proportion receiving immediate custody has only declined slightly during that time, from 41.7% to 40.7%, and average custodial sentences have increased noticeably, from 13.8 months in 1996 to 17.1 months in 2006 (Ministry of Justice 2007c: 10) (cf. the sentencing guidelines set out in *McInerney and Keating* [2003] 2 Cr App Rep (S) 240).

Domestic burglary now has a maximum sentence of 14 years' imprisonment, compared with the 10 years' maximum imprisonment for non-domestic burglary, after the Criminal Justice Act 1991. Clarkson (2005) would argue that the differences in maximum sentence have been introduced to reflect the morally worse behaviour of breaking into a building where someone is living, and the increased threat to public safety and security that this poses. However, average sentences for domestic burglaries and non-domestic burglaries do not differ significantly in either magistrates' or Crown Courts. Section 4 of the Crime (Sentences) Act 1997 introduced a mandatory minimum sentence of three years' imprisonment for a third conviction for domestic burglary for adult offenders, although data show that courts rarely give these sentences in practice – only 229 received this sentence in 2006 (Ministry of Justice 2007c: 39). Courts have the discretion not to give the mandatory sentence where they believe that 'exceptional circumstances apply to either the offence or the offender', and this discretion appears to be extensively used in practice.

Research into the experiences of victims of burglary (especially victims of domestic burglary) has increased in the past 25 years (Mawby 2001) since the pioneering study by Maguire and Bennett (1982), which highlighted the psychological effects that burglary had on its victims. Maguire and Bennett found that the emotional impact on victims of domestic burglary was often severe, and perceived as being worse than the financial loss they suffered. Over 25% of victims in the study said that they had suffered serious or quite serious shock, and two-thirds had had their lives affected for some weeks after the offence, despite very little evidence of violence. Thornton et al. (2003) found that 40% of older victims of distraction burglary and those who repelled distraction burglary reported that the incident had had a significant impact on their quality of life. Maguire and Bennett found that many victims of burglary who reported their offence to the police were further distressed by the police's failure to keep them in touch with what was happening in their case, as well as the feelings of mistrust and suspicion towards people generally when no suspect was identified by the police.

British Crime Survey research into the causes of domestic burglary has tended to focus on individual characteristics and behaviour that is perceived to increase the risk of being victimised, and situational crime prevention. For example, Taylor et al. (2007: 77) found that that property with no home security measures, like window locks and door deadlocks, had a 22.5% chance of being burgled compared with the average risk of 2.5%, and other increased risk factors, such as leaving the property unoccupied for five hours or more per day, also fit in with the ideas of Felson (2002) about the absence of 'suitable guardians' leading to increased opportunities to commit crime, and promote the suitability of a crime control and risk assessment approach to responding to burglary. Maguire and Bennett's (1982) findings, which emphasised the importance of factors like unoccupied properties, how easy it was to enter properties, and whether properties had a hidden point of entry in burglars choosing their targets, support a risk assessment approach, as does evidence of the effectiveness of so-called 'cocoon hardening', which encourages the neighbours of a burgled house to watch out for further attempts to break in (Kent 2007). In terms of non-residential burglaries, research in one area found a 20% higher rate of non-residential burglary than for residential burglary, and recommended targeting crime prevention measures particular at educational and sports facilities, which were found to suffer higher rates of victimisation than other types of non-residential sites (Bowers et al. 1998).

However, research from burglars themselves draws attention to the roots of burglary in issues relating to social harm. Hearnden and Magill (2004) found that the need to get money to buy drugs was the main reason given by convicted burglars for their most recent burglary, while Bennett and Wright (1984) highlighted the complex relationship between individual choice to commit burglary and wider social factors. In their study, alcohol and drug use sometimes provided encouragement to commit 'spur of the moment' burglaries, but on other occasions, addiction to alcohol or drugs provided the main motivation to offend, in order to obtain more money to feed these addictions. Wright and Decker (1994), in a study from the USA, found that most of the burglary discussed by the offenders in their study was motivated by financial need, either directly due to financial debt, or indirectly through the costs of alcohol and drug addiction.

Finally, although there are some 'professional burglars' who specialise in burglary as a criminal career (e.g. Maguire and Bennett 1982: chapter 4), Shover's (1991: 87–8) overview of research from the UK and the USA suggests that most burglars do not specialise in committing burglary, and actually commit a range of other crimes as well. This and other evidence suggests that measures based on individual crime control and risk assessment which are specifically targeted at burglars, both inside the criminal justice process (tougher sentences) and outside it (situational crime prevention), while potentially effective, are not sufficiently focused on reducing the social harm that both drives the commission of burglary and results in a reduced quality of life for its victims. Mawby (2001: chapter 7) points out that successful burglary reduction programmes, such as the Kirkholt Project and the Burglary Reduction Initiative in Plymouth, combined situational target-hardening measures with targeting of resources on the social problems which were identified as being key causes of burglary locally, particularly drug abuse and debt.

STUDY EXERCISE 9.8

Read Hearnden and Magill's (2004) research findings. Do you think, after reading them, that situational factors (e.g. strong locks on doors and windows) or social factors (e.g. drug abuse and unemployment) are more important in trying to reduce the amount of burglaries that occur?

Example IV: criminal damage and criminal justice

Criminal damage, or vandalism as it is commonly referred to in criminal justice statistics, comprised 30% of all of the crime recorded by the police in 2006/07, jointly the most common offence (with all non-vehicular theft taken together). Vandalism was also the most common offence reported to the BCS in 2006/07, making up 34% of all recorded offences (Taylor et al. 2007: 74). In terms of longer-term trends, from the peak of BCS-reported vandalism in 1995, when 3,366,000 incidents were estimated, the BCS estimated in 2006/07 that vandalism had declined by 11%, to 2,993,000, although there had been a 10% rise in estimated incidents compared with 2005/06. Police records of criminal damage had also declined since the mid-1990s, although the rate had stabilised by 2006 (ibid.: 82). Vandalism also had the lowest rate of reporting to the police by victims of any offence category in 2006/07, at just 32% (Thorpe et al. 2007: 25).

In terms of arson, there was a 6% fall in the number of arson offences recorded by the police in 2006/07 (43,103 offences) compared with 2005/06. Fire Service statistics recorded a higher number of deliberate fires (72,600) than the police in 2006, although that number did include fires where deliberate fire-starting was only 'suspected' as well as where there was clear proof of this. Again, though, this figure represented a 9% fall in incidents compared with 2005, and a 40% fall compared with the peak figure of 123,300 incidents in 2001 (Department for Communities and Local Government 2008: 4).

The BCS found that there was an average 7% risk of vehicle vandalism, and an average 2.8% risk of home or property vandalism, in England and Wales in 2006/07. However, the factors identified as increasing the risk of vandalism seemed to vary across different social classes. For example, the unemployed were most at risk of vehicle vandalism, which suggests that those from a lower-class background are most at risk. On the other hand, those who owned three or more vehicles were most at risk of being victims of vandalism overall, a factor which suggests a middle- or upper-class background (Taylor et al. 2007: 85).

In terms of sentencing for criminal damage, the number of people being sentenced for a criminal damage offence has increased from 9,754 in 1996 to 12,518 in 2006. However, the proportion of those cases receiving immediate custody has decreased slightly from 11% to 10.6% over that time, while the proportion receiving community sentences has increased from 33.7% to 48.3%. The average length of custodial sentence has also declined from 18 months to 12.9 months between 1996 and 2006 (Ministry of Justice 2007c: 10). However, these data cannot be relied on completely, not least because of the range of criminal damage offences covered by these statistics, from minor vandalism through to arson intentionally endangering life. The division of criminal damage offences in mode of trial terms between criminal damage with a value of up to £5000, which is a summary offence, and criminal damage exceeding this value, which is a triable either way offence, reflects the range of offences covered (Ministry of Justice 2007c: 139).

It is argued, in fact, that criminal justice has struggled to provide a consistent approach to the wide range of social behaviour covered by the category of criminal damage. At the most serious end of the harm scale, there is the social damage caused by arson. Herring (2006: 657) reports data which suggest that in an average week, arsonists in the UK start 3,600 fires which result in two deaths, 60 casualties and £40m worth of damage. Faced with this level of damage, it is difficult to argue against a criminal justice approach based on punishment. But criminal damage also includes a range of other types of behaviour whose criminality and social harmfulness is less obvious. Graffiti is clearly regarded as criminal damage by criminal justice. For example, two students, Charlotte Backhouse and Ian Town, were convicted of 26 counts of criminal damage at Liverpool Crown Court following a 'graffiti campaign' lasting over two years. They were sentenced to nine months' imprisonment suspended for two years, avoiding immediate custody mainly because of the character evidence given by one of their university lecturers testifying to their artistic talent (BBC News 2007). Yet the art created by artists such as Banksy, which often consists of stencils spray-painted on to (other people's) walls, regularly sells for thousands of pounds at auction, and has apparently never resulted in its author even being arrested, at least since he became famous (Vallely 2006).

STUDY EXERCISE 9.9

Should some graffiti be classed as art, and therefore not be punished as criminal damage by criminal justice? If so, where would you draw the line between damage and art? Would you prosecute Banksy, for example?

Example V: robbery and criminal justice

Robbery, at least according to available crime statistics, is a much less common crime than other property offences, such as theft and criminal damage. It comprised 2% of crimes recorded by the police, and 3% of BCS-recorded crime, in 2006/07 (Thorpe et al. 2007: 17). The BCS victimisation risk rate for robbery in 2006/07 was only 0.5% (ibid.: 35), and although the number of robberies recorded by the police rose by 3% in 2006/07 (to 101,370 offences) compared with 2005/06, this still represented a 16% reduction compared with the peak of 121,359 offences in 2001/02 (Jansson et al. 2007: 49). Of the 8,169 people sentenced for robbery in 2006 in all courts, 4,802 received immediate custody, so that there was a custody rate of 58.8%, and the average custodial sentence length was 32.3 months. This compares with a custody rate of 71.1%, and an average sentence of 38.1 months, in 1996 (Ministry of Justice 2007c: 10).

These statistics portray an image of robbery as being a very serious crime, but also a rare one. However, as with other criminal statistics, they do not tell the whole story about robbery. On the most basic level, when robberies which are not reported, not recorded and not cleared up are taken into account, the offence has an attrition rate of about 97%. In other words, only 3% of known robberies are sentenced in the courts (Ashworth 2002: 854). Secondly, as Ashworth (ibid.: 857–60) shows, there have been moves towards deterrence in robbery sentencing, which have been driven more by the small minority of serious armed offences than by the normal pattern of offending. He also shows that there has been considerable confusion about the appropriate level of sentencing, even in the most serious cases, which has led to inconsistency.

Thirdly, because robbery, as it is legally defined, is a combination of a property offence (theft) and any violent offence, it covers a very wide range of behaviour, from professionally organised armed robberies involving kidnap or serious injury through to children demanding small amounts of money from one another in school playgrounds. There is also a great deal of overlap between minor robbery and theft from the person (Jansson et al. 2007: 52), even though robbery is an offence which can only be dealt with at the Crown Court and carries a maximum sentence of life imprisonment. This overlap is especially important because most robberies are so-called 'muggings' involving personal possessions being snatched from V without much force being used. Only 3.8% of robberies recorded by the police in 2006/07 involved the use of guns (ibid.: 64). As Matthews (2002) explains, improvements in crime prevention measures from businesses which were traditionally targets of robbery (e.g. banks and post offices), such as intruder alarms and closed-circuit TV, meant that there were fewer professional armed robbers at the start of the twenty-first century than ever before. This helps to explain why most robberies are committed by badly organised individuals for small amounts of money.

Fourthly, robbery offending and victimisation are both unusually clustered in terms of where offenders and victims live, and who they are. In 2006/07, the BCS found that 45% of recorded robbery offences occurred in London alone, and that the 18 local authority areas with more than three times the national recorded robbery rate accounted for 8% of the population, but 38% of the recorded robbery offences – a greater concentration of offences than for any other type of crime (Higgins and Budd 2007: 113–14). The robbery 'hot spots' were all in areas more likely to be socio-economically deprived. Harrington and Mayhew (2001) found that nearly half of all victims in their study were under 18, and that 77% of incidents were male-on-male. Smith (2003: 15–29) found that 71% of robberies in his study were male-on-male, 42% involved both offenders and victims under the age of 21, and also found over-representation of Afro-Caribbeans as suspects in areas such as Lambeth and Westminster in London. Crucially, however, Smith made the point that the Afro-Caribbean population in these areas was larger than the national average, and that Afro-Caribbeans are more likely to be younger, unemployed and living in inner-city areas than the national average – all factors which make people more likely to be victimised regardless of their ethnicity (2003: 29).

Lastly, although the rate of recorded robbery has declined in the past five years or so, it increased steadily between 1990 and 2002, and by 26% between 2001 and 2002 alone (Smith 2003: 9). One factor which has been identified as being important in this trend has been the increased availability of portable electronic goods such as iPods and mobile phones, which are both valuable and easy to steal. Harrington and Mayhew (2001) found that the number of robberies involving mobile phones being stolen increased from 8% of all recorded robberies in 1998/99 to 28% in 2000/01. These data, when combined with the moves towards deterrence in custodial sentencing practice, indicate a move towards individual responsibility for robbery (both from offenders and victims) and a risk-based criminal justice approach. However, Matthews (2002: 37) found that a significant number of the armed commercial robbers in his study were either drunk or on drugs at the time of their robbery, and in a large percentage of cases the robbers were desperate for money, either to clear debts or to fund a drug habit. This meant that many of the robbers in Matthews' study only had a vague idea of how much money was available from their victims, and an even vaguer idea of what security measures were there to prevent them from committing robbery. Wright et al.'s (2006) study into street robbers again rejects the rational choice approach to explaining why robbery is committed. Instead, the research found that the robbers interviewed were heavily involved in 'street culture', which often meant that they felt desperate and had an immediate need for cash, to which robbery offered a solution. However, most of the robbers did not think about the consequences of their actions as individualist crime prevention supporters would predict. Instead, robbery had a range of cultural causes for the study's participants, from maintaining personal reputation, through obtaining money for alcohol or drugs, to seeking informal justice for earlier harm suffered.

Overall, the criminal justice response to robbery has been characterised by a move towards individual responsibility, risk assessment and deterrence in recent times. However, this is a move which once again hides the social harm and cultural context which influences the commission of robbery, in terms of deprivation, drug abuse and unemployment. It is also arguable that BCS assessments of victimisation not only place too much emphasis on individual crime prevention, but also understate the fear and psychological trauma suffered by victims of serious robbery, as reported in Matthews (2002).

STUDY EXERCISE 9.10

Presdee (2005) argues that robbery is best understood as an expression of young people's need for excitement in their lives, as a form of rebellion against social control, and as a response to the increasingly consumerist society we live in. If Presdee is right, what implications would this have for the way in which criminal justice should respond to robbery?

Discussion and Conclusions

Despite the range of offences covered in this chapter, it is possible to identify some trends in the response of the criminal law to these types of behaviour as well as in the response of criminal justice in enforcing that law.

In the criminal law, the first trend has been one of widening the scope of criminal behaviour, focusing on individual responsibility and risk-based criminality, in terms of both *actus reus* and *mens rea* requirements. In the context of theft,

DPP v *Gomez* and *Hinks* extended the concept of appropriation, the key element in theft's *actus reus*, to include situations where D takes V's property with V's consent, where D touches V's property with V's consent (e.g. in V's shop), and even situations where property has been legally transferred to D by V under civil law, which, as Simester and Sullivan (2007) point out, creates the property ownership rights which criminal law is supposed to enforce (cf. Shute 2002). The new fraud offences created by the Fraud Act 2006 could be said to have the same tendency of widening the scope of criminal law on the basis of risk-based criminality. As Ormerod (2008) points out, the new offences do not need proof of any causal link between D's deception and D's obtaining of V's property, or of the effects of D's false representation on V. In fact, the offences do not need D to have obtained V's property at all, as long as D intends to make a gain, cause loss to V, or expose V to the risk of loss, using one of the methods covered by the 2006 Act. The focus on *mens rea* rather than *actus reus* risks breaching Article 6 of the ECHR (the right to a fair trial). The inclusion of exposing V to the risk of a loss also means that reckless fraud is criminalised, a feature which again extends the scope of the criminal law. As Lacey et al. (2003: 388) point out, some people are careless or ignorant about the state of their bank or credit card accounts, and enter into transactions for goods realising that they might not have the authority to pay for them, but intending to sort the problem out with their bank or credit card company later on – situations like this could be criminalised under the new law.

The widening of the scope of the *actus reus* in both theft and fraud has meant more of an emphasis on the *mens rea* requirement of dishonesty. The law has given dishonesty a 'common sense' legal definition by allowing the magistrates or jury to decide whether D's behaviour was dishonest in each case, and by defining dishonesty (under the *Ghosh* test) as anything which the community would think was dishonest. In this way, the law claims to reflect moral views on what is and is not dishonesty, which everyone in the community shares. However, as Norrie (2001: 41–3) shows, there is no agreement in society about what counts as dishonesty. To give one example, downloading music via the Internet without paying for it is seen as theft by criminal justice, yet Yar (2006: 66) estimates that 81.5m people, in England and Wales and elsewhere, illegally downloaded music in 2003. Yet the law chooses to cover up the social conflict on this issue by claiming that the community always agrees on what dishonesty is. This problem is made even worse by legal decisions since *Ghosh*, where the courts have disregarded the subjective part of the test (i.e. that D must believe that the community would think what they have done is honest) and based dishonesty entirely on the objective standard (Halpin 1996). The current state of the law in this area challenges Article 7 of the ECHR (the right to legal certainty) by making the concept of dishonesty so vague.

In burglary, the *actus reus* requirements of trespass and entry have been steadily reduced in terms of actual criminal behaviour in cases such as *Jones and Smith* and *Ryan*, leading to an increasing emphasis on *mens rea*. In robbery, an offence which carries a maximum sentence of life imprisonment, the scope of the offence's *actus reus* means everything from snatching and then dropping a bag from V's arm to a well-organised, professional armed raid causing economic and physical harm can be included. This again can be seen as a challenge to Articles 6 and 7 of the ECHR, by making the legal category of robbery so wide.

In criminal damage, the criminal law has again gone too far towards a risk-based model of criminal law and justice. One legal result of this direction, the aggravated 'endangering life' criminal damage offence under s. 1(2) of the Criminal Damage Act 1971, which is punishable with a maximum of life imprisonment, convicts people on the basis of their *mens rea* (recklessness as well as intention) rather than any actual damage done (Elliott 1997). This offence also moves towards risk-based criminality by allowing people to be convicted, and potentially punished severely, for damaging property with the owner's permission, even if the risk is created for a short period and D eliminates it immediately, as happened in *Merrick* (Lacey et al. 2003: 408). As Lacey et al. (ibid.: 406) also point out, the image created by the legal definition of criminal damage is one of the destruction of tangible goods – the smashed bus shelter or the indelible inner-city graffiti, for example – but it does not label the damage caused by the pollution of air and water, offences which are far more likely to be committed by middle- and upper-class offenders, as being 'criminal' in the same way. Criminal law has also interpreted the defences to criminal damage in a way which suggests social bias, as *Hill and Hall* and *Jones and Milling*, both cases of 'political' criminal damage in response to legally questionable governmental and political decisions, show. All of this evidence suggests that the legal response to criminal damage sends out very mixed messages, taking a punitive and risk-based approach to responding to damage committed by individuals which threaten the social order, while effectively ignoring arguably more harmful conduct by those who are not seen as being socially dangerous.

In criminal justice terms, the responses to theft and fraud reveal a range of different criminal justice approaches. There are some indications that at the policy level, criminal justice wants to use a due process approach to reduce the number of people who are sent to prison for theft, at least in terms of sentencing guidelines. But in practice, a crime control approach seems to be more influential, especially in the magistrates' court. Even the increasing use of fixed penalty notices for shoplifting, apparently a sign of increased diversion, could be seen as a move towards informal justice, which prioritises admissions of guilt, crime control and bureaucracy through efficiency in dealing with cases over due process and the thorough proof of criminal responsibility in terms of *actus reus* and *mens rea* (Hillyard and Gordon 1999).

Crime and conviction statistics also do not reveal the social context of attitudes towards theft generally, and shoplifting in particular. Walsh (1978: 6) shows how it was the increasing cost of shop workers' wages and the need to increase profits which led to the introduction of self-service and self-selection shops after the Second World War, which increased the opportunities for shoplifting. Some writers have argued that there is a contradiction between the society in which we live, which is increasingly materialistic and organised by the need to buy and consume more and more personal possessions, and the moral disapproval of shoplifting shown by the criminal law and criminal justice (Presdee 2005). Overall, the response to shoplifting by criminal justice is more characterised by individualistic ideas of crime control and the harm caused to the powerful in society than by due process and the reflection of the social harm and inequality which drives the commission of shoplifting, such as unemployment and drug abuse (Cook 2006). Research such as Ditton's (1977), by contrast, shows how much theft from the workplace by employees is tolerated in terms of escaping liability, but also how great the economic cost of such theft is.

The response to fraud seems to be quite different, however. Critical criminologists have used the low rate of serious fraud prosecutions and convictions to argue that the criminal justice response to fraud is characterised by the power model, so that, for example, the Serious Fraud Office's 'soft' response is aimed at protecting and maintaining the power and wealth of those who commit serious fraud (e.g. Tombs 2005: 279). This is a convincing argument, and there is some clear evidence of differences in criminal justice's response based on the social class of the fraudster (Cook 1989). But it ignores the fact that most victims of serious fraud are also powerful people in society, and so fraud is not in their interests (Levi 1987: 79), or in the interests of capitalism and making more profit generally (Nelken 2007). Nor does the approach reflect the fact that many fraud victims' first priority will be to recover the money they have lost, rather than to see their offender being punished harshly (Levi and Pithouse 1992), and that businesses rely on having a good reputation which is damaged just by the process of publicly appearing in court (Fisse and Braithwaite 1985), both factors which may explain why sentencing patterns differ for higher-class fraudsters. There may also be some other explanations for the differences in approach which do not depend completely on power, such as the socially harmful knock-on effects of others losing their jobs due to fraudulent employers being sent to prison, for example. Finally, jury trials and their role in acquitting defendants where they are unsure about legal guilt is more characterised by due process concerns than power relations.

These data indicate that there is no one model of criminal justice which is in control in this area of the criminal law. Instead, there seems to be a complex mixture of crime control and risk-based responses attempting to respond to the social harm caused by these crimes, due process responses which perhaps try to counterbalance the increasing scope of the criminal law by reflecting the minor nature of most offences in less harsh sentencing, and bureaucratic responses concerned with processing cases as efficiently as possible. As argued previously in this book, the discretion of police, prosecutors, court fact-finders and sentencers in deciding whether or not to take action against individuals remains key in understanding how criminal justice operates, despite the moves of the criminal law towards risk and power-based approaches.

The evidence on the theoretical basis of criminal justice's response to property crime is therefore mixed. However, the evidence on the social harm caused by it remains strong. This harm is shown by the research done into the extensive economic and psychological harm suffered by victims of offences like burglary and robbery, as well as the evidence of the widespread public tolerance of handling stolen goods – a factor which also makes the argument that the criminal law reflects common ideas on morality in this area doubtful. Criminal justice has responded to information on harm caused, particularly what has emerged from BCS reports, by acknowledging the limits of what it can do to address social harm caused by crime, in the form of promoting crime prevention measures which go beyond the police and the courts. However, these measures have tended towards individual responsibility for preventing crime, while overlooking the continuing evidence of the influence of alcohol and drug abuse, unemployment, and social divisions on the chances of becoming both a perpetrator and a victim of one of these offences.

FURTHER READING

Card, R. (2008), *Card, Cross and Jones' Criminal Law* (18th edn): chapters 10 and 12. Oxford: Oxford University Press.

Jefferson, M. (2007), *Criminal Law* (8th edn): chapters 15 and 16. Harlow: Pearson.

Lacey, N., Wells, C., and Quick, O. (2003), *Reconstructing Criminal Law* (3rd edn): chapter 4. London: Butterworths.

Levi, M., and Burrows, J. (2008), 'Measuring the Impact of Fraud in the UK: A Conceptual and Empirical Journey', *British Journal of Criminology*, 48(3): 293–318.

Mawby, R.I. (2001), *Burglary*. Cullompton: Willan.

Part Three

Conclusions

Conclusions

| Chapter Aims |

After reading Chapter 10 you should be able to understand:

- Which of the theoretical models in Chapter 1 play a part in criminal law in practice, and what part they play
- Which of the theoretical models in Chapter 1 play a part in criminal justice in practice, and what part they play
- Current trends in the development of criminal law and criminal justice
- Key ideas on how criminal law and criminal justice could be reformed in the future

Introduction

This final chapter of the book returns to the key questions posed in Chapter 1. It summarises the evidence on what the criminal law's functions are in society, what criminal justice's functions are in society, and how big is the gap between them, referring back to the theoretical models put forward in Chapter 1. It will then move on to make some suggestions about how both criminal law and criminal justice could work more effectively in future. First, current trends in the criminal law and criminal justice are summarised.

Where are Criminal Law and Criminal Justice Going Now?

Where is criminal law going?

As shown in the discussion of general principles of criminal law in Chapters 2–5, the criminal law is apparently based around principles of liberalism and the classical 'law and economics' approach. As Norrie (2001) has pointed out, many of the criminal law's key principles are based around these ideas. For example, *actus reus*, the behaviour required to be criminally liable for a particular offence, was seen to be defined by the law as about voluntary acts which the offender has played a part in causing through their behaviour. The different types of *mens rea* – especially intent and recklessness (after the decision in G [2003]) – were shown to support principles of subjective planning, foresight and risk-taking with regards to criminal consequences. The discussion of criminal defences again pointed to liberal principles by showing the different circumstances in which the law removes criminal liability from people, even though they have the required *actus reus* and *mens rea* for an offence because they were not fully responsible for their actions – because they were insane or acting in self-defence, for example. Finally, the implementation of the ECHR into the law in England and Wales through the Human Rights Act 1998 means that all criminal law should be interpreted in line with basic human rights such as the right to life and the right to have a fair trial, and as a result should mean further liberal protection against unfair criminal laws.

However, a recent trend has appeared across a range of issues in the criminal law which has displaced liberalism – the trend of risk-based criminal law. This approach involves attempts to reduce the risk of criminal behaviour occurring, especially by those who are seen as being dangerous in society, using managerialist techniques of assessment. But it also involves a punitive, harsh approach to criminalising what is seen as socially unacceptable or risky behaviour, as the analysis in the previous chapters showed. This trend has been developing in the criminal law over the past 30 years, making impossible attempts a criminal offence under the Criminal Attempts Act 1981 even though no crime can be committed being just one example. However, the trend has accelerated in recent years. To give just three examples:

- The decision on the meaning of appropriation in theft in *Gomez*, which makes any touching of property with the right *mens rea* an offence;
- The imposition of strict liability on Sexual Offences Act 2003 rape offences involving children of a similar age where the defendant has a reasonable belief that the victim is over 13 years old in G [2008];
- The extension of fraud in the Fraud Act 2006 to cover situations where the defendant does not actually obtain any property from the victim but only has the intention to do so.

The criminal law has moved away from liberal ideas about punishing harm and towards intervening at an earlier stage to try to reduce the risk of that harm occurring by punitive means. Even the 1998 Human Rights Act (HRA) has not guaranteed liberal criminal law. A range of examples of law which could be seen as breaching the ECHR have been discussed in this book. As the decision in *Concannon* made clear, the courts have not been prepared to say that the substantive criminal law's fairness can be questioned by the HRA. Only procedural criminal law – fairness in criminal trials, for example – can be regulated by ECHR principles. Even here, defendants have rarely been able to use the HRA to challenge the law's decisions against them, as shown most recently by the House of Lords' decision in G [2008]. Dennis (2005) has pointed out that even in the area of strict liability offences, where the burden of proof moves on to the defendant, the law has effectively decided that in almost all cases there is no inconsistency with the ECHR. The HRA's impact on the criminal law has therefore been more in line with Buxton's (2000) view of intervention only in extreme circumstances than with Ashworth's (2000a) view of substantive change to improve the fairness of the criminal law itself.

But as Norrie (2005) has shown, there is still more discretion in the criminal law than either risk-based or liberal principles suggest. For example, the concept of intent goes further than just planning or aiming to do something, to cover situations where someone only has foresight of the illegal outcome being virtually certain to occur. But it is the jury's decision whether or not evidence of this level of foresight counts as intent. The scope of the defences of consent to offences of violence against the person, and provocation and diminished responsibility to offences of murder, has been decided by court decisions, and the concept of dishonesty, which is fundamental to proving theft and other property offences, also has to be decided by the magistrates or jury in each case.

It is therefore clear from this overview that judges, magistrates and juries have a great deal of scope to inject their own values into the criminal law. As a result, the criminal law can be about the imposition of morality in terms of blaming 'bad' people (*Brown* [1994] on consent) and excusing 'good' people (*Steane* on motive), the patriarchal protection of people who are viewed as being vulnerable in society (*Stone and Dobinson* on omissions liability), the deterrence of economically inefficient acts (*Corcoran v Anderton* on the wide scope of robbery), or the maintenance of social order (the denial of a defence to criminal damage in political cases like *Jones and Milling*) at different times. All of these are common law decisions, but different values can clearly be seen in statute law as well, such as the Sexual Offences Act 2003 where there is a con-clusive presumption or a rebuttable presumption that consent was not given in offences of rape, for example, where deceit as to identity is seen to be morally 'worse' than spiking someone's drink, and both are 'worse' than having non-consensual sex while voluntarily intoxicated; and the limited effectiveness of the corporate manslaughter offence created by the Corporate Manslaughter and Corporate Homicide Act 2007 to regulate deaths caused by corporate wrongdoing.

▨▨▨▨▨▨▨▨▨▨▨▨▨▨▨▨▨▨▨▨▨▨ STUDY EXERCISE 10.1 ▨▨▨▨▨▨▨▨▨▨▨▨▨▨▨▨▨▨▨▨▨

Find three examples of new statutory criminal offences which have been introduced since 1997 and which could be described as risk-related criminal offences. For each one, explain why you think the offence tries to reduce the risk of future offending behaviour.

▨▨

Where is criminal justice going?

The story of criminal justice's development is similar to the story of criminal law's. Again, the basis of criminal justice principles lies in liberal ideas about due process, whereby punishment can only be imposed in cases where the defendant's liability has been proved beyond reasonable doubt. The police can only stop, search and arrest on the basis of 'reasonable suspicion'. The Crown Prosecution Service can only prosecute where doing so is in the public interest, and where there is a reasonable chance of obtaining a conviction. In court, there is a presumption in favour of releasing defendants on bail; defendants have the right to choose to have their case heard in either the magistrates' or the Crown Court if the offence is triable either way; convictions can only be made if there is proof of guilt beyond reasonable doubt; and custodial sentences can only be given if the court gives justification for the offence(s) being 'so serious' that only custody can be justified. Community punishment should involve rehabilitation and reparation as well as punishment based on responsibility, and the stated aim of prison is to help inmates to lead a good and useful life after release. In theory, the criminal justice process gives a series of rights to defendants and only punishes them when individual responsibility is proved, and in proportion with their responsibility.

As with criminal law, though, recent developments have signalled a move towards a risk-assessment model of criminal justice, based on managerialist risk assessment and an increasingly harsh and punitive criminal justice response to crime. These developments have included the following:

- The acceptance of forward-looking reductivist sentencing aims such as deterrence and protection of the public, and the introduction of indeterminate custodial sentences on the grounds of protecting the public, both under the Criminal Justice Act 2003, as well as the doubling of the prison population since 1992 due to more and longer prison sentences (Cavadino and Dignan 2007) and the increasing harshness of sentencing generally (Morgan 2003);
- The introduction of new civil and criminal orders which restrict liberty and threaten to punish people based on the risk of dangerous behaviour rather than a criminal conviction in court, such as ASBOs, Sexual Offences Prevention Orders, and Drinking Banning Orders under the Violent Crime Reduction Act 2006;
- The expansion of police powers to extend the 'normal' period of detention before charge to 36 hours and remove the need for 'reasonable suspicion' when searching for items relating to terrorism under the Terrorism Act 2000;
- More specifically, the circumstances surrounding the shooting of Jean Charles de Menezes at the Stockwell underground station in London on 22 July 2005 by Metropolitan

Police officers who had mistaken him for a known terrorist suspect, in the aftermath of the terrorist bomb attacks in London on 7 July 2005. Menezes was killed by seven bullets to the head, but was innocent of any involvement in terrorism in any way, and was not challenged at any time on his 33-minute journey to the Stockwell station. Moreover, he was not carrying a bag or wearing clothing which would have allowed him to conceal explosives, and the surveillance officers following him could not communicate any doubts about de Menezes being the wrong man to the armed officers who shot him because their radios would not work underground (Taylor 2006). In this case, the prevention of risk seemed to override effective communication between police officers, or 'due process' caution in terms of doubts as to de Menezes' true identity.

These developments pose challenges to the ECHR human rights (especially the rights to life under Article 2 (in the de Menezes case), liberty under Article 5, a fair trial under Article 6, and legal certainty under Article 7) just as recent developments in the criminal law do. However, as with criminal law, discretion still exists at every stage of the criminal justice process. The exercising of police powers is inherently low-profile, and the 'discretion gap' is sometimes filled using crime control values, or even using the aim of maintaining social order (McConville et al. 1991). The CPS *Code for Crown Prosecutors* has little influence on CPS discretion in terms of whether or not to prosecute (Hoyano et al. 1997). Hucklesby's (1997) work indicated that local 'court cultures' or decision-making patterns influenced by particular combinations of magistrates deciding cases were more important in understanding variations in usage of bail than the legislative principles of the Bail Act 1976. Courts still have a great deal of discretion over which evidence to allow during trials, especially after the increased range of hearsay evidence introduced by the Criminal Justice Act 2003, and even after the restrictions imposed on sexual history evidence in rape trials by the Youth Justice and Criminal Evidence Act 1999 (Temkin and Krahe 2008).

In terms of sentencing, despite the introduction of proportionality as a guiding sentencing principle in the Criminal Justice Act 1991, its retention as an overall sentencing principle (alongside other sentencing aims) in the Criminal Justice Act 2003, and increased sentencing guidelines and guidance from the Sentencing Guidelines Council, there is still evidence of inconsistency in sentencing in the magistrates' court (Tarling 2006) and discretion in Crown Court sentencing which can, in some cases, allow courts to increase social divisions by sentencing on the grounds of racism (Hood 1992). In terms of punishment, discretion over how punishment is carried out remains important, as shown by the continuing commitment to rehabilitation in probation practice (Raynor and Robinson 2005), and the ability of some prisons to treat prisoners with humanity (Liebling and Arnold 2004) and others to treat them with repressive brutality and control (Scraton et al. 1991).

As a final point about the presence of discretion, the Jean Charles de Menezes case (discussed above) makes an excellent case study in terms of how prevalent it is in criminal justice. Following the shooting of de Menezes, the Independent Police Complaints Commission (IPCC) investigated the actions of the police – an investigation which the then Commissioner of the Metropolitan Police, Sir Ian Blair, tried to block immediately after the shooting (Dodd 2007) – and condemned the confusion and lack of communication characterised by the police's actions, both in the run-up to the shooting, and after the shooting, when Blair was not informed for at least 24 hours about suspicions that the police had shot the wrong person. However, the IPCC used its discretion to choose not to recommend criminal prosecution or disciplinary action against the officers involved in the death of de Menezes. Although the Metropolitan Police were convicted of health and safety breaches as a result of the Stockwell shooting (ibid.), the Crown Prosecution Service used its discretion to decide not to criminally prosecute any individual police officer involved in the case (Pidd 2009). More use of discretion was evident in the inquest into de Menezes' death. The coroner presiding over the inquest prevented the jury from returning a verdict of unlawful killing (which would have implied criminal liability). As a result, the jury were forced to either label the case as lawful killing or return an open verdict. The jury chose to return a open verdict, going as close as it could to blaming the police for the death, but prevented from going further by the coroner's use of discretion to narrow the verdict options available (Wistrich 2008). This case illustrates the many ways in which discretion is used to promote a range of competing values and principles in criminal justice practice.

STUDY EXERCISE 10.2

In the light of the de Menezes case, should there be more or less discretion in the criminal justice process than there currently is? Explain your answer.

The next section of the chapter looks at how criminal law and criminal justice can move in a more progressive direction in the future, offering a series of recommendations based on the evidence presented in this and earlier chapters.

Where should Criminal Law and Criminal Justice go from here?

Reorganisation on principled grounds

Ashworth (2000b) argued that the scope of the criminal law needs to be limited by clear principles relating to what it should do in order to comply substantively with human rights. Ashworth went on to argue that the criminal law should be limited to censuring people who have committed substantial wrongdoing. On Ashworth's view, for example, ASBOs would not play a part in the criminal law because they can be used for minor acts of anti-social behaviour which are not officially defined as crimes, and which make the definition of anti-social behaviour very vague (Ramsay 2004). As Reiner (2007a: 28) points out, there is no consensus on what counts as 'substantial wrongdoing'. But the advantage of Ashworth's approach is that it would force those who have a say in developing criminal law and criminal justice to think not only about what they do now, but also what they should do – a normative view, in other words. The approach is also flexible enough to apply to the very wide range of behaviour which the criminal law regulates. The ECHR human rights, which are already part of the criminal law in England and Wales under the Human Rights Act, could provide one way of implementing Ashworth's principle of limiting criminal law. For example, Article 8 (the right to privacy) could justify overturning the decision in *Brown* [1994] relating to the causing of consensual physical violence. This would mean, however, that the criminal law would have to stop limiting itself to using the HRA to regulate criminal procedure and start using it to regulate the fairness of the substantive criminal law itself.

Cavadino and Dignan (2007: chapter 11) argue for a similar re-orientation process in criminal justice, again based on the principles of human rights and maximum possible liberty and autonomy for all of those in the criminal justice process, including prisoners. This leads Cavadino and Dignan (ibid.: 386) to make a series of recommendations for reforming criminal justice, such as a move back towards just deserts and away from incapacitation in sentencing, restrictions on the use of custodial remands, and enforceable ceilings on individual prison numbers. They also recommend greater use of restorative justice, in ways which could make offenders face up to the responsibility and motivations for their offending, while giving victims a say in how to respond to offending, and giving the opportunity to reintegrate offenders back into society following their 'shaming' (Braithwaite 1989). These reforms would again have the advantage of injecting humanity and decency back into criminal justice throughout the process (Rutherford 1993). As with criminal law, the reforms could be achieved by a 'strong' implementation of human rights which are already part of criminal justice in theory. However, these changes could not only be implemented by legislative and policy changes. There would need to be a change in criminal justice practice too, which forms the subject of the next recommendation.

Accepting that discretion is inevitable

A key feature of current government policy on the criminal law and criminal justice is the attempts increasingly to control what happens in both processes from central government. The huge amount of new legislation affecting criminal law and criminal justice since 1997 and the increase in centralised monitoring of probation and prison practice are the clearest examples of this trend. The government has tried to remove discretion from criminal law and criminal justice completely. It has, on this view, expanded the size and socially controlling scope of criminal law and criminal justice at the same time, as managerialism and punitivism mix together (Sullivan 2001), through the use of private and non-state organisations to increase social control over day-to-day life, inside and outside criminal justice (Braithwaite 2000).

However, despite this increase in 'top-down' managerialist control over criminal law and criminal justice in practice, the evidence in this book clearly shows that discretion remains at every stage in the criminal justice process, from investigation by police or other agencies to policies on how prisons are organised and run. Similarly, despite all the new statutory legislation, key decisions on the development of the criminal law are still made by the Court of Appeal and the House of Lords in England and Wales, based on individual judges' values and principles. The cases of *Attorney-General for Jersey v Holley* and G [2003], which both changed key criminal law principles, are just two examples of this.

Why is it that even the full force of rapid and frequent legislative and policy change cannot remove discretion in criminal law and criminal justice? The answer is that so many people are involved in their management and development, as shown in Chapters 1 and 2. Despite the moves towards increased centralisation, managerialism and regulation, it would still be almost impossible for a democratic government to control everything that happens in both processes. Young and Matthews (2003) have argued that New Labour have failed to tackle the causes of crime because they have managerially reformed the response to crime, based on increased bureaucracy and risk assessment, as shown above, but have not undertaken transformative reforms of the response to crime, which involve 'deeper' cultural changes in the attitudes of those involved in criminal law and criminal justice.

These 'cultural' changes take time, however, and as recent legislation and policy has tended to be a 'knee-jerk' response to misinformation about crime and criminal justice in the mass media rather than carefully considered and principled developments (Reiner 2007b), the government has been too impatient when it has introduced new legislation and policy. It is argued that the government needs to recognise that discretion is inevitable in both criminal law and criminal justice, and do more to understand how that discretion operates in practice (Gelsthorpe and Padfield 2003), and how it leads to conflicts in the values of criminal law and criminal justice, instead of trying to remove it. Such attempts might even have the reverse effect of criminal justice agencies fighting harder to hold on to the local discretion that they have, therefore reducing the impact of policy (Shapland 1988).

Moving beyond criminal law and criminal justice

The recommendations so far have concentrated on how criminal law and criminal justice could be improved, but there is only so much that either of them can do about crime, even if they are organised in a fairer way. Cavadino and Dignan (2007: 382–3) argue that it is foolish as well as inhumane to look to punitive and risk-based criminal justice approaches to solve the problems of crime, given that such a small percentage of crime results in a criminal conviction and that the real amount of crime in today's society is unknown. The gap between criminal law and criminal justice remains wide, and how wide it is remains unknown, due to the limits of what is known about the extent of crime through police and British Crime Survey data. On the other hand, without criminal justice to enforce it, the criminal law would have little impact in daily life.

STUDY EXERCISE 10.3

List three ways in which you think the gap between criminal law and criminal justice could be narrowed.

The work of Norrie (2001) has illustrated the conflicting values which compete with each other for influence over how the criminal law develops, and the inconsistency in development and content which occurs as a result. This book has reached similar conclusions about criminal law and criminal justice. However, the major trends in both criminal law and criminal justice are based around individual responsibility and punishment on that basis. As Zedner (2004) has argued, the liberal and risk-based approaches are both individualistic, so that the move from liberalism to risk assessment is not really a radical move on to a totally different view of what law and justice should do. As a result, Hillyard and Tombs (2007) claim that criminal law and criminal justice pay too much attention to behaviour which does not cause significant social harm in most cases, such as minor anti-social behaviour. On the other hand, law and justice do not pay enough attention to behaviour which causes far more social harm, such as crime which is committed by states and corporations, such as war crimes, torture, genocide, tax fraud or deaths in the workplace (Cohen 2001; Green and Ward 2004; Tombs and Whyte 2007). Worse still, other preventable social conditions that have the ability to damage or destroy people's lives, such as poverty, political exclusion and a wide gap between rich and poor in society (Cook 2006), are completely ignored by criminal law and criminal justice because they are not seen as being criminal at all. This leads Hillyard and Tombs to argue that in order to understand how to make criminal law and criminal justice fairer, it is necessary to look beyond what is officially defined as 'crime' and examine the whole range of what Hulsman (1986) calls 'problematic situations' in society, where individuals or groups of people are suffering preventable physical, psychological, social, political and/or economic harm.

This is not to argue that changes should be made to criminal law and criminal justice alone. Reiner (2007a: chapter 4) offers a range of evidence which shows a strong link between rising rates of crime (especially violent crime), harsher punishment and socio-economic conditions. Reiner argues that it is a complex combination of so-called 'neo-liberal' economic policies, which emphasise minimum regulation of financial markets and freedom for big business to make as much profit as possible, and social and cultural changes, which emphasise selfishness, greed and success through owning material goods, that explain the expansion and harshness of criminal law and criminal justice since the 1970s. This socio-cultural mix promotes material gain as the primary measure of success in society, but does not allow everyone the opportunity to achieve this material success, thereby encouraging selfishness and crime. It encourages corporate crime at the top of society because state regulation of financial business is weakened in order to allow people to achieve financial wealth. But it also encourages crime at the lower levels of society, through making people more selfish and more desperate to achieve material success that society and culture encourage them to want, but will not let them have (ibid.). This argument can be backed up with a range of statistical evidence from social scientists who are not criminologists, such as Dorling (2004), which also points to the links between social and cultural inequality, more crime, and increasingly harsh punishment.

As a result, if both criminal law and criminal justice are to be made fairer and more effective, it is necessary not just to change them (as shown above), but also to change economic and social policies in ways which reduce social inequality and exclusion, and increase community cohesion and trust between individuals and groups in society – something that risk-based approaches fail to do (Walklate 2000). Further, these changes need to be made in a transformative way, bringing 'deep' social and cultural changes, rather than in a superficial managerial way, as the New Labour government has limited itself to so far (Cook 2006). Only this transformation can really make a positive difference to criminal law and criminal justice.

STUDY EXERCISE 10.4

If you could make five changes to criminal law as it currently is in England and Wales, and five changes to criminal justice, what would those changes be, and why?

FURTHER READING

Cook, D. (2006), *Criminal and Social Justice*. London: Sage.

Garland, D. (2001), *The Culture of Control: Crime and Social Order in Contemporary Society*. Oxford: Oxford University Press.

Hillyard, P., Pantazis, C., Tombs, S., and Gordon, D. (eds) (2004), *Beyond Criminology: Taking Harm Seriously*. London: Pluto Press.

Hudson, B.A. (2003b), *Justice in the Risk Society: Challenging and Re-affirming Justice in Late Modernity*. London: Sage.

Young, J. (1999), *The Exclusive Society: Social Exclusion, Crime and Difference in Late Modernity*. London: Sage.

Glossary of common legal terms

Actus reus   legal phrase meaning the 'guilty act', or the physical/external element of a crime.

Automatism   a legal defence sometimes available where the defendant, for various reasons defined in the criminal law, is judged not to be in control of his or her actions.

Common law   law which is made and developed by judges, in line with the rules on **precedent** (see below).

Complete defence   a defence which, if successfully used, leads to the acquittal of the defendant. Examples include self-defence.

Complicity   the area of criminal law dealing with crimes where two or more people are involved in planning and/or commission of the criminal acts.

Conduct crime   a crime where the illegality relates to conduct which is not allowed. An example is the *actus reus* for the offence of perjury (lying while giving evidence in court).

Doli incapax   the principle in the common law of England and Wales (now abolished by the Crime and Disorder Act 1998) under which young children were presumed not to be capable of committing crime with the necessary *mens rea*, unless it was proved otherwise by the prosecution.

Duress   a **justificatory defence** (see below) available for some crimes, where a defendant has committed the crime as a result of particular threats or pressure, from a human or non-human source. Includes duress *per minas* (through threats) and duress through circumstances.

Excusatory defence   a defence available because of internal factors which are affecting the defendant. Examples include infancy and insanity.

Homicide — the unlawful killing of another person, committed with the required *mens rea*. Homicide includes the offences of murder and various types of manslaughter.

Inchoate offence — an offence under which the required *actus reus* and *mens rea* of a full offence have not been completed, but certain acts defined by the criminal law have been carried out, with the appropriate *mens rea*, in preparation for the full offence taking place. There are three types of inchoate offence in the criminal law: attempt, incitement and conspiracy.

Indictable offence — an offence which can only be dealt with at the Crown Court, by a judge and jury (e.g. murder, rape).

Justificatory defence — a defence available because of external factors which are affecting the defendant. Examples include **duress** (see above) and self-defence.

Lacuna — a loophole in the law. Often used when discussing the *Caldwell* [1982] AC 341 test for objective recklessness.

Mens rea — legal phrase meaning the 'guilty mind', or the mental/internal element of a crime.

Obiter (dictum/dicta) — things said by judges which are not part of the deciding principle in a particular case, and are therefore not binding on later court decisions.

Partial defence — a defence which, if successfully used, reduces the seriousness of the charge against the defendant. Examples include provocation and diminished responsibility, both of which are only defences to murder, and if successfully used reduce the offence from murder to manslaughter.

Precedent (or *stare decisis*) — the system by which a court has to follow decisions made on the same issue earlier by a higher court, and (usually) also decisions made at the same level as itself.

Ratio (decidendi) — the legal principle which is used to decide a particular case, and which is binding (subject to **precedent** – see above) on later court decisions.

Result crime — a crime where the illegality relates to a result which is not allowed to occur. An example is the *actus reus* for the offence of murder (the causation of someone else's death).

Statute law (legislation) — the law which is introduced by Acts of Parliament. It is often used to decriminalise old offences, create new offences, redefine or modify offences which already exist, or consolidate (bring together) old pieces of legislation on the same topic.

Strict liability — a crime under which only a certain defined *actus reus* is required – no accompanying *mens rea* is needed.

Summary offence — an offence which can only be dealt with at the magistrates' court (e.g. drink-driving).

Triable either way offence — an offence which can be dealt with either at the magistrates' court or at the Crown Court, depending on a number of factors, including magistrates' and defendants' opinions on where the case should be dealt with.

Table of cases

Table of statutes

References

Allen, M.J. (2007), *Textbook on Criminal Law* (9th edn). Oxford: Oxford University Press.

APACS (2007), *Fraud: The Facts 2007.* London: Association for Payment and Clearing Services.

Ashworth, A. (1989), 'The Scope of Criminal Liability for Omissions', *Law Quarterly Review,* **105**(3): 424–59.

Ashworth, A. (2000a), 'The Human Rights Act and the Substantive Criminal Law: A Non-Minimalist View', *Criminal Law Review*: 564–7.

Ashworth, A. (2000b), 'Is the Criminal Law a Lost Cause?', *Law Quarterly Review,* **116**(2): 225–56.

Ashworth, A. (2002), 'Robbery Re-assessed', *Criminal Law Review*: 851–72.

Ashworth, A. (2005), *Sentencing and Criminal Justice* (4th edn). Cambridge: Cambridge University Press.

Ashworth, A. (2006), *Principles of Criminal Law* (5th edn). Oxford: Oxford University Press.

Ashworth, A. (2007), 'Sentencing', in Maguire, M., Morgan, R., and Reiner, R. (eds), *The Oxford Handbook of Criminology* (4th edn). Oxford: Oxford University Press.

Ashworth, A., and Blake, M. (1996), 'The Presumption of Innocence in English Criminal Law', *Criminal Law Review*: 306–17.

Ashworth, A., and Redmayne, M. (2005), *The Criminal Process* (3rd edn). Oxford: Oxford University Press.

Attorney-General's Office (2005), *Attorney-General's Guidelines on the Acceptance of Pleas and the Prosecutor's Role in the Sentencing Exercise (2005 edition).* London: Attorney-General's Office.

Baldwin, J. (1997), 'Understanding Judge Ordered and Directed Acquittals in the Crown Court', *Criminal Law Review*: 536–55.

Baldwin, J., and McConville, M. (1977), *Negotiated Justice.* London: Martin Robertson.

Barnish, M. (2004), *Domestic Violence: A Literature Review.* London: HM Inspectorate of Probation.

BBC News (2001), 'Catalogue of Blunders That Led to Death', 19 April.

BBC News (2007), 'Graffiti Vandals Spared Jail Term', 16 April. Available online at: http://news.bbc.co.uk/1/hi/england/merseyside/6561357.stm (last accessed 18th May 2009).

Bennett, T., and Wright, R. (1984), *Burglars on Burglary: Prevention and the Offender.* Aldershot: Gower.

Birch, D.J. (2000), 'A Better Deal for Vulnerable Victims?', *Criminal Law Review*: 223–49.

Bix, B. (1993), 'Assault, Sadomasochism and Consent', *Law Quarterly Review,* **109**(4): 540–4.

Blom-Cooper, L., and Morris, T. (2004), *With Malice Aforethought: A Study of the Crime and Punishment for Homicide.* Oxford: Hart.

Bottoms, A.E. (1983), 'Neglected Features of Contemporary Penal Systems', in Garland, D., and Young, P. (eds), *The Power to Punish: Contemporary Penality and Social Analysis.* London: Heinemann.

Bottoms, A.E. (1995), 'The Philosophy and Politics of Punishment and Sentencing', in Clarkson, C.M.V., and Morgan, R. (eds), *The Politics of Sentencing Reform.* Oxford: Clarendon Press.

Bowers, K.J., Hirschfield, A., and Edwards, S.D. (1998), 'Victimisation Revisited: A Study of Non-residential Repeat Burglary on Merseyside', *British Journal of Criminology,* **38**(3): 429–52.

Bowling, B. (1999), *Violent Racism: Victimisation, Policing and Social Context*. Oxford: Clarendon.

Box, S. (1983), *Power, Crime and Mystification*. London: Tavistock.

Braithwaite, J. (1989), *Crime, Shame and Reintegration*. Cambridge: Cambridge University Press.

Braithwaite, J. (2000), 'The New Regulatory State and the Transformation of Criminology', in Garland, D., and Sparks, J.R. (eds), *Criminology and Social Theory*. Oxford: Clarendon Press.

Bridges, L. (2002), 'The Right to Representation and Legal Aid', in McConville, M., and Wilson, G. (eds), *The Handbook of the Criminal Justice Process*. Oxford: Oxford University Press.

Broeders, A.P.A. (2007), 'Principles of Forensic Identification Science', in Newburn, T., Williamson, T., and Wright, A. (eds), *Handbook of Criminal Investigation*. Cullompton: Willan.

Bronitt, S. (1994), 'Spreading Disease and the Criminal Law', *Criminal Law Review*: 21–34.

Brookman, F. (2005), *Understanding Homicide*. London: Sage.

Brookman, F., and Maguire, M. (2005), 'Reducing Homicide: A Review of the Possibilities', *Crime, Law and Social Change*, **42**: 325–403.

Brown, D. (1997), *PACE Ten Years On: A Review of the Research*. Home Office Research Study No. 155. London: Home Office.

Brown, S. (1991), *Magistrates at Work*. Buckingham: Open University Press.

Brown, S. (2005), *Understanding Youth and Crime: Listening to Youth?* (2nd edn). Maidenhead: Open University Press.

Burney, E. (2003), 'Using the Law on Racially Aggravated Offences', *Criminal Law Review*: 28–36.

Burney, E. (2005), *Making People Behave: Anti-social Behaviour, Politics and Policy*. Cullompton: Willan.

Burton, M. (2003), 'Sentencing Domestic Homicide upon Provocation: Still "Getting Away with Murder"', *Feminist Legal Studies*, **11**(3): 279–89.

Burton, M., Evans, R., and Sanders, A. (2006), 'Implementing Special Measures for Vulnerable and Intimidated Witnesses: The Problem of Identification', *Criminal Law Review*: 229–40.

Buxton, R. (2000), 'The Human Rights Act and the Substantive Criminal Law', *Criminal Law Review*: 331–40.

Cammiss, S. (2007), 'Deciding upon Mode of Trial', *Howard Journal of Criminal Justice*, **46**(4): 372–84.

Campbell, S. (2002), *A Review of Antisocial Behaviour Orders*. Home Office Research Study No. 236. London: Home Office.

Card, R. (2008), *Card, Cross and Jones' Criminal Law* (18th edn). Oxford: Oxford University Press.

Card, R., Gillespie, A., and Hirst, M. (2008), *Sexual Offences*. Bristol: Jordans.

Carlen, P. (1980), 'Radical Criminology, Penal Politics and the Rule of Law', in Carlen, P., and Collison, M. (eds), *Radical Issues in Criminology*. Oxford: Martin Robertson.

Cavadino, M., and Dignan, J. (2007), *The Penal System: An Introduction* (4th edn). London: Sage.

Centre for Corporate Accountability (2007), 'Statistics on Convictions of Companies, Directors etc. for Corporate Manslaughter as of 10 December 2007'. Available online at: www.corporateaccountability.org/manslaughter/cases/convictions.htm (last accessed 18th May 2009).

Chalmers, J., Duff, P., and Leverick, F. (2007), 'Victim Statements: Can Work, Do Work (For Those Who Bother to Make Them)', *Criminal Law Review*: 360–79.

Chambers, G., and Millar, A. (1983), *Investigating Sexual Assault*. Edinburgh: HMSO/Scottish Office Central Research Unit.

Chambers, G., and Millar, A. (1987), 'Proving Sexual Assault: Prosecuting the Offender or Persecuting the Victim?', in Carlen, P., and Worrall, A. (eds), *Gender, Crime and Justice*. Milton Keynes: Open University Press.

Chapman, B., and Niven, S. (2000), *A Guide to the Criminal Justice System in England and Wales*. London: Home Office Research, Development and Statistics Directorate.

Charles, N., Whittaker, C., and Ball, C. (1997), *Sentencing without a Pre-Sentence Report*. Home Office Research Findings No. 47. London: Home Office.

Choongh, S. (1997), *Policing as Social Discipline*. Oxford: Clarendon Press.

Christie, N. (1977), 'Conflicts as Property', *British Journal of Criminology*, **17**(1): 1–19.

Christie, N. (2000), *Crime Control as Industry: Towards Gulags, Western Style* (3rd edn). London: Routledge.

Christie, N. (2004), *A Suitable Amount of Crime*. London: Routledge.

Christie, S. (2003), *Introduction to Scots Criminal Law*. Harlow: Pearson.

Clarkson, C.M.V. (2005), *Understanding Criminal Law* (4th edn). London: Sweet and Maxwell.

Clarkson, C.M.V., Cretney, A., Davis, G., and Shepherd, J.P. (1994), 'Assault: The Relationship between Seriousness, Criminalisation and Punishment', *Criminal Law Review*: 4–20.

Cohen, S. (1985), *Visions of Social Control*. Cambridge: Polity Press.

Cohen, S. (2001), *States of Denial: Knowing about Atrocities and Suffering*. Cambridge: Polity Press.

Coleman, C., and Moynihan, J. (1996), *Understanding Crime Data: Haunted by the Dark Figure?* Buckingham: Open University Press.

Connell, R.W. (1987), *Gender and Power: Society, the Person and Sexual Politics*. Cambridge: Polity Press.

Cook, D. (1989), *Rich Law, Poor Law: Different Responses to Tax and Supplementary Benefit Fraud*. Milton Keynes: Open University Press.

Cook, D. (2006), *Criminal and Social Justice*. London: Sage.

Corbett, C. (2003), *Car Crime*. Cullompton: Willan.

Crawford, A. (2003), 'The Pattern of Policing in the UK: Policing Beyond the Police', in Newburn, T. (ed.), *The Handbook of Policing*. Cullompton: Willan.

Cretney, A., and Davis, G. (1995), *Punishing Violence*. London: Routledge.

Cretney, A., and Davis, G. (1997), 'Prosecuting Sexual Assault: Victims Failing Courts, or Courts Failing Victims?', *Howard Journal of Criminal Justice*, **36**(2): 146–57.

Croall, H. (2001), *Understanding White Collar Crime*. Buckingham: Open University Press.

Crow, I., Richardson, P., Riddington, C., and Simon, F. (1989), *Unemployment, Crime and Offenders*. London: Routledge.

Crown Prosecution Service (2004), *Code for Crown Prosecutors (2004 edition)*. London: Crown Prosecution Service.

Crown Prosecution Service (2007), *Crown Prosecution Service Annual Report and Resource Accounts 2006–07*. London: Crown Prosecution Service.

Cunningham, S. (2005), 'The Unique Nature of Prosecutions in Cases of Fatal Road Traffic Collisions', *Criminal Law Review*: 834–49.

Davies, M., Croall, H., and Tyrer, J. (2005), *Criminal Justice* (3rd edn). Harlow: Pearson.

D'Cruze, S., Walklate, S., and Pegg, S. (2006), *Murder*. Cullompton: Willan.

Dell, S. (1984), *Murder into Manslaughter: The Diminished Responsibility Defence in Practice*. Oxford: Oxford University Press.

Dennis, I.H. (2005), 'Reverse Onuses and the Presumption of Innocence: In Search of Principle', *Criminal Law Review*: 901–36.

Department for Communities and Local Government (2008), *Summary Fire Statistics, United Kingdom 2006*. London: Department for Communities and Local Government. Available online at: www.communities.gov.uk/publications/fire/firestats2006summary (last accessed 18th May 2009).

Department for Constitutional Affairs (2006), *Judicial Statistics for England and Wales, 2005* (revised edn). London: Department for Constitutional Affairs.

Department for Transport (2007), *Road Casualties, Great Britain 2006*. London: Department for Transport/HMSO.

Devlin, P. (1965), *The Enforcement of Morals*. Oxford: Oxford University Press.

Dignan, J. (2005), *Understanding Victims and Restorative Justice*. Maidenhead: Open University Press.

Ditton, J. (1977), *Part-Time Crime: An Ethnography of Fiddling and Pilferage*. London: Macmillan.

Dixon, D. (1997), *Law in Policing*. Oxford: Oxford University Press.

Dobash, R.E., and Dobash, R.P. (1979), *Violence against Wives*. New York: Free Press.

Dobash, R.E., and Dobash, R.P. (1992), *Women, Violence and Social Change*. London: Routledge.

Dodd, V. (2007), 'Met Chief's Attempt to Block Investigation Made Bad Situation Worse, Says IPCC', *The Guardian*, 9 November.

Dorling, D. (2004), 'Prime Suspect: Murder in Britain', in Hillyard, P., Pantazis, C., Tombs, S., and Gordon, D. (eds), *Beyond Criminology: Taking Harm Seriously*. London: Pluto Press.

Duff, P. (2004), 'Changing Conceptions of the Scottish Criminal Trial: The Duty to Agree Uncontroversial Evidence', in Duff, R.A., Farmer, L., Marshall, S., and Tadros, V. (eds), *The Trial on Trial: Volume 1 – Truth and Due Process*. Oxford: Hart.

Duff, R.A. (1997), *Criminal Attempts*. Oxford: Clarendon.

Easton, S., and Piper, C. (2008), *Sentencing and Punishment: The Quest for Justice* (2nd edn). Oxford: Oxford University Press.

Elliott, D. (1997), 'Endangering Life by Destroying or Damaging Property', *Criminal Law Review*: 382–95.

Farrall, S. (2002), *Rethinking What Works with Offenders: Probation, Social Context and Desistance from Crime*. Cullompton: Willan.

Faulkner, D. (2006), *Crime, State and Citizen: A Field Full of Folk* (2nd edn). Winchester: Waterside Press.

Feeley, M., and Simon, J. (1994), 'Actuarial Justice: The Emerging New Criminal Law', in Nelken, D. (ed.), *The Futures of Criminology*. London: Sage.

Feinberg, J. (1984), *Harm to Others*. New York: Oxford University Press.

Felson, M. (2002), *Crime and Everyday Life* (3rd edn). Thousand Oaks, CA: Pine Forge Press.

Fielding, N. (2006), *Courting Violence: Offences against the Person Cases in Court*. Oxford: Clarendon Press.

Finch, E. (2002), 'Stalking the Perfect Stalking Law: An Evaluation of the Efficacy of the Protection from Harassment Act 1997', *Criminal Law Review*: 703–18.

Finney, A. (2004), *Alcohol and Intimate Partner Violence: Key Findings from the Research*. Home Office Research Findings No. 216. London: Home Office.

Fisse, B., and Braithwaite, J. (1985), *The Impact of Publicity on Corporate Offenders*. Albany, NY: State University of New York Press.

Ford, R. (2008), 'ASBOs Quietly Dropped as Most Young Offenders Ignore Them', *The Times*, 9 May.

Ford, R., and Strange, H. (2008), 'Bellfield Joins List of Those to Die in Jail', *The Times*, 26 February.

Garland, D. (1985), *Punishment and Welfare*. Aldershot: Gower.

Garland, D. (1990), *Punishment and Modern Society: A Study in Social Theory*. Oxford: Clarendon Press.

Garland, D. (2001), *The Culture of Control: Crime and Social Order in Contemporary Society*. Oxford: Oxford University Press.

Gelsthorpe, L., and McIvor, G. (2007), 'Difference and Diversity in Probation', in Gelsthorpe, L., and Morgan, R. (eds), *Handbook of Probation*. Cullompton: Willan.

Gelsthorpe, L., and Morgan, R. (eds) (2007), *Handbook of Probation*. Cullompton: Willan.

Gelsthorpe, L., and Padfield, N. (eds) (2003), *Exercising Discretion: Decision-making in the Criminal Justice System and Beyond*. Cullompton: Willan.

Genders, E. (1999), 'Reform of the Offences against the Person Act: Lessons from the Law in Action', *Criminal Law Review*: 689–701.

Genders, E., and Player, E. (1995), *Grendon: A Study of a Therapeutic Prison.* Oxford: Clarendon Press.

Gibb, F. (2005), 'Jealousy is No Longer an Excuse for Murder', *The Times*, 28 November.

Gobert, J. (2008), 'The Corporate Manslaughter and Corporate Homicide Act 2007: Thirteen Years in the Making, but Was It Worth the Wait?', *Modern Law Review*, **71**(3): 413–33.

Gobert, J., and Punch, M. (2003), *Rethinking Corporate Crime.* London: Butterworths LexisNexis.

Goodey, J. (2005), *Victims and Victimology: Research, Policy and Practice.* Harlow: Pearson.

Green, P., and Ward, T. (2004), *State Crime.* London: Pluto Press.

Gregory, J., and Lees, S. (1999), *Policing Sexual Assault.* London: Routledge.

Grubin, D. (1998), *Sex Offending against Children: Understanding the Risk.* Police Research Series Paper No. 99. London: Home Office.

Gunn, M.J., and Ormerod, D. (1995), 'The Legality of Boxing', *Legal Studies*, **15**(2): 181–203.

Hadfield, P. (2006), *Bar Wars: Contesting the Night in Contemporary British Cities.* Oxford: Oxford University Press.

Haines, K., and Drakeford, M. (1998), *Young People and Youth Justice.* Basingstoke: Macmillan.

Hall, N. (2005), *Hate Crime.* Cullompton: Willan.

Halpin, A. (1996), 'The Test for Dishonesty in Theft', *Criminal Law Review*: 283–95.

Hamilton, P., and Harper, J.R. (2008), *A Fingertip Guide to Criminal Law.* Edinburgh: Tottel.

Harrington, V., and Mayhew, P. (2001), *Mobile Phone Theft.* Home Office Research Study No. 235. London: Home Office.

Harris, J. (2000), *An Evaluation of the Use and Effectiveness of the Protection from Harassment Act 1997.* Home Office Research Study No. 203. London: Home Office.

Harris, J., and Grace, S. (1999), *A Question of Evidence: Investigating and Prosecuting Rape in the 1990s.* Home Office Research Study No. 196. London: Home Office.

Hart, H.L.A. (1963), *Law, Liberty and Morality.* Oxford: Oxford University Press.

Hart, H.L.A. (1968), *Punishment and Responsibility.* Oxford: Oxford University Press.

Hart, H.L.A., and Honoré, T. (1985), *Causation in the Law* (2nd edn). Oxford: Oxford University Press.

Hawkins, K. (2002), *Law as Last Resort: Prosecution Decision-making in a Regulatory Agency.* Oxford: Oxford University Press.

Hearnden, I., and Magill, C. (2004), *Decision-making by Burglars: Offenders' Perspectives.* Home Office Research Findings No. 249. London: Home Office.

Hedderman, C., and Sugg, D. (1996), *Does Treating Sex Offenders Reduce Offending?* Home Office Research Findings No. 45. London: Home Office.

Henham, R. (1998), 'Sentencing Sex Offenders: Some Implications of Recent Criminal Justice Policy', *Howard Journal of Criminal Justice*, **37**(1): 70–81.

Herring, J. (2006), *Criminal Law: Text, Cases and Materials* (2nd edn). Oxford: Oxford University Press.

Hester, M., and Westmarland, N. (2005), *Tackling Domestic Violence: Effective Interventions and Approaches.* Home Office Research Study No. 290. London: Home Office.

Higgins, N., and Budd, S. (2007), 'Geographic Patterns of Crime', in Nicholas, S., Kershaw, C., and Walker, A. (eds), *Crime in England and Wales 2006–07.* London: Home Office.

Hillyard, P., and Gordon, D. (1999), 'Arresting Statistics: The Drift to Informal Justice in England and Wales', *Journal of Law and Society*, **26**(4): 502–22.

Hillyard, P., Pantazis, C., Tombs, S., and Gordon, D. (eds) (2004), *Beyond Criminology: Taking Harm Seriously.* London: Pluto Press.

Hillyard, P., and Tombs, S. (2007), 'From "Crime" to Social Harm?', *Crime, Law and Social Change*, **48**(1): 9–25.

von Hirsch, A., Bottoms, A.E., Burney, E., and Wikström, P.-O. (1999), *Criminal Deterrence: An Analysis of Recent Research.* Oxford: Hart.

Hirst, M. (1999), 'Assault, Battery and Indirect Violence', *Criminal Law Review*: 557–60.

HM Crown Prosecution Service Inspectorate (2005), *HM Chief Inspector's Annual Report 2004-5*. London: HM Crown Prosecution Service Inspectorate.

HM Inspectorate of Constabulary and HM Crown Prosecution Service Inspectorate (2007), *Without Consent: A Report on the Joint Review of the Investigation and Prosecution of Rape Offences*. London: Her Majesty's Inspectorate of Constabulary.

Hoare, J., and Jansson, K. (2008), 'The Extent of Intimate Violence, Nature of Partner Abuse and Serious Sexual Assault: 2004/5, 2005/6 and 2006/7 BCS', in Povey, D. (ed.), *Homicides Firearm Offences and Intimate Violence 2006/7*. London: Home Office.

Hogan, B. (1987), 'Omissions and the Duty Myth', in Smith, P. (ed.), *Criminal Law: Essays in Honour of JC Smith*. London: Butterworths.

Home Office (2005a), *PACE Code of Practice A (2005 edition)*. London: Home Office.

Home Office (2005b), *PACE Code of Practice G (2005 edition)*. London: Home Office.

Home Office (2005c), *DNA Expansion Programme 2000-2005: Reporting Achievement*. London: Home Office Forensic Science and Pathology Unit.

Home Office (2006), *The National DNA Database Annual Report 2005-6*. London: Home Office.

Home Office (2007), *CDRP Survey including ASBO Statistics, from October 2003 up to December 2006*. London: Home Office. Available online at: www.crimereduction.homeoffice. gov.uk/asbos/asbos02b.xls (last accessed 18th May 2009).

Hood, R. (1992), *Race and Sentencing*. Oxford: Oxford University Press.

Hope, T., and Sparks, J.R. (2000), 'Introduction: Risk, Insecurity and the Politics of Law and Order', in Hope, T., and Sparks, J.R. (eds), *Crime, Risk and Insecurity: Law and Order in Everyday Life and Political Discourse*. London: Routledge.

Horder, J. (1994), 'Rethinking Non-fatal Offences against the Person', *Oxford Journal of Legal Studies*, **14**(3): 335-51.

Horder, J. (1999), 'Between Provocation and Diminished Responsibility', *Kings College Law Journal*, **9**: 143-66.

Hoyano, A., Hoyano, L.C.H., Davis, G., and Goldie, S. (1997), 'A Study of the Impact of the Revised Code for Crown Prosecutors', *Criminal Law Review*: 556-64.

Hoyle, C. (1998), *Negotiating Domestic Violence: Police, Criminal Justice, and Victims*. Oxford: Oxford University Press.

Hoyle, C., and Zedner, L. (2007), 'Victims, Victimization and Criminal Justice', in Maguire, M., Morgan, R., and Reiner, R. (eds), *The Oxford Handbook of Criminology* (4th edn). Oxford: Oxford University Press.

Hucklesby, A. (1997), 'Court Culture: An Explanation of Variations in the Use of Bail by Magistrates' Courts', *Howard Journal of Criminal Justice*, **36**(2): 129-45.

Hucklesby, A. (2002), 'Bail in Criminal Cases', in McConville, M., and Wilson, G. (eds), *Handbook of the Criminal Justice Process*. Oxford: Oxford University Press.

Hudson, B.A. (2003a), *Understanding Justice: An Introduction to Ideas, Perspectives and Controversies in Modern Penal Theory* (2nd edn). Buckingham: Open University Press.

Hudson, B.A. (2003b), *Justice in the Risk Society: Challenging and Re-affirming Justice in Late Modernity*. London: Sage.

Hulsman, L. (1986), 'Critical Criminology and the Concept of Crime', *Contemporary Crises*, **10**(1): 63-80.

Huxtable, R. (2002), 'Separation of Conjoined Twins: Where Next for English Law?', *Criminal Law Review*: 459-70.

Innes, M. (2003), *Investigating Murder: Detective Work and the Police Response to Criminal Homicide*. Oxford: Oxford University Press.

INQUEST (2009), 'Statistics: Deaths in Custody'. Available online at: http://inquest.gn. apc.org/statistics.html (last accessed 15th May 2009).

Jansson, K., Povey, D., and Kaiza, P. (2007), 'Violent Crime', in Nicholas, S., Kershaw, C., and Walker, A. (eds), *Crime in England and Wales 2006-07*. London: Home Office.

Jefferson, M. (2007), *Criminal Law* (8th edn). Harlow: Pearson.

Jewkes, Y. (2004), *Media and Crime: A Critical Introduction*. London: Sage.

Jewkes, Y. (ed.) (2007), *Handbook on Prisons*. Cullompton: Willan.

Johnstone, G. (2001), *Restorative Justice: Ideas, Values, Debates*. Cullompton: Willan.

Jones, S. (2000), *Understanding Violent Crime*. Buckingham: Open University Press.

Jones, S. (2005), *Criminology* (3rd edn). Oxford: Oxford University Press.

Jones, T.H., and Christie, M.G.A. (2008), *Criminal Law* (4th edn). Edinburgh: Thomson/ W. Green.

Jordan, J. (2001), 'Worlds Apart? Women, Rape and the Police Reporting Process', *British Journal of Criminology*, **41**(4): 679–707.

Kelly, L. (1988), *Surviving Sexual Violence*. Cambridge: Polity Press.

Kelly, L. (1999), *Domestic Violence Matters: An Evaluation of a Development Project*. Home Office Research Study No. 193. London: Home Office.

Kelly, L., Temkin, J., and Griffiths, S. (2006), *Section 41: An Evaluation of New Legislation Limiting Sexual History in Rape Trials*. Home Office Online Report 20/06. Available online at: www.homeoffice.gov.uk/rds/pdfs06/rdsolr2006.pdf (last accessed 18th May 2009).

Kemshall, H. (2003), *Understanding Risk in Criminal Justice*. Buckingham: Open University Press.

Kemshall, H., Mackenzie, G., Wood, J., Bailey, R., and Yates, J. (2005), *Strengthening Multi-agency Public Protection Arrangements (MAPPAs)*. Home Office Development and Practice Report No. 45. London: Home Office.

Kent, A. (2007), *Identified Gaps: Domestic Burglary*. London: Home Office Crime Reduction Effectiveness Group.

Kibble, N.T. (2005), 'Judicial Perspectives on the Operation of s.41 and the Relevance and Admissibility of Sexual History Evidence – Four Scenarios: Part 1', *Criminal Law Review*: 190–205.

King, M. (1981), *The Framework of Criminal Justice*. London: Croom Helm.

King, M., Coxell, A., and Mezey, G. (2000), 'The Prevalence and Characteristics of Male Assault', in Mezey, G., and King, M. (eds), *Male Victims of Sexual Assault* (2nd edn). Oxford: Oxford University Press.

Koffman, L. (2006), 'The Use of Anti-Social Behaviour Orders: An Empirical Study of a New Deal for Communities Area', *Criminal Law Review*: 593–613.

Lacey, N. (1993), 'A Clear Concept of Intention: Elusive or Illusory?', *Modern Law Review*, **56**(5): 621–42.

Lacey, N. (1994), 'Introduction: Making Sense of Criminal Justice', in Lacey, N. (ed.), *Criminal Justice: A Reader*. Oxford: Oxford University Press.

Lacey, N. (1995), 'Contingency and Criminalisation', in Loveland, I. (ed.), *Frontiers of Criminality*. London: Sweet and Maxwell.

Lacey, N. (2007), 'Legal Constructions of Crime', in Maguire, M., Morgan, R., and Reiner, R. (eds), *The Oxford Handbook of Criminology* (4th edn). Oxford: Oxford University Press.

Lacey, N., Wells, C., and Quick, O. (2003), *Reconstructing Criminal Law* (3rd edn). London: Butterworths.

Lees, S. (1997), *Ruling Passions: Sexual Violence, Reputation and the Law*. Buckingham: Open University Press.

Leigh, D. (2005), 'Jury Protest Forces Trial Collapse after Two Years', *The Guardian*, 23 March.

Leng, R. (2002), 'The Exchange of Information and Criminal Disclosure', in McConville, M., and Wilson, G. (eds), *The Handbook of the Criminal Justice Process*. Oxford: Oxford University Press.

Leverick, F. (2002), 'Is English Self-defence Law Incompatible with Article 2 of the ECHR?', *Criminal Law Review*: 347–62.

Levi, M. (1987), *Regulating Fraud: White-collar Crime and the Criminal Process*. London: Tavistock.

Levi, M. (2002a), 'Suite Justice or Sweet Charity? Some Explorations of Shaming and Incapacitating Business Fraudsters', *Punishment and Society*, **4**(2): 147–63.

Levi, M. (2002b), 'Economic Crime', in McConville, M., and Wilson, G. (eds), *The Handbook of the Criminal Justice Process.* Oxford: Oxford University Press.

Levi, M., and Burrows, J. (2008), 'Measuring the Impact of Fraud in the UK: A Conceptual and Empirical Journey', *British Journal of Criminology*, **48**(3): 293–318.

Levi, M., Maguire, M., and Brookman, F. (2007), 'Violent Crime', in Maguire, M., Morgan, R., and Reiner, R. (eds), *The Oxford Handbook of Criminology* (4th edn). Oxford: Oxford University Press.

Levi, M., and Pithouse, A. (1992), 'The Victims of Fraud', in Downes, D. (ed.), *Unravelling Criminal Justice.* Basingstoke: Macmillan.

Liebling, A., and Arnold, H. (2004), *Prisons and their Moral Performance: A Study of Values, Quality and Prison Life.* Oxford: Oxford University Press.

McAlinden, A.-M. (2007), *The Shaming of Sexual Offenders: Risk, Retribution and Reintegration.* Oxford: Hart.

McBarnet, D. (1981), *Conviction: Law, the State and the Construction of Justice.* Basingstoke: Macmillan.

McCallum, F., Ross, G., and Oag, D. (2007a), *The Scottish Criminal Justice System: The Public Prosecution System.* Scottish Parliament Information Centre Subject Map 07/03. Edinburgh: Scottish Parliament.

McCallum, F., Ross, G., and Oag, D. (2007b), *The Scottish Criminal Justice System: The Criminal Courts.* Scottish Parliament Information Centre Subject Map 07/04. Edinburgh: Scottish Parliament.

McColgan, A. (1993) 'In Defence of Battered Women Who Kill', *Oxford Journal of Legal Studies*, 13(4): 508–29.

McConville, M. (2002), 'Plea Bargaining', in McConville, M., and Wilson, G. (eds), *The Handbook of the Criminal Justice Process.* Oxford: Oxford University Press.

McConville, M., Hodgson, J., Bridges, L., and Pavlovic, A. (1994), *Standing Accused.* Oxford: Oxford University Press.

McConville, M., Sanders, A., and Leng, R. (1991), *The Case for the Prosecution.* London: Routledge.

McConville, M., and Wilson, G. (eds) (2002), *The Handbook of the Criminal Justice Process.* Oxford: Oxford University Press.

McDiarmid, C. (2006), *Criminal Law Essentials.* Dundee: Dundee University Press.

McEwan, J.A. (2002), 'Special Measures for Witnesses and Victims', in McConville, M., and Wilson, G. (eds), *The Handbook of the Criminal Justice Process.* Oxford: Oxford University Press.

McEwan, J.A. (2005), 'Proving Consent in Sexual Cases: Legislative Change and Cultural Evolution', *International Journal of Evidence and Proof*, **9**(1): 1–28.

McLaughlin, E. (2007), *The New Policing.* London: Sage.

Mackay, R.D. (1993), 'The Consequences of Killing Very Young Children', *Criminal Law Review*: 21–30.

Mackay, R.D. (2000), 'Diminished Responsibility and Mentally Disordered Killers', in Ashworth, A., and Mitchell, B. (eds), *Rethinking English Homicide Law.* Oxford: Oxford University Press.

Mackay, R.D., Mitchell, B.J., and Howe, L. (2006), 'Yet More Facts about the Insanity Defence', *Criminal Law Review*: 399–411.

Mackinnon, C.A. (1983), 'Feminism, Marxism, Method and the State: Toward Feminist Jurisprudence', *Signs*, **8**(4): 635–58.

Macklem, T., and Gardner, J. (2001), 'Provocation and Pluralism', *Modern Law Review*, **64**(6): 815–30.

Macpherson, W. (1999) *The Stephen Lawrence Inquiry: Report of an Inquiry by Sir William Macpherson of Cluny.* London: Home Office.

Maguire, M. (2002), 'Regulating the Police Station: The Case of the Police and Criminal Evidence Act 1984', in McConville, M., and Wilson, G. (eds), *The Handbook of the Criminal Justice Process.* Oxford: Oxford University Press.

Maguire, M. (2007), 'Crime Data and Statistics', in Maguire, M., Morgan, R., and Reiner, R. (eds), *The Oxford Handbook of Criminology* (4th edn). Oxford: Oxford University Press.

Maguire, M., and Bennett, T. (1982), *Burglary in a Dwelling*. London: Heinemann.

Maguire, M., and Corbett, C. (1987), *The Effects of Crime and the Work of Victims Support Schemes*. Aldershot: Gower.

Mair, G. (2004), 'The Origins of What Works in England and Wales: A House Built on Sand?', in Mair, G. (ed.), *What Matters in Probation*. Cullompton: Willan.

Mair, G., Burke, L., and Taylor, S. (2006), '"The Worst Tax Form You've Ever Seen": Probation Officers' Views about OASyS', *Probation Journal*, **53**(1): 7–23.

Mair, G., and Canton, R. (2007), 'Sentencing, Community Penalties and the Role of the Probation Service', in Gelsthorpe, L., and Morgan, R. (eds), *Handbook of Probation*. Cullompton: Willan.

Mair, G., Cross, N., and Taylor, S. (2007), *The Use and Impact of the Community Order and the Suspended Sentence Order*. London: Centre for Crime and Justice Studies.

Marshall, P. (1997), *A Reconviction Study of HMP Grendon Therapeutic Community*. Home Office Research Findings No. 53. London: Home Office.

Mathiesen, T. (2005), *Prison on Trial* (3rd edn). Winchester: Waterside Press.

Matravers, A. (ed.) (2003), *Sex Offenders in the Community: Managing and Reducing the Risks*. Cullompton: Willan.

Matthews, R. (1999), *Doing Time: An Introduction to the Sociology of Imprisonment*. London: Macmillan.

Matthews, R. (2002), *Armed Robbery*. Cullompton: Willan.

Matthews, R. (2005), 'The Myth of Punitiveness', *Theoretical Criminology*, **9**(2): 175–201.

Mawby, R.I. (2001), *Burglary*. Cullompton: Willan.

Mayhew, P. (2007), 'Researching the State of Crime', in King, R.D., and Wincup, E. (eds), *Doing Research on Crime and Justice* (2nd edn). Oxford: Oxford University Press.

Ministry of Justice (2007a), *Judicial and Court Statistics 2006*. London: Ministry of Justice.

Ministry of Justice (2007b), *Criminal Statistics 2006*. London: Ministry of Justice.

Ministry of Justice (2007c), *Sentencing Statistics 2006, England and Wales*. London: Ministry of Justice/RDS NOMS.

Ministry of Justice (2007d), *Statistics on Race and the Criminal Justice System 2006*. London: Ministry of Justice.

Ministry of Justice (2008a), *Population in Custody, England and Wales: February 2008*. London: Ministry of Justice/NOMS.

Ministry of Justice (2008b), 'Number of Individuals Charged with Murder or Manslaughter and Out on Bail, 31 January 2008'. Available online at: www.justice.gov.uk/docs/foi-charged-on-bail.pdf (last accessed 18th May 2009).

Morgan, R. (1995), 'Damned If They Do, Damned If They Don't: *The Case for the Prosecution*', in Noaks, L., Levi, M., and Maguire, M. (eds), *Contemporary Issues in Criminology*. Cardiff: University of Wales Press.

Morgan, R. (2003), 'Thinking about the Demand for Probation Services', *Probation Journal*, **50**(1): 7–19.

Morgan, R. (2007), 'Probation, Governance and Accountability', in Gelsthorpe, L., and Morgan, R. (eds), *Handbook of Probation*. Cullompton: Willan.

Morris, N. (2008), 'More than 3,600 New Offences under Labour', *The Independent*, 4 September.

Muncie, J. (2001), 'The Construction and Deconstruction of Crime', in Muncie, J., and McLaughlin, E. (eds), *The Problem of Crime* (2nd edn). London: Sage/Open University Press.

Myhill, A., and Allen, J. (2002), *Rape and Sexual Assault of Women: The Extent and Nature of the Problem – Findings from the British Crime Survey*. Home Office Research Study No. 237. London: Home Office.

Nelken, D. (1987), 'Criminal Law and Criminal Justice: Some Notes on Their Irrelation', in Dennis, I.H. (ed.), *Criminal Law and Justice*. London: Sweet and Maxwell.

Nelken, D. (2007), 'Corporate and White Collar Crime', in Maguire, M., Morgan, R., and Reiner, R. (eds), *The Oxford Handbook of Criminology* (4th edn). Oxford: Oxford University Press.

Newburn, T. (2003), *Crime and Criminal Justice Policy* (2nd edn). Harlow: Pearson.

Newburn, T. (2007), *Criminology*. Cullompton: Willan.

Nicolson, D. (1995), 'Telling Tales: Gender Discrimination, Gender Construction and Battered Women Who Kill', *Feminist Legal Studies*, **3**(2): 185–206.

Norrie, A. (2001), *Crime, Reason and History* (2nd edn). London: Butterworths.

Norrie, A. (2005), *Law and the Beautiful Soul*. London: GlassHouse.

Ormerod, D. (2008), *Smith and Hogan's Criminal Law* (12th edn). Oxford: Oxford University Press.

Packer, H.L. (1968), *The Limits of the Criminal Sanction*. Stanford, CA: Stanford University Press.

Padfield, N. (2007), 'Ten Years of Sentencing Reform', *Criminal Justice Matters*, **67**: 36–7.

Padfield, N. (2008), *Text and Materials on the Criminal Justice Process* (4th edn). London: Butterworths/LexisNexis.

Parker, H., Sumner, M., and Jarvis, G. (1989), *Unmasking the Magistrates*. Milton Keynes: Open University Press.

Pathé, M., and Mullen, P.E. (1997), 'The Impact of Stalkers on Their Victims', *British Journal of Psychiatry*, **170**(1): 12–17.

Pattenden, R. (2002), 'Appeals', in McConville, M., and Wilson, G. (eds), *The Handbook of the Criminal Justice Process*. Oxford: Oxford University Press.

Peay, J. (2007), 'Mentally Disordered Offenders, Mental Health, and Crime', in Maguire, M., Morgan, R., and Reiner, R. (eds), *The Oxford Handbook of Criminology* (4th edn). Oxford: Oxford University Press.

Phillips, C., and Brown, D. (1998), *Entry into the Criminal Justice System*. Home Office Research Study No. 185. London: Home Office.

Pidd, H. (2009), 'No Charges over De Menezes Shooting', *The Guardian*, 13 February.

Plotnikoff, J., and Woolfson, R. (2000), *Where Are They Now? An Evaluation of Sex Offender Registration in England and Wales*. Police Research Series Paper No. 126. London: Home Office.

Povey, D. (ed.) (2004), *Crime in England and Wales 2002/3: Supplementary Volume 1 – Homicide and Gun Crime*. London: Home Office.

Power, H. (2006), 'Provocation and Culture', *Criminal Law Review*: 871–88.

Presdee, M. (2005), 'Volume Crime and Everyday Life', in Hale, C., Hayward, K., Wahidin, A., and Wincup, E. (eds), *Criminology*. Oxford: Oxford University Press.

Quick, O. (2006), 'Prosecuting "Gross" Medical Negligence: Manslaughter, Discretion and the Crown Prosecution Service', *Journal of Law and Society*, **33**(3): 421–50.

Raine, J., Dunstan, E., and Mackie, A. (2004), 'Financial Penalties: Who Pays, Who Doesn't, and Why Not?', *Howard Journal of Criminal Justice*, **43**(5): 518–38.

Ramsay, P. (2004), 'What is Anti-Social Behaviour?', *Criminal Law Review*: 908–25.

Raynor, P. (2004), 'Rehabilitative and Reintegrative Approaches', in Bottoms, A.E., Rex, S., and Robinson, G. (eds), *Alternatives to Prison: Options for an Insecure Society*. Cullompton: Willan.

Raynor, P., and Robinson, G. (2005), *Rehabilitation, Crime and Justice*. London: Palgrave Macmillan.

Redmayne, M. (2004), 'Disclosure and its Discontents', *Criminal Law Review*: 441–62.

Reeves, H., and Mulley, K. (2000), 'The New Status of Victims in the UK: Opportunities and Threats', in Crawford, A., and Goodey, J. (eds), *Integrating a Victim Perspective within Criminal Justice*. Dartmouth: Ashgate.

Reiner, R. (2000), *The Politics of the Police* (3rd edn). Oxford: Oxford University Press.

Reiner, R. (2007a), *Law and Order: An Honest Citizen's Guide to Crime and Control.* Cambridge: Polity Press.

Reiner, R. (2007b), 'Media-made Criminality', in Maguire, M., Morgan, R., and Reiner, R. (eds), *The Oxford Handbook of Criminology* (4th edn). Oxford: Oxford University Press.

Roberts, P. (1997), 'Philosophical Foundations of Consent in the Criminal Law', *Oxford Journal of Legal Studies*, **14**(3): 389–414.

Roberts, P. (2002), 'Science, Experts, and Criminal Justice', in McConville, M., and Wilson, G. (eds), *The Handbook of the Criminal Justice Process.* Oxford: Oxford University Press.

Robinson, G. (2002), 'Exploring Risk Management in Probation Practice: Contemporary Developments in England and Wales', *Punishment and Society*, **4**(1): 5–25.

Rock, P. (1993), *The Social World of an English Crown Court.* Oxford: Clarendon Press.

Rumney, P.N.S. (2001), 'Male Rape in the Courtroom: Issues and Concerns', *Criminal Law Review*: 205–13.

Rumney, P.N.S., and Morgan-Taylor, M. (2004), 'The Construction of Sexual Consent in Male Rape and Sexual Assault', in Cowling, M., and Edwards, P. (eds), *Making Sense of Sexual Consent.* Aldershot: Ashgate.

Rutherford, A. (1993), *Criminal Justice and the Pursuit of Decency.* Oxford: Oxford University Press.

Sanders, A. (2002), 'Prosecutions Systems', in McConville, M., and Wilson, G. (eds), *The Handbook of the Criminal Justice Process.* Oxford: Oxford University Press.

Sanders, A., Hoyle, C., Morgan, R., and Cape, E. (2001), 'Victim Impact Statements: Can't Work, Won't Work', *Criminal Law Review*: 447–58.

Sanders, A., and Young, R. (2006), *Criminal Justice* (3rd edn). Oxford: Oxford University Press.

Scraton, P., Sim, J., and Skidmore, P. (1991), *Prisons under Protest.* Milton Keynes: Open University Press.

Seaton, M. (2002), 'The Unspeakable Crime', *The Guardian*, 18 November.

Sentencing Guidelines Council (2007), *Sexual Offences Act 2003 – Definitive Guideline.* London: Sentencing Guidelines Council. Available online at: www.sentencing-guidelines. gov.uk/docs/ooo_SexualOffencesAct1.pdf (last accessed 15th May 09).

Selfe, D.W., and Burke, V. (2001), *Perspectives on Sex, Crime and Society* (2nd edn). London: Cavendish.

Shapland, J. (1988), 'Fiefs and Peasants: Accomplishing Change for Victims in the Criminal Justice System', in Maguire, M., and Pointing, J. (eds), *Victims of Crime: A New Deal?* Milton Keynes: Open University Press.

Shapland, J., Atkinson, A., Atkinson, H., Chapman, B., Colledge, E., Dignan, J., Howes, M., Johnstone, J., Robinson, G., and Sorsby, A. (2006), *Restorative Justice in Practice: The Second Report from the Evaluation of Three Schemes.* Sheffield: University of Sheffield Centre for Criminological Research.

Shapland, J., and Bell, E. (1998), 'Victims in the Magistrates' Court and Crown Court', *Criminal Law Review*: 537–46.

Shapland, J., Willmore, J., and Duff, P. (1985), *Victims in the Criminal Justice System.* Aldershot: Gower.

Shover, N. (1991), 'Burglary', *Crime and Justice: A Review of Research*, **14**: 73–113.

Shury, J., Speed, M., Vivian, D., Kuechel, A., and Nicholas, S. (2005), *Crime against Retail and Manufacturing Premises: Findings from the 2002 Commercial Victimisation Survey.* Home Office Online Report 37/05. London: Home Office.

Shute, S. (2002), 'Appropriation and the Law of Theft', *Criminal Law Review*: 445–58.

Shute, S. (2004), 'Punishing Murderers: Release Procedures and the "Tariff", 1953–2004', *Criminal Law Review*: 873–95.

Sibbitt, R. (1997), *The Perpetrators of Racial Harassment and Racial Violence.* Home Office Research Study No. 176. London: Home Office.

Silverman, J., and Wilson, D. (2002), *Innocence Betrayed: Paedophilia, the Media and Society.* Cambridge: Polity Press.

Sim, J., Scraton, P., and Gordon, P. (1987), 'Introduction: Crime, the State and Critical Analysis', in Scraton, P. (ed.), *Law, Order and the Authoritarian State.* Milton Keynes: Open University Press.

Simester, A.P. (2005), 'Is Strict Liability Always Wrong?', in Simester, A.P. (ed.), *Appraising Strict Liability.* Oxford: Oxford University Press.

Simester, A.P., and Sullivan, R. (2007), *Criminal Law: Theory and Doctrine* (3rd edn). Oxford: Hart.

Sivarajasingam, V., Moore, S., and Shepherd, J.P. (2007) *Violence in England and Wales 2006: An Accident and Emergency Perspective.* Cardiff: Cardiff University.

Smith, J. (2003), *The Nature of Personal Robbery.* Home Office Research Study No. 254. London: Home Office.

Smith, R. (2007), *Youth Justice: Ideas, Policy, Practice* (2nd edn). Cullompton: Willan.

Smithers, R. (2006), 'Keep Jailing Shoplifters, Retailers Demand', *The Guardian*, 11 October.

Soothill, K., and Francis, B. (1997), 'Sexual Reconvictions and the Sex Offenders Act 1997 – Part One', *New Law Journal*, **147** (5 September): 1285–6.

Soothill, K., and Walby, S. (1991), *Sex Crime in the News.* London: Routledge.

Sparks, J.R., Bottoms, A.E., and Hay, W. (1996), *Prisons and the Problem of Order.* Oxford: Oxford University Press.

Speed, M., and Burrows, J. (2006), *Sentencing in Cases of Theft from Shops.* Sentencing Advisory Panel Research Report 3. London: Sentencing Advisory Panel/Morgan Harris Burrows.

Squires, P., and Stephen, D.E. (2005), *Rougher Justice: Antisocial Behaviour and Young People.* Cullompton: Willan.

Stanko, E.A. (1985), *Intimate Intrusions: Women's Experiences of Male Violence.* London: Routledge and Kegan Paul.

Stanko, E.A. (1994), 'Challenging the Problem of Men's Individual Violence', in Newburn, T., and Stanko, E.A. (eds), *Just Boys Doing Business? Men, Masculinities and Crime.* London: Routledge.

Stanko, E.A. (2001), 'The Day to Count: Reflections on a Methodology to Raise Awareness of the Impact of Domestic Violence in the UK', *Criminal Justice*, **1**(2): 215–26.

Stanko, E.A. (2003), 'Introduction: Conceptualising the Meanings of Violence', in Stanko, E.A. (ed.), *The Meanings of Violence.* London: Routledge.

Sullivan, R.R. (2001), 'The Schizophrenic Self: Neo-Liberal Criminal Justice', in Stenson, K., and Sullivan, R.R. (eds), *Crime, Risk and Justice: The Politics of Crime Control in Liberal Democracies.* Cullompton: Willan.

Tadros, V. (2005), 'The Distinctiveness of Domestic Abuse', in Duff, R.A., and Green, S. (eds), *Defining Crimes.* Oxford: Oxford University Press.

Tadros, V., and Tierney, S. (2004), 'The Presumption of Innocence and the Human Rights Act', *Modern Law Review*, **67**(3): 402–34.

Tarling, R. (2006), 'Sentencing Practice in the Magistrates' Courts Revisited', *Howard Journal of Criminal Justice*, **45**(1): 29–41.

Taylor, P. (2006), 'The Terrorist Who Wasn't', *The Guardian*, 8 March.

Taylor, P., Hoare, J., and Murphy, R. (2007), 'Property Crime', in Nicholas, S., Kershaw, C., and Walker, A. (eds), *Crime in England and Wales 2006–07.* London: Home Office.

Temkin, J. (2000), 'Prosecuting and Defending Rape: Perspectives from the Bar', *Journal of Law and Society*, **27**(2): 219–48.

Temkin, J. (2002), *Rape and the Legal Process* (2nd edn). Oxford: Oxford University Press.

Temkin, J. (2003), 'Sexual History Evidence – Beware the Backlash', *Criminal Law Review*: 217–42.

Temkin, J., and Ashworth, A. (2004), 'The Sexual Offences Act 2003: (1) Rape, Sexual Assaults and the Problems of Consent', *Criminal Law Review*: 328–46.

Temkin, J., and Krahe, B. (2008), *Sexual Assault and the Justice Gap: A Question of Attitude*. Oxford: Hart.

Thomas, T. (2005), *Sex Crime: Sex Offending and Society* (2nd edn). Cullompton: Willan.

Thomas, T. (2008), 'The Sex Offender "Register": A Case Study in Function Creep', *Howard Journal of Criminal Justice*, **47**(3): 227–37.

Thornton, A., Walker, D., and Erol, R. (2003), *Distraction Burglary amongst Older Adults and Minority Ethnic Communities*. Home Office Research Findings No. 197. London: Home Office.

Thorpe, K., Robb, P., and Higgins, N. (2007), 'Extent and Trends', in Nicholas, S., Kershaw, C., and Walker, A. (eds), *Crime in England and Wales 2006–07*. London: Home Office.

Tombs, S. (2005), 'Corporate Crime', in Hale, C., Hayward, K., Wahidin, A., and Wincup, E. (eds), *Criminology*. Oxford: Oxford University Press.

Tombs, S., and Whyte, D. (2007), *Safety Crimes*. Cullompton: Willan.

Travis, A. (2006), 'Criminals on Probation Murdered 98 in Two Years', *The Guardian*, 6 December.

Tur, R.H.S. (2003), 'Legislative Technique and Human Rights: The Sad Case of Assisted Suicide', *Criminal Law Review*: 3–12.

Uglow, S. (2005), 'The Criminal Justice System', in Hale, C., Hayward, K., Wahidin, A., and Wincup, E. (eds), *Criminology*. Oxford: Oxford University Press.

Vallely, P. (2006), 'Banksy: The Joker', *The Independent*, 23 September.

Walby, S., and Allen, J. (2004), *Domestic Violence, Sexual Assault and Stalking: Findings from the British Crime Survey*. Home Office Research Study No. 276. London: Home Office.

Walker, C., and Starmer, K. (eds) (1999), *Miscarriages of Justice: A Review of Justice in Error*. London: Blackstone Press.

Walklate, S. (2000), 'Trust and the Problem of Community in the Inner City', in Hope, T., and Sparks, J.R. (eds), *Crime, Risk and Insecurity: Law and Order in Everyday Life and Political Discourse*. London: Routledge.

Walklate, S. (ed.) (2007), *Handbook of Victims and Victimology*. Cullompton: Willan.

Walsh, D.P. (1978), *Shoplifting: Controlling a Major Crime*. London: Macmillan.

Ward, T., and Maruna, S. (2006), *Rehabilitation*. London: Routledge.

Wasik, M. (1991), *Crime and the Computer*. Oxford: Clarendon Press.

Weait, M. (2007), *Intimacy and Responsibility: The Criminalisation of HIV Transmission*. London: Routledge.

Wells, C. (1989), 'Otherwise Kill Me: Marginal Children and Ethics at the Edge of Existence', in Lee, R.G., and Morgan, D. (eds), *Birthrights: Law and Ethics at the Beginning of Life*. London: Routledge.

Wells, C. (2000), 'Provocation: The Case for Abolition', in Ashworth, A., and Mitchell, B. (eds), *Rethinking English Homicide Law*. Oxford: Oxford University Press.

Wells, C. (2001), *Corporations and Criminal Responsibility* (2nd edn). Oxford: Oxford University Press.

Wells, C., and Morgan, D. (1991), 'Whose Foetus Is It?', *Journal of Law and Society*, **18**(4): 431–47.

Whitehead, E. (2000), *Key Findings from the Witness Satisfaction Survey 2000*. Home Office Research Findings No. 133. London: Home Office.

Wilczynski, A. (1997), 'Mad or Bad? Child-killers, Gender and the Courts', *British Journal of Criminology*, **37**(3): 419–36.

Wilczynski, A., and Morris, A. (1993), 'Parents Who Kill Their Children', *Criminal Law Review*: 31–6.

Williams, J., and Taylor, R. (1994), 'Boys Keep Swinging: Masculinity and Football Culture in England', in Newburn, T., and Stanko, E.A. (eds), *Just Boys Doing Business? Men, Masculinities and Crime*. London: Routledge.

Wilson, D. (2004), 'The Politics and Processes of Criminal Justice', in Muncie, J., and Wilson, D. (eds), *The Student Handbook of Criminal Justice and Criminology*. London: Cavendish.

Wistrich, H. (2008), 'Verdict on a Whitewash', *The Guardian*, 13 December.

Wright, R., and Decker, S. (1994), *Burglars on the Job: Streetlife and Residential Break-ins.* Boston, MA: Northeastern University Press.

Wright, R., Brookman, F., and Bennett, T. (2006), 'The Foreground Dynamics of Street Robbery in Britain', *British Journal of Criminology,* **46**(1): 1–15.

Yar, M. (2006), *Cybercrime and Society.* London: Sage.

Young, J. (1999), The Exclusive Society: Social Exclusion, Crime and Difference in Late Modernity. London: Sage.

Young, J., and Matthews, R. (2003), 'New Labour, Crime Control and Social Exclusion', in Matthews, R., and Young, J. (eds), *The New Politics of Crime and Punishment.* Cullompton: Willan.

Zedner, L. (2004), *Criminal Justice.* Oxford: Clarendon Press.

Zedner, L. (2005), 'Securing Liberty in the Face of Terror: Reflections from Criminal Justice', *Journal of Law and Society,* **32**(4): 507–33.

Index

Supporting researchers for more than forty years

Research methods have always been at the core of SAGE's publishing. Sara Miller McCune founded SAGE in 1965 and soon after, she published SAGE's first methods book, *Public Policy Evaluation*. A few years later, she launched the Quantitative Applications in the Social Sciences series – affectionately known as the 'little green books'.

Always at the forefront of developing and supporting new approaches in methods, SAGE published early groundbreaking texts and journals in the fields of qualitative methods and evaluation.

Today, more than forty years and two million little green books later, SAGE continues to push the boundaries with a growing list of more than 1,200 research methods books, journals, and reference works across the social, behavioural, and health sciences.

From qualitative, quantitative and mixed methods to evaluation, SAGE is the essential resource for academics and practitioners looking for the latest in methods by leading scholars.

www.sagepublications.com